Praise for *Publicize Your Book!*

"Easily the most incisive and expert guide to book publicity ever. Deval covers every conceivable aspect of generating and participating in book publicity, from creating press materials to engaging in a publicity tour, from getting on *Oprah* to marketing on the Internet, from conducting media interviews to hiring a freelance publicist, and much more. And she gives advice that's applicable to both veterans and novices, authors with publishing houses backing them and those who are self-published. Her approach is direct and no-nonsense yet congenial, with the hard information enlivened by scores upon scores of anecdotes (including a most tantalizing section on so-called authors from hell). With all this information, plus an extensive resource section, this is the book for authors who want to expand publicity for their books, and there's not a publishing professional who won't learn something new and useful from it as well."

    —*Publishers Weekly*

"Want to see the title of your book in the media? And want that coverage to help you sell copies? Read this book. Whether you are an author who is using a publicist or working directly with the press, you'll learn how to pitch the right angle at the right time . . . and why that is essential. The media is hungry, but only for good stories. *Publicize Your Book!* covers all the publicity essentials."

    —Ellen Levine, editorial director, Hearst Magazines

"Here is everything your publisher, editor, and publicist will never tell you but you need to know. If there is something missing from these pages—either it's never been done before or it doesn't work."

    —M. J. Rose, author of nine novels including *The Reincarnationist*, two works
      of nonfiction including *Buzz Your Book* (coauthored with Douglas Clegg),
      and founder of AuthorBuzz.com

"For authors planning to go on the road, I recommend this book highly. Successful bookstore events take special planning and here is everything authors should know about making entertaining—and effective—appearances."

    —Sharon Kelly Roth, director of public relations, Books & Co., Dayton, Ohio

continued . . .

"Valuable advice here for both the first-time author and the seasoned pro. I loved this book—for the way it encourages the reader while packing in tons of vital information that every author should know before his or her book is published."

 —Douglas Clegg, author of *The Queen of Wolves* and *Buzz Your Book*
  (coauthored with M. J. Rose)

"Getting media coverage is a more competitive undertaking than ever before, and authors need every advantage they can get. This book gives them a head start—all the information they need to present themselves to the media as compelling and newsworthy. As an author, I highly recommend this book with its no-nonsense, take-charge advice."

 —Nancy Lindemeyer, founding editor, *Victoria* magazine

"A treasure house of essential wisdom for any author seeking to publicize their work. Jacqueline Deval serves as an inspired guide, inviting the reader to creative possibilities while remaining completely grounded in the real world of marketing. Her combination of exciting vision and hands-on experience make this book a tremendous resource."

 —Sharon Salzberg, author of *Faith* and *Lovingkindness*

Publicize Your Book!

AN INSIDER'S GUIDE TO GETTING YOUR BOOK THE ATTENTION IT DESERVES

Jacqueline Deval

A Perigee Book

A PERIGEE BOOK
Published by the Penguin Group
Penguin Group (USA) Inc.
375 Hudson Street, New York, New York 10014, USA
Penguin Group (Canada), 90 Eglinton Avenue East, Suite 700, Toronto, Ontario M4P 2Y3, Canada
(a division of Pearson Penguin Canada Inc.)
Penguin Books Ltd., 80 Strand, London WC2R 0RL, England
Penguin Group Ireland, 25 St. Stephen's Green, Dublin 2, Ireland (a division of Penguin Books Ltd.)
Penguin Group (Australia), 250 Camberwell Road, Camberwell, Victoria 3124, Australia
(a division of Pearson Australia Group Pty. Ltd.)
Penguin Books India Pvt. Ltd., 11 Community Centre, Panchsheel Park, New Delhi—110 017, India
Penguin Group (NZ), 67 Apollo Drive, Rosedale, North Shore 0632, New Zealand
(a division of Pearson New Zealand Ltd.)
Penguin Books (South Africa) (Pty.) Ltd., 24 Sturdee Avenue, Rosebank, Johannesburg 2196,
South Africa

Penguin Books Ltd., Registered Offices: 80 Strand, London WC2R 0RL, England

While the author has made every effort to provide accurate telephone numbers and Internet addresses at the time of publication, neither the publisher nor the author assumes any responsibility for errors, or for changes that occur after publication. Further, the publisher does not have any control over and does not assume any responsibility for author or third-party websites or their content.

PRINTING HISTORY
First Perigee trade paperback edition / April 2003
Revised Perigee trade paperback edition / July 2008

Revised Perigee edition ISBN: 978-0-399-53431-7

The Library of Congress has cataloged the first Perigee edition as follows:

Deval, Jacqueline.
Publicize your book! : an insider's guide to getting your book the attention it deserves / Jacqueline Deval. —1st Perigee ed.
    p. cm.
    Includes index.
        ISBN 0-399-52863-6 (pbk.)
    1. Authorship—Marketing.   2. Books—Marketing.   I. Title.
    PN161 .D46   2003
070.5'2—dc21   2002035544

PRINTED IN THE UNITED STATES OF AMERICA

10 9 8 7 6 5 4 3 2

Most Perigee books are available at special quantity discounts for bulk purchases for sales promotions, premiums, fund-rising, or educational use. Special books, or book excerpts, can also be created to fit specific needs. For details, write: Special Markets, Penguin Group (USA) Inc., 375 Hudson Street, New York, New York 10014.

CONTENTS

ACKNOWLEDGMENTS

Thank you to everyone who assisted me during the research and writing of this book: Carl Sferrazza Anthony, James Barron, Nelvia Brady, Beth Bruno, Fauzia Burke, Charles Cook, Tami DePalma, Carol Fass, Carol Fitzgerald, Mark Fortier, Caitlin Friedman, Mark Gebbie, Tracey George, Lynn Goldberg, Katherine Wyse Goldman, Jane Heller, Lucine Kasbarian, Paul Krupin, David Lida, Justin Loeber, Diane Mancher, Brad Meltzer, Meryl Moss, Steve O'Keefe, Linda Palladino, Bill Parkhurst, Liz Perle, Kristen Powers, Diane Roback, M. J. Rose, Sharyn Rosenblum, Marly Rusoff, Michael Schrage, Andrew Sobel, Judy Spagnola, Bella Stander, Joan Stewart, Mariah Stewart, Bob Sutton, Laura Van Wormer, Lois Wyse, Kim Yorio, and Karyn Zoldan.

I would like to extend special thanks to Stuart Applebaum, a master of publicity strategy, who took me under his wing when I was a novice.

To Alberto Vitale, who once told me to think not like a publicist, but like a publisher. This was an important remark.

To Loretta Barrett, for her unswerving support.

To Jeanne Krier, for her flair as a publicist and insights as first reader.

To Kelvin Christopher James, for being a publicist's dream to work with and for thoughtful editorial comments.

To Jean and Bill Deval, for their very helpful comments on the manuscript.

To Jorden, who, when I was struggling to come up with an appropriate title for the book, helpfully suggested *The Mysteries of Science*, or else *The Brain*. Which suggests that book marketing is a science, or that I had not properly explained to my child exactly what I do for a living.

And now, of course, to Madeline.

INTRODUCTION

THE reality of book publishing is that there are too few resources to support every book. This means that some books will get publicity campaigns and budgets while others will go without. Additionally, most publishing houses are not staffed with enough publicists to mount a full-fledged campaign for every book. Because of this, editors must compete with one another to lobby the publisher, and the marketing and publicity departments, for the funds and staff attention to promote their books.

Some aspects of publishing boggle the minds of first-time writers. (That's okay. It boggles the minds of many veterans in publishing, too.) For example, you might wonder why the big-name authors get tons of money spent on their campaigns when their bestseller status would seem to be a foregone conclusion. Meanwhile, a new author could use some of those marketing funds to begin to build a reputation. The bald fact is that publishers need to protect their interest in the big authors and spending marketing dollars is one way to keep the author and agent happy. The harsher reality is that this dynamic is unlikely to change anytime soon.

The good news is that authors who know how to properly represent themselves to their publishers *can* find discretionary dollars for book promotion. Do not count on your agent to make this happen. Your agent may be terrific, but is truly unable to fight every battle on your behalf. You will need to become your own advocate with the right efforts at the right time.

Too many authors simply wake up too late to the problem of under-promotion. An author who can get involved creatively and make allies of the publishing staff can have the most impact on the marketing and publicity program and the best possible chance of reaching a readership.

It's never too soon to get started. These days, many proposals submitted to publishing houses are accompanied by a marketing plan written by the author in cooperation with his or her agent. This is particularly true of nonfiction in categories like self-help and how-to, which require a promotable author to publicize the book. In the absence of a marketing plan, which demonstrates the author's willingness to participate energetically in the book's successful publication, the publishing house has fewer reasons to publish the book. Therefore, you may find yourself writing a marketing plan before a publisher has signed up your book. Even if you didn't write a plan to submit along with your book proposal, count on starting your marketing efforts early. More than ever, an author's serious marketing efforts can truly shape the trajectory of a book's life, but it takes time and effort. Start planning your book's marketing a year before publication and you'll be glad for the time you've allowed yourself to get prepared.

You may have heard from other writers, or your agent, or your editor that writing the book is only half of your job and that the other half is marketing it. That statement is not entirely valid because the marketing of your book *never* has to end. The campaign can last as long as you like after your publicist has finished his or her job. You are limited only by the effort you put out. Even with successful books, the publisher eventually steps back to focus on bringing its other titles to market. By paying attention to the market and learning a few marketing and publicity tricks and techniques, you can keep the marketing effort for your book moving forward indefinitely.

While marketing at first may seem like drudge work—and there are tedious aspects like assembling mailing lists—you may instead find that marketing delivers an enormous amount of fun and pleasure, and brings you rewarding new relationships and—most important—into closer and even ongoing contact with your readers. Marketing is particularly thrilling when you come up with a bright idea, carry it through, and, as a result, enjoy a boost in your book's sales.

If your publisher intends to put some muscle behind your book, you will nevertheless need to get involved in shaping your book's campaign. The promotional opportunities that are available to your book might require some research—a task your in-house publicist might not be able to accomplish in the hours available to her. Nor is your role limited to providing viable leads for promotion. You are a valuable resource in many other ways when it comes to determining how to market your book.

While you may never have had a book published before, or been involved with the marketing or publicity surrounding any kind of product, you might view yourself as an adventurer. You are embarking on an unusual enterprise. You will face risk and excitement in your chance to reach fortune. My role is a guide of sorts: a companion with sound advice on how to make it through what can sometimes seem like rough going.

I finally decided to write this book because a friend needed my help. With his novel on the verge of publication, he found himself bereft of publishing support, his editor departed for another house, and his publicist was reluctant to meet him. I realized that our conversations were identical to many I'd had before with writers who felt either abandoned or unsure when their books were on the verge of publication, who wanted to promote their books, and yet lacked the deep pockets to afford a freelance publicist. Despite the ominous signs, my friend set about to create some publicity for his book and even managed to garner some resources from his publisher to do so. I wrote this book to help other writers like him.

Because I've been a publicity director, an author, and a publisher, my perspective encompasses the desires of the author (who wants to see the book sell and reach a readership) and the reality of the publisher (who is constrained by budgets, time, and other books competing for attention that may have more obvious opportunities in the marketplace). Those two sometimes competing interests can be reconciled, with some up-front management of expectations for both parties.

While I talk about all aspects of marketing a book, I've concentrated most on publicity opportunities—the realm in which an author has the greatest chance to make a significant difference. Because one size does not fit all in book publicity, not all of the advice here will be appropriate to your book. For example, fiction and nonfiction have different opportunities. So do children's books and books intended for adults. While you read this book, keep a notebook of the ideas that seem appropriate to your book's promotion.

This book will explain what you might reasonably expect from your publisher during the course of publication and how to get involved with the planning. It answers those nagging questions that might seem too petty to trouble your editor with and provides creative solutions to many issues that will arise. Most important, this book will show how you might work effectively with your publishing team to create marketing and publicity opportunities that can drive book sales.

Since the first edition of this book was published in 2003, book marketing has evolved dramatically, with online tools offering authors ever more sophisticated and immediate ways to reach readers, whether through blogs or social networking or book trailers. While traditional media outlets for books, like newspaper book review pages, are being eliminated or reduced, the new online forums for books have increased exponentially. And some of the online commentary about books is as engaging as anything you'll read in traditional print media. So the good news for authors is that the potential for direct access to readers has been vastly improved.

By getting involved in publicizing your book early, armed with the right information, you can get your book the publicity and promotion it deserves.

Jacqueline Deval
New York City

A COMMON MIDLIST SCENARIO TO AVOID AT ALL COSTS

WHAT follows is a scenario familiar to many published authors. What seemed like a promising start evaporates for no discernable reason and without warning. If you recognize your own situation in this scenario, the good news is that if you act in a timely fashion, you can fix it.

The publicist: Newly promoted to her position after one year in the business, Kate is bright and enthusiastic but untrained. Most of what she does she's figured out by the seat of her pants and from chatting with the other publicists. Kate is working actively on five to eight books at any one time—other books will be added to her list next month—and she has no assistant to help with mailings and other clerical work. She's relieved when she's assigned to authors who live outside New York City because they can't drop by the office to talk about their publicity campaigns. She's careful to avoid telling authors that they're getting a limited campaign. If she says the wrong thing, the authors might complain to their agents or editors and then she will get in trouble.

One of the books assigned to Kate is a debut literary novel by a writer named Jeremy. She enjoyed the novel, but is having trouble figuring out how to promote it because she hasn't publicized a novel before. The book's editor, Frank, is somewhat condescending to the younger publicists. She could tell he was unhappy she'd been assigned to the book, so she's intimidated to ask if he has any ideas about the book's campaign.

Kate also knows that if the publicity director thought the book was important, then she wouldn't have assigned the book to her. So, she's mailed copies of the book to reviewers, none of whom she's ever met because the publicity director is the one who meets with the key media. Jeremy calls almost daily, wanting to know where his book will be reviewed. Kate's getting anxious about what to say to him. She works from nine until at least seven every evening and is paid $28,000 a year.

The editor: Frank's been in the business for 10 years and has a large list of midlist authors—authors whose books have achieved only modest sales. He desperately needs a big breakout bestseller to get his career back on track. No longer the wonder boy he once seemed, he's impatient for that big winner. He's had some near hits—books that hovered frustratingly close to the *New York Times* bestseller list but never quite made it. Frank has a lot of enthusiasm and each acquisition, in his mind, has the potential to be the next big winner. When Frank presented Jeremy's novel at the launch meeting for the next season's new titles, he was disappointed by the group's reaction. Granted, Frank presented the title at 4:00 p.m. after the sales and marketing folks had been in the meeting all day. No one said anything about Jeremy's book and when Frank tried to prod the staff for any ideas, he didn't get much response. Since then, Frank's been battling uphill on behalf of Jeremy's book, but just can't seem to light a fire under anyone. He lobbied the sales rep for Barnes & Noble to get the book into the Discover program. While the book got a reading at the chain (great!), it was ultimately passed over for the special promotion and the bigger buy that goes with it (oh well). He lobbied the publicity director to put aside a small budget for the book, which she did. But a round of budget cuts initiated by the publisher and the business manager soon eliminated that. When Frank sees the all-too-familiar sales pattern—a slow trickle of small advance orders from bookstores—he starts to detach from his author. Frank's onto the next big book, and this time it's a project that he hopes will get people really excited.

The author: Jeremy can't understand why his editor isn't returning his calls. He enjoyed the editing process with Frank and their occasional lunches. His novel was published one month ago—7,500 copies were printed and most of those shipped, he's been told. The big reviews haven't happened yet, though there was a nice write-up in the hometown paper where Jeremy lived until he went away to college. Whenever he calls, the editorial assistant, who answers Frank's phone, is always very nice to him, but recently he's detected an embarrassed, evasive tone in her voice. Or is he imagining it? His publicist, Kate, returns his calls, though not necessarily on the same day. She's very pleasant but she's also overwhelmed and resists Jeremy's suggestion that she call the editor of the *New York Times Book Review* to see if a review has been scheduled. She can't tell him about the sales because, she says, she doesn't see the sales reports. To top it all off, Jeremy's agent, Francine, is becoming a little testy with him. After she spoke to Frank about the lack of publicity for the book, she reported that there's no budget for the book and not much more that Frank can do. Jeremy asks her why Frank paid him a $35,000 advance if the publishing house isn't promoting the book. Surely the publisher will lose its investment. Francine agrees but points out that that's the nature of this crazy publishing business. After a few more weeks go by, no one at the publishing house is thinking about Jeremy's book. Jeremy himself no longer calls. The book is pretty much dead.

The analysis: Jeremy's situation is by no means unique in the book publishing business, though he was lucky to get a higher advance than most midlist authors. However, a relatively large advance doesn't always guarantee a publisher's support. Many books with advances much higher than his have fallen by the wayside from lack of marketing and publicity attention. Jeremy's real problem is he realized too late that he was not getting the campaign he believed his book deserved. Had he asked the right questions during the months leading up to publication, he would have been in a much better position to influence the course of events. Once a book has been published, it is difficult to start a publicity campaign or hire a freelance publicist, because an unenthusiastic sales force has already distributed the book. In other words, few copies of the book exist in the marketplace, making it difficult for consumers to find the book even if they do read about it in the press. Once a book has been in the marketplace for a couple of months, making the book stand out from the pack is an imposing challenge because of the next wave of new books coming up behind.

An author who thinks like a marketer, and who starts thinking about marketing before the book is even completed, will help the book toward a successful publication. The author is in the best position to offer suggestions for marketing that the house might have overlooked, and sometimes to help bridge any difficult internal relationships among the publishing team that might impede the book's success. (In-house squabbles do happen in the business, and while in a just world they shouldn't interfere with a book's progress, sometimes they do.) Most important, the author can be the catalyst to motivate a house's enthusiasm about a book.

Jeremy could have provided critical information to his editor and publishing house by getting actively involved in his own marketing campaign. He could have come up with leads about speaking opportunities and reporters who cover subjects related to his book; developed sales and publicity angles for his book; set up a meeting for his editor, his publicist, and himself to brainstorm about publicizing the book; assisted with the development of his publisher's marketing materials to help raise his profile in-house; reached out to friends and family across the country to set up local promotions; devised an unusual presentation for bookstore and library appearances; developed an online presence in appropriate newsgroups to help build an audience; assembled a personal database or emailing list to market the book; researched any special audiences that might take a particular interest in the book; and so much more.

WHAT ONE AUTHOR DID RIGHT—A 7,000-COPY FIRST PRINTING LEADS TO 185,000 COPIES IN PRINT: A TRUE STORY

James Douglas Barron is the author of *She's Having a Baby—and I'm Having a Breakdown*, a funny and informative gift book for expectant fathers that started with an inauspicious 7,000 copies sold into bookstores. Barron devoted a significant amount of his time and imagination to helping the book succeed. Though his publishing house would not justify devoting significant resources to promote the book, he was very lucky that his publicist, Sharyn Rosenblum, had faith in the book's appealing message and in his own commitment. While Rosenblum set up some media interviews, the author set up some promotional events, special mailings, and special sales, and underwrote the expenses to travel to a few cities, which amounted to several thousand dollars. The result: Within three years the book was in its nineteenth printing and now has more than 185,000 copies in print. Once the book took off, the publisher paid for a larger publicity tour and some print advertising. Barron has since published two more books: *She's Had a Baby—and I'm Having a Meltdown* and *She Wants a Ring—and I Don't Wanna Change a Thing*.

"When I write a book and it's been accepted and all the editing is finished, then I'm only at the fifty-yard line and I have another fifty to go," says James Barron. "And I can't depend on anyone else to get me there. I work harder once I've handed in my manuscript."

For his campaign for *She's Having a Baby*, Barron understood that his publisher simply did not have the time and resources to promote the book to the extent he desired. He decided to invest a certain amount of money as well as an enormous amount of time in creating his own campaign, sometimes logging as many as 11 hours a day on marketing. "I'd worked for years to get a book published," Barron says, "so I wasn't going to stop there."

He sought endorsements from several noted people to put on the book cover. Among them were Michael J. Fox, whom he'd met at a barbecue and to whom he pitched his book; the author of a parenting book bestseller, S. Adams Sullivan; and the actor Tony Randall, who, at 77, had been in the news when his wife gave birth to their first child. Barron did not know any of these people beforehand; he reached Sullivan and Randall simply by writing to them.

Barron wrote or called everyone he knew and told them about the book. He stopped by specialty stores like maternity shops, toy shops, and hospital gift shops to persuade them to order the book from his publisher to sell to their customers, and provided them with a ready-made sales order form. Barron offered to buy the books back if they could not sell them—but he never had to buy back one copy. He guesses that somewhere between 40 and 75 stores chose to order the book, sold out, and reordered again and again.

Tapping into his charitable involvement with the Children's Museum of Manhattan, he organized a book launch party there. He found a donor to contribute money for the museum's fee for renting the space for the party, and the museum notified its mailing list of 40,000 about the event as well as his own list of 2,000 names. Knowing that the head of Barnes & Noble was also involved with the museum, he wrote him an appealing letter about the book and the event, which translated into significantly increased support for the book from Barnes & Noble.

For a second book event, he worked with a gallery owner whom he knows—Barron is by profession a private art dealer—to throw a party and was able to use the gallery's 8,000-name mailing list. Then he persuaded his publisher to buy a mailing list from ACOG (American College of Obstetricians and Gynecologists) and to send out a complimentary book to doctors. (At a subsequent book event, one doctor reported how he alone was responsible for selling 250 copies of the book.)

Then Barron selected two markets outside of New York City to promote the book: Chicago, his original hometown, and Atlanta, where his wife grew up. He hired publicists in those cities to help set up media and book signings, as well as to go to the same kinds of specialty stores as he did in New York.

Barron called many strangers during his campaign. He simply picked up the phone and made his pitch to people involved with organizations or groups likely to take a natural interest in his book. "I work under the assumption that I'm going to get twelve rejections for every yes," he says. He doesn't mind the rejections because he views them as part of the process of getting to that one yes.

Though Barron puts in an extraordinary amount of effort to promote his books, he also believes that publishers can be great collaborators. He advises that if you work with them in a positive way, you can garner an enormous amount of support. Bottom line, though, he says, is that you have to be realistic about what the publisher is capable of and willing to do, given its limited resources. Your publisher views your book as a business investment, he says, and you should, too. Ask yourself, what time and money are you willing to put into your business venture?

Barron's other promotional activities on behalf of *She Wants a Ring—and I Don't Wanna Change a Thing* included book signings at jewelry stores in Los Angeles and Las Vegas. That's a very smart marketing idea.

What other authors can learn from Barron is how he used his personal and professional affiliations to market his book, how he understood his target audience and figured out how to reach them, and that he made a conscious decision to commit a certain amount of his time and a little money to try to make his book succeed in the marketplace.

1

BOOK MARKETING BASICS

BOOK marketing is, quite simply, determining how to sell books as fast as possible to as many people as possible. Specifically, book marketing is defining and reaching your potential readership, and then coming up with ways to convince them to buy your book—the more copies they buy and the faster they buy them the better.

Faster is better because when a book achieves a certain level of sales momentum, bookstores steadily reorder copies and, in some cases, will automatically replenish inventory. Also, books that sell in high quantities in a short amount of time have a greater opportunity to hit bestseller lists than books that might sell the same number of copies but over a longer period of time. This is because bookstores report sales on a weekly basis to the bestseller lists.

If your book can't achieve high-speed sales, it still benefits from ongoing small though steady sales. Regular demand for your book will prompt a bookstore to reorder your book from your publisher. A bookstore that has ordered one or two copies of your book is perfectly happy when those books sell out. But the store won't automatically reorder the book. Therefore it is your ardent desire, as well as your publisher's, that the marketing of your book drives consumer demand, which in turn stimulates bookstore reorders.

Advertising, promotions, and publicity are the three core areas of book marketing. Advertising—which refers to paid ads in any form of media—is not particularly effective in driving book sales, and few books receive advertising campaigns. Unless the publisher plans to spend a significant amount of money, an ad campaign alone simply cannot reach enough consumers. When a publisher advertises a book, the strategy is generally meant to accomplish one of two things: to alert readers that a big-name author with a known fan base has just published a new book, or to boost visibility for a book that has already been successfully publicized.

Promotions are the discounts, displays, and co-op funds that publishers offer booksellers. Co-op funds are earned marketing dollars that publishers give to booksellers to promote their books. The amount of co-op available to a bookseller is based on its volume of business with the publisher the previous year. If you're going on a book tour, then booksellers might spend co-op money on posters and newsletters to promote your appearances in their stores. The promotional materials that a publisher might produce include corrugated book displays, posters, bookmarks, and postcards.

Publicity—getting your book mentioned in any form of media—earns you the legitimacy of a third-party editorial endorsement, can reach large audiences, and requires relatively little spending. Publicity is where your greatest opportunity lies to contribute to the shape and scope of your campaign. The right media coverage for your book can stimulate measurable sales results that turn your book into a success.

The challenge for many writers is to think of themselves as marketers. Marketing might at first seem at odds with the creator's side of the business. But with close to 200,000 books published a year—and one recent industry report puts the number at closer to 300,000—every book needs help to find its market, whether the book is the latest release by a well-known author, an unknown writer's first novel, or the paperback edition of a book that enjoyed decent though modest sales in hardcover. While your relationship with your editor may focus almost entirely on the editorial quality of the work itself, every good editor is engaged in the act of selling every day, advocating the works of his or her writers. The earlier you engage your editor in conversations about selling the book, the earlier you help your editor promote your work effectively in-house. In other words, editing your book is only one of your editor's jobs: He or she is also responsible for generating in-house enthusiasm for your work and getting the publisher to view the book as worthy of time and money.

Coming up with innovative marketing ideas—or *any* marketing ideas—may at first seem to require a special set of thinking skills. Do not be discouraged. You can acquire and practice this kind of thinking. First, try to recall the skills of persuasion that you used when you got a job you really wanted, or talked your way out of an awkward situation. In those scenarios, most likely, you drew from a deep well of conviction, an important asset that you will tap into throughout your campaign to persuade your publicist and editor to help you.

Other qualities that you need to help you create a marketing success of your book are an open mind, curiosity, polite persistence, and a certain level of boldness. There's no room for shyness in a publicity campaign, a characteristic that some authors have to combat. One helpful idea is to form a small circle of trusted friends, family, and colleagues who would draw you out, and serve as a sounding board for mock interviews or readings.

What you *do not* require is a lot of money. Of course, money helps if you want to hire a freelance publicist or send yourself on a book tour. But you can market your book effectively, or work with your publisher to market your book effectively, without spending an abundance of cash. (Even if you do not intend to spend a lot of money on your marketing campaign, keep an expense log of tax-deductible phone calls, postage, book-related business travel, express mail, Internet service provider fees, and so on.) The resource that you *will* spend extravagantly is your time. Be prepared. If you work a full-time job, save your personal days and vacation time to contribute toward marketing the book as needed.

The best way to start planning your marketing is to develop a well-thought-out marketing plan. Normally a publishing house creates a formal marketing plan only for the top books on its list. Your written marketing plan will help your publisher focus on your book, will prove your own commitment, and will become a valuable reference tool throughout the publishing process. If your publisher elects not to use your marketing plan, then you have created a blueprint to promote the book yourself, or to turn over to a freelance publicist. If you are a self-published author, you should still write a marketing plan. A marketing plan helps any author focus on what needs to be done to reach readers and to organize priorities in the book campaign.

THINK LIKE A MARKETER

What does your book offer readers? Who are those readers? How do you reach them and convince them to spend money on your book? Any marketer has to answer these questions at the start of any campaign. Put in marketing terms, you provide the product, you locate the audience, and then you persuade them to buy.

Actually, you will have several audiences to persuade about the appeal of your book. First, you want the audiences inside your publishing house—the editor, your publicist, the sales reps, and other publishing staff—to get excited about your book's potential. The staff will then convey its enthusiasm to your other target audiences: the booksellers, the media, and then finally, consumers. Considering that each audience has particular interests, your job is to address them in a way that ultimately sells your book.

Here's how it works: Your editor convinces the publishing staff that your book has potential in the market. Following the in-house planning meetings, the marketing, publicity, and sales people begin working on various tasks to launch your book. The subsidiary rights staff sells direct marketing rights to book clubs, like Book-of-the-Month Club, and to foreign publishers. The sales reps promise booksellers that your book will be covered in the media to encourage them to buy large quantities of your book. (And if you're a writer of fiction or quality nonfiction, the reps may also successfully convince the booksellers to read your book. If they like it, you will benefit from hand-selling, which is when booksellers recommend your book to their customers.) The publicists work with book reviewers and other media to begin to arrange media coverage for your book, which in turn may create ongoing favorable conversations and recommendations among your readers—and stimulate ongoing book sales. At various stages all along the way, you can contribute ideas and enthusiasm.

The Internet gives you access to the news of publishing no matter where you live. To get inside the heads of the people you're now in business with, read what they read. *Publishers Weekly* is the trade magazine for the industry, and you can subscribe to the print edition or read it online at www .publishersweekly.com, where you should also check out the archives of the magazine's free daily e-newsletter called *PW Daily*. You will learn what the trade press is interested in covering, which will help you come up with media angles for your publicist later. Another source that you might find helpful: an e-newsletter called *Publishers Lunch* that summarizes the daily news in publishing (www.publisherslunch.com). To get a feel for the library market, read *Library Journal*, which you can subscribe to at www.libraryjournal .com or read at your local library. If you're the author of a children's book, read *School Library Journal*, which you can find online at www.slj.com.

Get to know your local booksellers and ask them what books are selling and why. In your visits to the bookstore, notice the books that you are drawn to. Did the vivid jackets and compelling titles catch your eye? Or was it the books' eye-level positioning on bookshelves and special displays? Going to bookstores will teach you about the competition that your book will face. It "is like boot camp for new authors" says marketing expert and literary agent Marly Rusoff, who has masterminded many book campaigns in her career. She sees the visit to the bookstore as an opportunity for authors to recognize the challenge before them in terms of the sheer volume of information and competing books.

Your local bookstores will include branches of the national chains, such as Barnes & Noble, Borders, and the regional southern chain, Books-A-Million, as well as independent booksellers, which are generally single-store businesses. The local chain store receives its books through orders placed with publishers at store headquarters. Store managers do have some discretionary buying power, so becoming familiar to local chain store managers can help you when your book is published. The independent booksellers may place their orders through a publisher's sales rep, who comes to the store, or through a publisher's telemarketing rep or wholesalers. Not all independent booksellers see publishers' reps so they must count on trade reviews and other sources of book news to decide which books to order.

As you become immersed in the marketing of your book, you may be surprised to find that the world views your book as a product. Some authors find this notion difficult to understand and accept, particularly writers of literary fiction. But, for example, in the world of the media, the author is just one more individual competing for airtime (or for ink) to sell a service or a product. A book is simply a form of entertainment or a source of information that a consumer might choose over another entertainment product, such as a movie or computer game. (Yes—your book is competing with *all* other forms of information and entertainment.) And while your publisher may treat your prose with all due respect, the house is also very concerned with your book's net units sold and its contribution to the company's bottom line. The earlier in the publishing process that you understand this thinking, the better, as you will become closer to learning the mind-set of the people you're working with. (It may also surprise you to overhear your publicist or editor referring to you as "my author." It's just the lingo of the trade, so do not be concerned by the implied possessiveness. Instead, be flattered!)

To give yourself the best head start, think about your marketing campaign while you write your book. Keep a separate notebook and jot down marketing ideas or reasons why your book stands out from others in its field. When you are ready to create a formal marketing plan, the notes will be valuable.

You may also include marketable ideas within your book itself. For example, print media will often use "Top 10" lists or other excerpts from how-to books. Include them in yours and you have provided desirable and accessible copy that's easily reproduced by the media. Another example of a marketing hook embedded in a book: One bestselling novelist always includes in his books a character who is a graduate of his alma mater, a school that happens to have an active alumni organization that supports all of his books in the form of promotional events.

Then there is *The Bulgari Connection*, by Fay Weldon, the *ne plus ultra* of product placement in fiction. The Bulgari jewelry company paid Weldon for prominent mention of the brand in the novel. The media's coverage of the book as the commercialization and co-option of art created buzz and controversy. The same thing happened a few years later when it was revealed that Proctor & Gamble agreed to promote a teen novel called *Cathy's Book*, by Jordan Weisman and Sean Stewart, on its website in exchange for some of its Cover Girl makeup products being mentioned in the book. Literary purists will balk at the notion of placing marketing angles within the text, feeling that it compromises artistic integrity, and that's a legitimate position to hold. You will need to make your own determination about what you think is acceptable within the context of your own book and your own field. Despite the media controversy, the marketing promotions for *Cathy's Book* were resoundingly successful: The book became a *New York Times* bestseller. The P&G tie-in was only one of many things going for the book: The authors set up MySpace.com profiles for the characters, websites for some of the companies in the book, as well as active phone numbers for some of the characters that readers could call to hear recorded messages. (For more on MySpace, see page 240 in Chapter 11.)

A thoroughly respectable way to embed a marketing angle within your book is to invite a noted person in a related field to contribute a foreword. Your book's sales will benefit from the additional draw that his or her name offers.

BRAINSTORM

The most fruitful way to begin to generate marketing ideas is to talk to other people. You must brainstorm with your friends and others about how they think your book will appeal to other readers. You are so close to your book that you may not see marketing opportunities that are obvious to others. Also, as any marketing person knows, the best ideas often emerge from conversation with others.

In my many conversations with authors for this book, the ones who had involved themselves in a writers' group, or other informed support group, seemed confident about their prospects and willing to try their hand at marketing. Beth Bruno, the self-published author of a book on parenting called *Wild Tulips*, credits the Connecticut Authors and Publishers Association (www.aboutcapa.com) as an important source of ideas and support. Search for "writers' groups" online to find organizations in your area, such as the Writers' League of Texas or Rocky Mountain Fiction Writers. They offer regular forums for writers to talk about their craft and to exchange ideas about getting published and finding an audience. Look also at the Shaw Guides, a free online guide to writers' conferences and workshops throughout the United States, at www.shawguides.com/writing.

Like Bruno, romance novelist Mariah Stewart says that the local chapter of Romance Writers of America (www.rwanational.com) was essential to her start as a writer. "They were very generous about sharing information," Stewart says, and cites the organization's ongoing contests as an excellent way to reach her core audience. Look for local chapters of national organizations that focus on your genre, whether romance, mystery (such as Mystery Writers of America, www.mysterywriters.org), science fiction (Science Fiction and Fantasy Writers of America, www.sfwa.org), horror (Horror Writers Association, www.horror.org), thrillers (International Thriller Writers, www.thrillerwriters.org), and more.

If you can't find any relevant local writers' organization, you can start your own, which is not as hard as it sounds. Your local bookstore or library would be more than happy to help you reach out to other writers in your community or host monthly meetings. Don't want to go to that trouble? Then you can reach out to brainstorming communities online. Browse the Internet and you'll come across active online writers' groups that you can join. (Search for writers' groups under Yahoo! or Google Groups.)

A helpful workbook, called *Buzz Your Book*, by M. J. Rose and Douglas Clegg, is available as a downloadable e-book (www.buzzyour.com). The book describes top marketing techniques for traditional media and for the Internet, offers advice from PR professionals who specialize in book marketing, links to many useful author websites and web-based services for authors, and much more.

The bottom line is this: Find people to talk to and ask them questions. Then find even more people and ask them questions, too. Don't stop doing this even after your book has been published.

SHARPEN YOUR MARKETING MIND

Learning to think like a marketer is a commonsense process that takes place over time. It is accomplished largely by paying attention to the

media and to the marketplace and thinking about how your book fits in.
Here's how to start:

- Read the newspaper with the intent to figure out which interest
group(s) had a hand in shaping or pitching the story. Nearly every article has one or more advocates behind it who were pushing a particular point of view. Yes, even governments have publicists in the form
of lobbyists—everyone has a message to convey, whether it's the author of a new book or the Chinese government.

- Watch television interviews and listen to radio interviews. Which
guests effectively convey their points? Which do not, and why?

- Scan for references to books in *Time* or *Newsweek*, in your local
newspaper, in *USA Today*, other media—particularly media that you
are not already familiar with. Books are covered in feature articles,
opinion columns, editorial pages, everywhere—not only in the book
review sections, which with few exceptions cover only serious fiction
and nonfiction. If your book will not fit well on the book review pages,
can you identify other opportunities elsewhere in these publications?

- Pay attention to how all media covers books to learn why the media
might take an interest in yours. Does the book offer news or information that's useful or important to consumers? Is the book funny or
controversial? Or does it represent a special achievement on the part
of the author?

- Pay attention to the names of reporters who regularly cover books
outside of the book review sections and make note of their names to
share with your publicist later. Start to develop a sense of the reporters' interests. Based on your growing knowledge of their beat,
would your book interest them?

- Attend author readings at local bookstores and libraries. Talk to the
authors about their campaigns.

- Talk to friends and associates to find out if you can tap into their
contacts to market or sell your book. Do you know someone with

access to an inexpensive party space? Or who has access to organizations that might be willing to sponsor a lecture, or buy your book as a premium to attract new customers?

■ Use the Internet to listen to radio interview programs and podcasts.

■ Go online to check out newspapers around the United States and Canada, and to research reporters interested in your book topic. (I will tell you about some great sites to do this in Chapter 6.)

■ Look for websites and blogs relevant to your book topic. (Blogs are online journal entries, many updated daily, and are often part of a website though they can also be stand-alone sites.) Start to make contact with the online community interested in your subject to build an online marketing base for your book. (There is a protocol to promoting your work online, which I will address in Chapter 11.)

■ If you think you belong on *The Oprah Winfrey Show*—the ultimate dream for many authors—or *The View*, *Live with Regis and Kelly*, *Today*, *Good Morning America*, *The Colbert Report*, or *The Jon Stewart Show*, then watch the shows faithfully to understand how to position your book to appeal to the shows' producers.

A WRITTEN MARKETING PLAN

If you have never written a marketing plan before, do not be intimidated, but take the challenge seriously. Your final plan need not follow any specified format—you may use the format suggested in the next chapter, or else come up with your own. What's important is that you convey your ideas about how your book will reach and sell to its audience. (If you submitted a marketing plan at the time your book was acquired, then you should plan on updating it, since your thinking will have evolved in the interim.)

If you've got a professional background in marketing at, say, a consumer goods company, then a book marketing plan is less formal than the ones you're accustomed to. It's more like a commonsense memo about how to reach your book's audience. You can find marketing plan templates on the Internet, though I've not come across one that's geared toward book promotion. Instead, they use a form of business school–influenced language that is unsuited to book publishing. Avoid them and concentrate instead on getting some smart ideas down on the page.

Publishers have a standard set of promotional tools, some or all of which they will put into use depending on the level of commitment to your book. These might include extra discounts to booksellers, advertising, a publicity tour, signage for bookstores, an unusual and eye-catching jacket, and so on. It's not your job to try to list all of these tools in the marketing plan. What you offer the publisher is more valuable—inside information about your book's potential, and how to define and possibly reach markets that they may not have thought of. The publisher may already be willing to promote your book and have set aside some funds to do so, but perhaps the staff cannot come up with a specific, individualized marketing or publicity plan that makes sense for your book. If the right idea doesn't materialize, then they may spend the money on ideas that do not make sense for your book, or else will divert the funds elsewhere.

The marketing plan will take you a significant amount of time and thought to prepare, but the effort is worthwhile. As you get closer to the publication date, other ideas will strike you as essential to include in your plan. As your plan evolves, alert your editor and publicist about any late-breaking brainstorms.

You will discuss your finished plan with your editor. Ask if he or she thinks it's on target, if your expectations are realistic, if you've missed anything appealing or interesting about the book. Enlist your editor in support of the plan and even to contribute ideas to the plan. Your editor's support will give you leverage in getting your ideas adopted later by others on the publishing team.

Your publisher can use your plan in a variety of ways. Your editor can draw from your book description to write jacket copy for the book, the tip sheet (also called the fact sheet or title information sheet), which encapsulates information about the book for the sales force, and catalog copy. The publicity department can use your marketing plan to create a publicity plan, press releases, and press pitches. Points you raise in the plan might later become the basis of media interviews and provide ways for the sales reps to pitch your book to booksellers. The marketing department might draw on your ideas to create promotions for booksellers, to write catalog marketing copy, and to alert the appropriate sales reps about any local connections you have in their territories. The subsidiary rights department may share parts of the plan with book clubs and foreign publishers to demonstrate the book's potential in the marketplace.

As you begin writing your marketing plan, you will probably be unaware of your relative position on the publisher's list. At this early stage your publisher has probably not decided upon your book's potential in the marketplace. Present the plan about six to seven months before your book's publication. You can present it closer to publication than that, but take advantage of the time you have to build support. To be certain to deliver the plan when it can do the most good, check with your editor about the key publishing dates at your publishing house. You want to deliver the plan to your editor before he or she participates in any key launch or strategy meetings.

BOOK MARKETING BASICS—A SUMMARY

The good news is that your marketing plan can have a genuine impact on the way your publisher decides to publish your book. Learning to think like a marketer for your books means that you will:

- Identify the many target audiences for your book.

- Read the book publishing trade press to understand your publisher's point of view.

- Read and watch all media with an eye to figuring out how your book fits in.

- Brainstorm with others about marketing opportunities; seek out as many brainstorming opportunities as possible.

- Make a commitment to writing a marketing plan.

2

How to Write a Marketing Plan

A MARKETING plan tells the publishing staff what's interesting, unusual, and special about you and your book and how you think the book can be promoted. To get an idea of your publisher's sensibilities, ask your editor for a copy of the latest catalog. From a thorough reading, you can find out how the publisher presents and describes their books. You might use this as a guide for writing about yours.

Don't plan on writing the plan in one sitting. A useful tactic is to begin your plan as a rough draft that you embellish over the course of several weeks, as you develop more ideas about how to market your book. For best results, start your plan a full year before your publication. For instance, I'm editing a book we're publishing 10 months from now: Our sales force requires my fact sheet about the book this week to start the presales process. Now my company works with a particularly long lead time, but don't assume your publishing house is much different. (Don't panic if you're reading this and your book's publication date is only four months away. You can still come up with terrific marketing ideas within a shorter time frame.)

Make your plan a thrifty one. Focus on promotional ideas that do not require your publisher (or you) to spend a lot of money. If your title is a "midlist" book (i.e., any book not at the top of the publisher's priorities), then you stand little chance of persuading your publisher to spend the kind of money required for print ads and other paid media. Where you stand a better chance of getting some money is for publicity, which is relatively inexpensive. "Publicity" refers to the array of strategies that generate positive (and free) media coverage of your book. This coverage can create the ever desirable word-of-mouth attention—when your book becomes the topic of conversation between friends and colleagues as they recommend your book to one another.

While you're thinking about appropriate publicity strategies, be honest with yourself. You know your own comfort level in public forums. If you are wildly uncomfortable with the idea of doing live interviews or bookstore appearances, then do not force yourself. On the other hand, if you're uncomfortable with the idea of giving interviews, but think that with some media or speech training that you could become an effective communicator, then perhaps push for a publicity tour.

A publicity tour—a trip to several cities where you will be interviewed by the media and appear in bookstores—is warranted if your book is topical and makes for interesting conversation on talk shows, which then might draw audiences to attend bookstore signings or talks. A tour also makes sense if your book is controversial, if you have an unusual life story to tell, or followed an unusual path to becoming a writer. On the audience side of the equation, having friends and family in other cities who can help drum up support is an important factor in determining whether you should tour.

If you want to go on a book tour, then let your editor know when your book is acquired or at least before you've turned in a marketing plan. That way your editor can begin to advocate for this in early conversations with the publisher and director of publicity. Do you have friends and family in other cities and free places to stay on tour? That alone is a convincing argument for a book tour. One author (whose books are now *New York Times* bestsellers) traveled with her father on his many business trips when she was launching her early novels. While her publishing house paid for her flights, her dad let her crash in his hotel room to help defray the costs of the tour. Many authors stay with friends as a way to decrease hotel expenses for the publisher and divert the savings into the rest of the campaign.

A book tour is merely one tool to promote a book. You will become familiar with many other ways to get the word out about yours. Among them are concentrated press pitches to the national press in New York and

Washington, DC, local book signings and publicity in your hometown, giving talks for local organizations, postcard mailings or emails to your contacts and growing list of readers, radio interviews conducted by phone, blogging and website activities, and online interviews. The beauty of the Internet is that when you engage an interested reader, a book purchase can be merely a click away.

Some sections of your marketing plan will duplicate the author's questionnaire that your editor may ask you to complete. However, as the marketing plan more specifically addresses how to sell your book, redundancies are expected and forgiven. The marketing plan should include:

- Book title, your name, and contact information

- Goal

- Book description

- Target audience(s)

- A positioning statement or pitch—the one or two sentences that capture the essence and appeal of your book

- Why you wrote the book—the background story

- Marketing strategy and campaign

- Sales handles and media angles

- Biography

- Competitive titles/comparative titles

- Personal and professional contacts (who might help in the book launch or who might give you a "blurb" or endorsement)

- Prior public speaking and media experience

- Sales leads

- Your top 10 media and marketing wish list and ideas how to target them (this last item is optional, but it's really impressive and puts you way ahead of your competition on your publisher's list)

THE TITLE

The title of your book is essential to its effective marketing. Its job is to tell and sell: It needs to tell what the book's about and sell it to your audience.

If your title and subtitle are not satisfactory, your editor will work with you to get them right before the book is first presented to key sales reps and other publishing staff. Your title should be set before catalog copy is finalized. While you can still change your title after the catalog has been printed, you've lost an important opportunity to make the right impression on booksellers and the media. Wrong titles in the catalog have a sneaky way of getting into bookstore computers, which causes confusion once the book is published when booksellers try to reorder.

Consider the titles of these novels: *All the Pretty Horses*, *The Curious Incident of the Dog in the Night-Time*, and *The Mysteries of Pittsburgh*. Or these works of nonfiction: *Angela's Ashes*, *The Best and the Brightest*, *The Cake Mix Doctor*, *The Dangerous Book for Boys*, *Good to Great: Why Some Companies Make the Leap and Others Don't*, *The Liars' Club*, and *Einstein's Dreams*. These books all have great titles that pique a reader's interest to explore further. A good title, in combination with the book jacket, will prompt the bookstore browser to pick up the book. Book reviewers sift through mail sacks filled with books by unknown writers: The book with an intriguing title or cover design is likely to get pulled out of the pile first.

In some cases the title and subtitle might define the audience, making it clear to the prospective customer that this book is for them. For example, a book by Eileen Behan called *Eat Well, Lose Weight While Breastfeeding* targets new mothers who want to lose the weight they gained during pregnancy; and Sarah Schlesinger's *500 Fat-Free Recipes* targets home cooks looking for no-fat dishes whether for health or dietary reasons. Both books performed exceptionally well.

DEFINE YOUR GOAL

The first important step in writing a plan is to understand and articulate your goal for the book. A goal helps you focus your expectations and forces the publishing team to address its own expectations.

Essentially you need to explain why you wrote your book in one or two lines.

Perhaps you want your book to become a bestseller, or to influence public policy. You might hope to create enough attention with the book's publication to attract paid speaking engagements and consulting assignments, or perhaps earn enough money from your royalties to quit your day job. Perhaps you want to leave something for posterity, or to share your expertise with people who need it. You may even intend to build a long-term writing career.

Make your stated goals realistic so that you appear credible. If you've written a book on a narrow topic and you expect a bestseller, then you've got to produce a convincing marketing plan. It bears repeating: Do not push unrealistic expectations on your publisher.

A DESCRIPTION OF YOUR BOOK

Many people working on promoting or selling your book may never have the time to read it. It is to your absolute advantage to carefully convey what your book is about in two to three tightly written paragraphs. What you write will become the basis of how the publishing staff will describe your book when they go out to sell it. Your description may even be used verbatim throughout the course of your book's publication in all manner of promotional materials—from tip sheets and catalog copy to flap copy and press releases.

DEFINE YOUR TARGET AUDIENCE

Michael Schrage, author of *Serious Play*, *No More Teams!*, and *Shared Minds* says that anything you can do to reduce the ambiguity in your book's marketing is very helpful to your publisher. One approach, he says, is coming up with a reader profile, literally writing down who you think your readers are, their age group, their personal and professional interests, and so on. Your definition of your audience will help you and your publisher to concentrate resources on reaching your largest groups of readers. To determine who these treasured folks are, ask yourself these questions:

- While you were writing your book, did you envision a particular kind of reader?

- Which individuals will benefit from reading your book? Think broadly, as your book likely has more than one target audience. (For example, the individuals who might benefit from this book include authors; editors and agents, who help their authors figure out how to market themselves; publicists, who need or want additional training; publicity directors, who can give the book to their authors to help make them an effective part of the publicity process; and small publishers, who need publicity and marketing advice.)

- Who do you think will buy your novel? If your answer to that is "all readers of general fiction" then try to further refine your thinking. Among readers of fiction, are they women who enjoy the Oprah-favored hardship-to-recovery novels, men who enjoy techno-thrillers, readers of mysteries with crossover mainstream themes, readers of family dramas, and so on? Beyond fiction readers, could other readers take an interest in your book? For example, *Ship Fever*, a short story collection by Andrea Barrett, has characters based on historic individuals in science. The harrowing and brilliant title story is about the infectious diseases carried by Irish immigrants to America escaping the famine back home. Several audiences exist for this book: readers of literary fiction, readers and practitioners of the biological and ecological sciences, readers of history and historians, and Irish Americans. Other examples: Tom Clancy's techno-thriller novels are clearly of potential interest to past and present members of the armed forces. Publishers of legal thrillers often market books successfully to the legal community. Less obvious: Your novel has a lovable cat in it? Then let *Cat Fancy* magazine know about it so that you can reach cat lovers. Or you've written a novel of political intrigue set in Berlin? Have your publicist send your book to the foreign correspondents based in the Berlin bureaus in case you can score a mention in their columns or at least get some good word of mouth in their circle. Your novel features recipes? Get the book into the hands of the food editors at the top papers as well as the book reviewers to reach readers interested in food. As you begin to define your audience, ways to reach them will begin to suggest themselves to you.

■ Can your book attract readers of books from other genres? For example, Jonathan Harr's nonfiction book, *A Civil Action*, was of interest to readers of crime, law, and politics. Yet the publisher also positioned the book to attract readers of fiction, as it had a strong narrative style.

■ What age groups might take interest in your book? If you're writing about midlife themes, then younger readers are less likely to be interested so don't spend time figuring out how to reach them. Try to focus on the core groups that will be engaged by your subject matter.

■ Are your potential readers located in a particular geographic region? If your book takes place in Iowa, for example, then Iowans should be a particular target of your marketing and publicity campaign.

■ Does your book speak to men or to women or both? For example, to define the audience for your diet book, do some research to find out the size and characteristics (or demographics) of the dieting marketplace. You might then target women of certain age groups, who are the most frequent dieters and buyers of diet books and diet products. And share the statistics you discover in the marketing plan: Your publisher can use that information to help convince booksellers of the need for your book.

■ Would your book interest people of a particular ethnic background, whether because of the themes you address or because of your own identity?

■ Would your book appeal to consumers of certain media? If you're unsure how to define your audience, then your intuitive sense of the media that your potential readers consume can provide a clue. For example, if you've written literary fiction, then perhaps your audience is to be found among the highbrow and educated listeners of National Public Radio. Or if you've written a joke book, a sex book, or a book about popular culture, then perhaps reach your readers through the zany, zoo morning-drive radio shows. (To really refine your understanding of these listeners, access the stations' media kits online to find out the demographic breakdown of your potential readership. Do the listener demographics as outlined in the media kits conform to your sense of who your audience might be?)

Remember: By defining your audience, you can figure out which media to approach—or suggest that your publicist approach—to get publicity coverage for your book that will reach your readership.

POSITIONING STATEMENT (OR PITCH)

When sales reps pitch your book, they need a concise way to talk about your book's content and audience, and why it stands out from all others. The positioning statement is one or two appealing sentences that make the listener highly curious about the book. The idea behind the positioning statement is to create a way to talk about the book that will appeal to booksellers, the media, and the reading audience. The finely honed positioning statement will become the basis of how everyone in your publishing house can talk about the book with their various constituencies, and it's how you'll talk about the book, too.

One way to understand positioning is to consider movie advertising. For example, the successful independent film *Billy Elliot* was positioned as a feel-good movie for general audiences about a young boy from a tough northern English mining town who beats all odds to become a dancer. Actually, the film contained more violence than the advertising suggested, with a plot about labor unrest, as well as a homoerotic subplot. Had the film been positioned as a gritty film about union busting, or as a film for gay audiences, then it probably would not have been as broadly successful with general audiences.

To come up with the positioning statement for your book, think about how you would briefly answer the questions "What's your book about?" and "Who will read it?" *The Hot Zone*, by Richard Preston, was positioned as a true-to-life medical thriller about the ravages of the

Ebola virus and its potential threat to us all. The positioning was intended to frighten us into reading the book as well as to capture general fiction readers, and those of quality nonfiction. The book became a bestseller.

A book's positioning might also be tied to the author's authority in the subject, or the topicality or controversial nature of the subject. Comparisons to other authors also help position a book by suggesting that the readers of one author will like the work of the other author. For example, the publisher of a young writer whose work is reminiscent of, say, John Irving's early work might position the novel as a similarly impressive debut. When Doubleday published *Faerie Tale* and wanted fantasy novelist Raymond Feist to reach a broad mainstream audience, the house compared his crossover potential to Clive Barker's, who had recently achieved bestseller status. (The publicity department extended the idea even further and booked a segment on ABC's *Good Morning America* with both Clive Barker and Feist.)

In an interview with *New York Magazine*, Little, Brown publisher Michael Pietsch described the strategy behind the marketing campaign for *Infinite Jest*, a literary novel by David Foster Wallace. Addressing the challenge of marketing such a long book—it was more than 1,000 pages— Pietsch had two strategies: to spur jealousy and therefore intense interest among the literary writing community through a word-of-mouth campaign, and to challenge readers of literary fiction with the premise "Are you reader enough?" The campaign worked beautifully, with news of the book first creating a stir in the publishing industry, and then going on to become a *New York Times* bestseller.

Why should we care about your book? The positioning statement answers this question.

It may be difficult for you to distill your entire work into the one or two sentences of a positioning statement. But it's worth going through the exercise to get the pitch right as this can be such a valuable tool to your publisher. When your editor presents your book to the sales force and publicity departments, the thought going through those sales reps' and publicists' heads is "How am I going to sell this book?" They get busy coming up with pitches of their own (or they remain skeptical about their chances of success with your book), but if you can give them something good to work with, all the better for you and your book.

Publishing consultant Bella Stander (www.bookpromotion101.com) gives seminars for published or soon-to-be-published authors to teach them how to come up with ways to promote their book. More specifically, a good part of her workshops focus on how to come up with the "elevator pitch" for a book. What does she mean by that? Say you're on an elevator and have, perhaps, 30 seconds to describe to a stranger what your book is about. The elevator pitch is your quick, succinct description of your book that makes that person want to read it. It answers the questions: So what? and Who cares? (Full disclosure: I have spoken at a number of Stander's workshops.) Stander also offers one-on-one consultations for authors about their publicity and marketing.

WHY YOU WROTE THE BOOK—THE BACKGROUND STORY

A short background piece—a couple of paragraphs or a couple of pages long—about how and why you wrote the book can be extremely useful information for publicists and sales reps. Your path to publication—whether it included 50 rejections before you found a publishing home, or was a beeline from your English professor to your editor—can become part of the promotional story surrounding your book. (Do not assume that an interesting story surrounding the book's acquisition is known or remembered by anyone else in the publishing house other than your editor. Include it in your written materials.) The piece might also include any unusual events in the research and writing of the book or specific influences on your work. (And the media loves a good rags-to-riches story, or tales of overnight success, or of many years of dedicated hard work suddenly paying off. If this applies to you, say so.)

If you're unsure about what qualifies as interesting material to include in this section of the plan, start reading profiles of individuals—not just writers—in your local paper, in magazines, online. Pay attention to how the subject talks about his or her work. Now think about the information or impressions that you were trying to convey to readers through your own work. Did the book require any special research? Did you work part-time jobs while raising your children and yet still managed to find time to write? The details of your writing career might seem mundane to you, but may interest your publicist or the media. Unsurprisingly, one of the most common questions that audiences ask writers at bookstore appearances is "When do you write?" or "How do you find the time to write?" Readers have an endless interest in the process of being or becoming a writer.

During publicity interviews for his memoir, David Crosby said that he became a musician because he wanted to meet women. (Actually he put it *way* more graphically than that!) Which is to say that as you write the back story on becoming a writer, you might inject a little humor or self-awareness to leaven what might otherwise come off as ponderous and self-absorbed. Simply put, be aware of the general impression that you create.

What all the background information attempts to get at is what marketer and agent Marly Rusoff calls the "story" about your book, or the way that the book is talked about—both in-house and, it is hoped, among consumers. Your editor will use your "story" to pitch the sales force; your publicist will use it to pitch the media. Bear in mind as you're writing this section of the plan that what you may view as uninteresting may intrigue those working on your marketing campaign.

If an author does not provide information about how the book came to be, a publicist will sometimes talk to the author in an effort to extract an idea of who they are and of the book's background. But by the time the publicist gets to you, your book has most likely already been discussed with the sales force and perhaps even presold to some booksellers, which means that you've missed some chances to share some interesting background details about your book. So don't wait until you're called on!

THE MARKETING STRATEGY AND CAMPAIGN

The marketing strategy section of your marketing plan addresses how you or your publisher will reach your readership, and will probably require the most time and thought and continual refinement on your part. This section is really the heart of your campaign—the blueprint for how you will reach your target audience. Here are many ideas and examples of successful strategies that you can draw on to develop your own marketing strategy. Not all examples will apply to every book, but they should serve to stimulate the marketing side of your brain.

- Can your book tie in to local or national political campaigns? One publishing house, Addison-Wesley, went right to the core market for a book called *Reinventing Government*, by David Osborne. Intending to get the book in the hands of reporters covering the New Hampshire primaries, the publisher sent staff to New Hampshire to put complimentary copies of books in the local bars where the national political reporters were hanging out. Many of the snowbound journalists wrote about the book. The subsequent coverage and sales launched the book onto the *New York Times* bestseller list.

- Could your book interest policy makers? Then suggest that your publisher send copies of the book to public opinion leaders and opinion columnists, who can become important mouthpieces for your book. For example, you could send a book that touches on political or social matters to influential government leaders who are interested in your subject matter. For a promotion for *The Tenth Justice*, the bestselling novel by Brad Meltzer about a group of fictional clerks at the Supreme Court, the publisher sent books to the current clerks and other members of the Justice Department, knowing that this audience could help build interest in Washington, DC.

- Does your book contain a strong spiritual or social message, in which case a church or other religious congregation can help spread the word? Send copies of a self-empowerment book to the church leaders, for instance, and invite them to share it with their congregations.

- Is your book aimed at a specific self-help readership? Then you might try working through the national media, which offers many service stories. For instance, a diet book, by definition geared to any American who thinks he or she is overweight, might be launched by national television media appearances, as well as excerpts or coverage in women's magazines and websites.

■ Does your book have a niche readership and, if so, what media vehicles reach that readership? For example, the publisher of a basic early childhood parenting book would target first-time parents by trying to sell excerpts to parenting magazines, offering free excerpts to parenting sections of newspapers (which often can't afford to pay for excerpts) or online parenting sites, and setting up media interviews for the authors. A few lucky authors have had their books excerpted in the promotional brochures of the baby formula manufacturers Similac and Enfamil. Other books have been bought by HMOs, which offer information about preventive medicine to their members.

■ Does your subject matter appeal to a dedicated group of journalists and other professionals who can generate exposure and buzz for your book? For instance, a sports book could be promoted to sportscasters who might mention the book during on-air broadcasts of games. Your publisher might also contact the public relations people at local sports arenas to see if they will put copies of the book in the pressroom at game time.

■ Should you take a grassroots approach to building an audience? Laurie Beth Jones, author of *Jesus, Inc.* and *Jesus CEO*, toured the United States in her RV to reach more cities than a traditional tour could finance (www.lauriebethjones.com).

■ Can you team up with other writers in your genre? Mystery and romance writers sometimes go on the road with other writers to help build one another's audiences and to save on expenses. To launch short story writer Helen Simpson, her publisher teamed her up with better known writers for a series of bookstore readings. (Doesn't this remind you of a rock concert's lesser-known act appearing before the headliner event? The music industry may still be reeling from the effect of free online music sharing but we can still learn from the marketing end of the music business, and better late than never.)

■ Can your book tie in with a local or national event? The publication of a book about the fashion industry called *Model*, by Michael Gross, coincided with Fashion Week in New York City, when the new collections are launched. The publisher delivered press packets to the hotel rooms of fashion reporters who were in town for the shows. The author was ubiquitous at Fashion Week parties and events, and was widely quoted everywhere in the fashion press. The publisher also worked with Saks Fifth Avenue, which mounted window displays that were themed around the book.

■ Can you link your book to events in the news? When former First Lady Hillary Clinton professed an admiration for Eleanor Roosevelt, publishers of Roosevelt biographies reprinted works by and about Roosevelt, and positioned their authors as experts on first ladies. More recently, emails about the planned dismissals of several U.S. attorneys sent by prominent members of the U.S. Department of Justice and the White House were made public. Will Schwalbe, the coauthor with David Shipley of *SEND: The Essential Guide to Email for Office and Home*, took the opportunity to write a memo to former U.S. Attorney General Alberto Gonzales about the risks inherent in emails; the memo was cleverly written in the form of an email and appeared on the *Huffington Post*, a prominent political blog. Political campaigns, the latest crime statistics, teacher shortages, reading scores, teenage behaviors, caring for aging parents, the economy—whether declining or booming—the environment: Reporters cover all these issues on a continuing basis and need to interview experts. Keep current with what's going on in the world, and if you see an opportunity to tie into the news headlines, then let your publicist know. If you are doing your own publicity, call or email the appropriate reporters to let them know about your book.

> ## *Linking to News Events—A Word of Caution*
>
> Link to the news in a tasteful manner. A publishing newsletter that appeared a few days after the destruction of the World Trade Center urged readers who had written books about grief, airport security, or skyscraper architecture to get in touch with news organizations to make themselves available for interviews—all legitimate topics. But before you tag onto a catastrophic event, ask yourself if you are providing a public service by letting the media know of your expertise, or merely straining to connect your book to the event. Many public relations people caught flak from the press for attempting far-fetched connections to 9/11 on behalf of their clients. Perhaps there are just some occasions when you shouldn't be thinking about book sales.

- Could your book be part of cultural programs organized by your local department store? For example, Macy's stages hundreds of special events a year and will invite authors to participate as guest lecturers. The store will also offer the authors' books for sale.

- The people that you interviewed for your book may help you promote it. Confirm your sources' willingness to help out and state that fact in the marketing plan. For example, James Hirsch's *Hurricane* is an authorized biography of Rubin "Hurricane" Carter, for which Carter appeared in interviews with the author. A writer of fiction might call upon any intriguing individuals he or she interviewed in doing background research for the novel.

- Can you link your book to a holiday or an anniversary? Check out a directory published every fall called *Chase's Calendar of Events*, which lists all kinds of quirky events, birthdays, celebrations, and anniversaries, such as National Pie Day and American Education Week, among many others. You may find an event to connect to your book's marketing.

- Are you an effective or charismatic public speaker? Then emphasize public appearances and media interviews as a key part of your campaign.

An Author Creates Marketing Events for Her Own Books

Bestselling author Lois Wyse was the author of 65 books. A marketer by profession, her success offers lessons for would-be marketers who want to sell their books to readers. Her books all have ready-made, built-in marketing angles. For a book called *How to Take Your Grandmother to the Museum*, she traveled with her coauthor, who happened to be her young granddaughter, to a number of tour cities where the local museums provided the press-worthy local settings for publicity interviews. For *Women Make the Best Friends*, the publisher set up friendship teas and parties in bookstores where women were encouraged to bring a friend. And for *Funny, You Don't Look Like a Grandmother*, Wyse had the idea to set up power breakfasts for grandmothers. The concept created a lot of buzz and print coverage and the book reached number one on the *New York Times* bestseller list.

Wyse's advice for new authors is to look at all your contacts and spend some time brainstorming with them. Ask your friends who they think is the audience for the book, and what in your book will make someone want to buy it. And then, who is that someone?

- Does your book's success depend on favorable and widespread book review coverage? A campaign for a literary novel or work of serious nonfiction might focus on getting galleys into the hands of book reviewers and influential critics on the board of the National Book Critics Circle, which awards an annual literary prize. To accomplish this you might urge your publisher to print a higher printing of galleys or advance readers copies (ARCs) than usual. (Galleys—a bound paperback-style edition of your book printed three to five months before its publication—allow reviewers who have a long lead time to read and review the book in time for the book's publication.) Some online social networking sites are putting galleys or prepublication advance copies of books into the hands of interested readers and inviting them to post their reviews: Library Thing (www.librarything .com) was among the first to develop such a program. Similarly,

Amazon—while not (yet) a social networking site—created an early reader program called Amazon Vine to allow customers to post opinions, a good way to stimulate sales. Research the social networking sites to see which one might be interested in offering early copies of your book to members and so stimulate prepublication buzz for your book among its intended audience.

■ Are you good-looking or unusual-looking or are you an eccentric? Some publishers promote the author's good looks (Michael Chabon for his first book, *The Mysteries of Pittsburgh*) or outrageous personality (David Sedaris for his collection of essays *Naked*) alongside the book's literary merits.

■ Can you create a trend story around your book by conducting informal surveys or polls? You do not have to be Gallup. As long as you poll people in a credible way, your results can form the basis of a press pitch for your book. The survey might even provide the basis for your book, as well as offering a marketing angle. For a book called *Married Lust* from Redbook magazine, the author Pamela Lister conducted research through surveys on the very active *Redbook* website and got 10,000 responses. What men and women reported about their feelings about sex and marriage became both part of the book's content and its press coverage. If you have a website and attract sufficient traffic, then you can conduct your surveys online. For a book in development on the counterintuitive findings about parenting, authors Po Bronson and Ashley Merryman offered a survey about child rearing attitudes on their blog and websites (www.pobronson.com.) They have also collected email names to notify interested respondents about the book when it comes out.

■ Does your book have any strong visuals? A photo insert with just a few stunning photographic images can create significant publicity for a book. State in your marketing plan the nature of the images that are available to help market the book. Strong visuals can become the basis not only for press coverage but also for striking window displays for booksellers. For David Halberstam's book *The Fifties*, the publisher created sets of easel-backed photographs of iconic images from the 1950s for displays.

■ Can you create a photo opportunity around the subject of your book? You might stage an event with a compelling visual that local or even national press will want to shoot. A shot of you handing a check to the president of a local charity is not an exciting photo. But a shot of the prizewinners at your costume party to raise money for that charity is a good photo op.

■ Does your book tie into current social trends and concerns? For example, a recent parenting book posited the idea that parents are less important than peers in determining a child's values and behavior. The argument generated a media interest because it tapped into parental anxieties about whether we're raising our children right.

A Book Campaign Connected to News Events That Did Not Sell Books

Shortly after Heidi Fleiss and Sidney Biddle Barrows had been arrested for running call-girl rings, we published a book by Hollywood's Madame Alex. I booked her on a major national talk show for which she procured several call girls for an on-air appearance. (Actually, she provided the phone numbers but I had to do the actual procuring—one of my more bizarre publicity assignments.) The women, some of them in disguise, were interviewed in the New York City studio while Madame Alex appeared live remote from Los Angeles. Well, the Madame couldn't hear the talk show host very well through the studio earpiece, so when he asked her if her girls were "ambitious," she misheard and replied indignantly, "My girls are not bitches." As book promotion segments go, it was hugely funny, but didn't sell many books. In this case the subject matter was interesting to the audience as an amusing media story, but not as a book. The point is, you can reach the potential consumer, but is your book something that they really want? That is the gamble that publishers make every day with every book.

■ For any project-based book, you might show finished projects. For a crafts book bring the finished crafts on-air on a television demo; for a floral arranging book you might present different styles of floral arrangements. The publicist might offer free excerpts of a project and illustrations to newspapers, websites, and blogs.

■ Does your book offer controversial information? If so, you can withhold information until publication date to build interest and suspense among your target audience. The idea behind embargoing a book until publication is that upon release, the information will instantly create news headlines that will in turn drive instant book sales. If the information leaks out before publication, then the news value is lost since books are not available for consumers to buy at the very moment when they're most interested in it. Typically books that are published like this are gossipy celebrity books, or exposés. But if your book contains never-before-known information within your field, then alert your publisher to that fact: They are not experts in your subject area and may not recognize the news value in your work. That's not to say they have to embargo your book, but they should treat the information carefully to take maximum advantage of its news-making potential.

■ Does your book offer a contrary point of view? Then stir up controversy through public or journalistic debate over your position.

■ Will your book provoke curiosity among people who think they are in the book? A publicity technique that sometimes works nicely to promote popular biographies and autobiographies, as well as books of a sensational nature, is sending a copy of the book's index to the individuals who are mentioned in the book. This tease gets them talking about the book—just what you want.

■ Can you attract guests to a book party who will start serious buzz about your book? Parties can also be useful in the context of an industry trade show, where your publisher can introduce you to key booksellers. They can also work as sales opportunities say, if a friend is throwing you a party and your publisher or a local bookseller brings books to sell to the guests. However, unless a party can achieve some real word of mouth or sales for a book, do not expect your publisher to pay for one just for the sake of it. (Of course, if you simply want to have fun and celebrate your book's publication, then by all means party on. As Peter Osnos, former book publisher and now senior fellow for media at The Century Foundation says, "Always have a book party. Surrounded by friends, family, and colleagues, this is the moment when the satisfaction of a completed book is shared with people who acknowledge the accomplishment.")

The Worthwhile Book Party

Some people in the business think it gauche to sell books at a party; other pragmatic folk will take a sale anytime and anywhere (that's me!); others suggest that friends should buy books at bookstores, not at parties, to help build bookstore reorders. I'm in the "sale is a sale" school of thought, because I'd like to capture the sale for a book at the moment the consumer is interested. You will simply have to make up your own mind about what to do. If you sell the books at your parties or any other events, then buy them at your author discount rate, charge full retail price for the book, and you get to keep the profit. (And depending on your contract, you might get paid a royalty on those copies.) Many authors will have a friend help sell the books so that they can meet their guests instead of handling a cash box. If your publisher is involved with your party, then your publicist can bring books either to sell or give away.

To keep party costs down (and therefore have access to more funds for other elements of your campaign), call a liquor company. Ask to speak to its public relations account manager or publicist about contributing the liquor for a promotional event. Explain what the party is for and offer to fax the guest list including your guests' professional titles. If the size and caliber of the guest list are suitably impressive, you may get a free case of wine or champagne. Ask your book publicist to make this call, if she is willing.

If you throw yourself a party, ask your publicist for the names of the appropriate staff to invite including any book club editors or paperback and audiotape publishers who might be interested in your book. Likewise ask your publicist for a media mailing list, or to send invitations to the media. Even if your publisher is not paying for the party, publicists are often willing to absorb the cost of printing and sending invitations in their budgets.

▪ Can you come up with a celebrity angle or a connection to celebrities? If you've got the time and energy, you can try to seek and obtain endorsements from celebrities. Be warned: This task may involve many months of relentless pursuit through celebrity publicists and agents. But there are better ways to create a celebrity angle. For instance, let's say a high-profile heiress goes to jail for drunk driving. Your book about the hard road to sobriety in young people is perfectly positioned to make you an expert commentator in the media.

▪ Can you create an award? When his novel *Secrets* was published, Kelvin Christopher James created an annual writing contest with a cash prize that he presented to three New York City high school students for their essays about "Getting Along in New York." The award gave me the angle to book him on NPR's *Talk of the Nation* along with the first-prizewinning student, as well as to get a column in the *New York Daily News*. The next year, his publicist used the award angle to get a column in the *New York Times*. All this for a literary short story writer and novelist. Another example: Novelist Rona Jaffe created a foundation through which she gave grants to women writers for fiction, poetry, and creative nonfiction. Every year the award's presentation is covered in the media. (While Jaffe died in 2005, her eponymous award contines.)

▪ Can you host a fund-raiser or other charity event to raise your profile? Create a local cause–based event for any institution in need: the public library, a children's day care center, a museum, a literacy program, any organization that has some reasonable connection with the message or intent of your book. Can you get local dignatories involved in your fund-raisers to help attract more media attention? A friend of mine, Lana Turner, has organized many fund-raising events, including house tours in Hamilton Heights, a prosperous area in Harlem, New York, followed by dinners with authors as the star attraction at each home. The fund-raising campaign received press attention, as well as exposure for the authors. Can you create this kind of event in your community and invite other authors to participate?

▪ Can you stage a stunt? No, you do not have to dress up like a bunny or a clown. But if you're willing to make yourself the center of attention, and if you make the stunt a visual one, then you've improved the chances that television news crews will want to tell your story. The attention-getting event could be a contest, a fashion show, or a pet parade—anything out of the norm for your community.

▪ Can you create a quiz around your book's theme? A quiz can provide entertaining material for radio discussion about your book, or else for pickup in the media. For example, a publisher of a first-aid book created a quiz to test the readers' first-aid knowledge that was picked up in the *New York Daily News* as well as other publications. A quiz can be serious or light entertainment depending on the nature and tone of your book. To promote *Don't Know Much About the Civil War*, author Kenneth Davis created quizzes and a crossword puzzle. Many of his radio interviews for the book took the form of "Stump the Author" with callers to the shows asking tough questions about the Civil War (www.dontknowmuch.com). Taking the appealing concept of testing your knowledge a few steps further, the publishers of the American Heritage Dictionary created "Define-a-Thon" events, run much along the lines of a spelling bee. Similarly, National Geographic hosts an annual contest testing kids' geographical knowledge.

Still having trouble figuring out your strategy? Try some serious brainstorming with your editor, who may even introduce you to a publicist or the publicity director at this early stage. (Later, you will have more brainstorming sessions with the publicist who is formally assigned to your book.) The editor and publicist will have a sense of which stories will interest the media, while you provide insight about your book. But don't stop there. Tackle your friends and family and colleagues to try out your marketing ideas on them. Sometimes the best ideas come out of collaboration: Getting other people's point of view will help you shape your media pitch.

Advertising Versus Publicity: Why Publicity Is More Cost Effective Than Paid Advertising

Your marketing plan should focus on publicity rather than advertising. Most advertising is too expensive to warrant spending on most books. For instance, one small black-and-white ad in the *New York Times, Washington Post, San Francisco Chronicle,* or the *New Yorker* may cost $10,000 to $15,000. Those short book ads that you hear on National Public Radio? Recently, they cost upward of $13,000 for a minimum commitment to twelve 15-second spots. Other types of book advertising include bus or subway ads (pricey), television ad campaigns (you've got to spend at least $25,000 on production and then another $50,000 minimum if you're buying network time; less if you're focusing on cable), and radio advertising (around $20,000 or more). True, online banner ads are another opportunity, but while less expensive a form of advertising, as an isolated marketing tactic they won't create buzz. Publishers can rarely afford to spend enough on advertising to create a sufficient number of impressions among the target consumers to deliver sales, and most book advertising is bizarrely obscure. Take a look at the book ads that appear in the *New York Times,* a favorite advertising vehicle for many publishers, where you will frequently see book ads that never actually explain what the book is about: How, then, will the target audience know that the book is for them?

In contrast, you have a much greater chance of reaching and, more important, engaging readers through a publicity campaign. A 10-city tour might cost $20,000 to $30,000. A tightly focused national media campaign—requiring travel to New York and Washington, DC, will cost your publisher $500 to $4000, depending where you live. If Canada is part of the book's market, then the national media in Toronto might also be included in the national campaign. Typically, book tours cost your publisher between $1,200 and $2,500 a city. Expenses include the hotel room, airfare, ground transportation, and food. The media coverage you can get through publicity is more extensive than what you can buy with the equivalent dollars spent in advertising.

SALES HANDLES AND MEDIA ANGLES

During the sales call with a bookseller, the sales rep will talk about the book's sales handles to clinch "the buy." The rep may have to present the entire publishing season in one sales call so there's not much time to convey the heart of your book—perhaps a few minutes or less. This is where the sales handles in your marketing plan will come in. Sales handles are the specific facts that prove the book's appeal to its market and why the book will do well.

Sales convey what's new and different about your book—your authority as the writer, the marketplace for your book's topic, its advantages over the competition, and its marketability. For example, for a new hypothetical dog-care book that focuses on natural health, the sales handles might be as follows (and do not be dismayed by the fact that I've thrown in the kitchen sink for this nonexistent book, as most books do not have quite so much going for them):

1. With the recent crisis in tainted pet food, pet owners more than ever want information about healthy food and nutrition.

2. The author's last book sold 85,000 copies.

3. The author is an established expert on dog care and is a frequent guest on national television.

4. The author is planning to underwrite an aggressive marketing campaign and already writes a dog-care blog and gets 400 visitors a day.

5. The book reveals for the first time how a dog owner can increase his or her dog's life span by changing its diet.

6. More than 60 percent of U.S. households own at least one dog and the number grows every year.

7. The book has been endorsed by celebrity animal activist Brigitte Bardot as well as Monty Roberts, the author of *The Man Who Listens to Horses*.

8. The *Washington Post* has compared the author to bestselling author and veterinarian James Herriot.

9. The book includes easy-to-read diagnostic flow charts.

10. The book includes a resource section telling readers where to buy natural dog care products.

If you can come up with a solid three or four sales handles, you are helping your publisher (and yourself) considerably.

Sometimes the sales handles can also serve as media angles, the key points your publicist will use to convince the media to interview you or to cover your book. In coming up with your media angles, think about what your book offers to consumers. Does your book:

- Make people's lives easier?

- Help them make more money?

- Entertain them?

- Get them a date or save their marriage?

- Help them accomplish a goal?

- Enlighten them?

- Help them save time, or decrease stress, or raise their kids?

- Help them improve their health?

By focusing on the end benefit to the consumer, you can come up with the angles that will help your book get media coverage. For example, for the same hypothetical dog-care book, the media angles might be:

- The author can bring animals from his practice onto television shows.

- The author can demonstrate how to prepare your dog's food (and so avoid any risk of purchasing packaged food that might be tainted or otherwise unhealthy).

- The author can talk about how changing the health and diets for the dogs in his practice has changed their lives and the lives of their owners.

In other words, the sales and marketing angles are merely ways to communicate to your core audiences: booksellers and media. Even if your publisher finds your sales and marketing handles a little off the mark, they are a helpful starting point for a conversation with your publisher about your book's publishing strategy.

One approach to coming up with media angles for your book is to ask yourself the questions you'd like to be asked in your media interviews and then figure out how you would answer them. A twist on this is to ask yourself what PR pro Justin Loeber of Mouth Public Relations asks all the authors he works with: Name the three reasons the media should interview you. If you can name them, then you've probably just come up with the media angles for your book.

YOUR BIOGRAPHY

Your publisher will use your biography in promotional materials including the book's jacket. Interesting aspects of your past may become the entire basis of the marketing strategy, which is why you've probably heard the story of J. K. Rowling's life as a cash-strapped single mother before she hit it big with Harry Potter. Mention your professional credits, any previously published books, personal achievements, notable events in your life, your birthplace, other places where you've lived, and where you attended college.

When she begins a campaign, publicist Meryl Moss of Meryl L. Moss Media Relations has several conversations with her clients to understand the person she is pitching. She tells the writers she works with, "I want to know you in ways that you don't think I want to know you." What she means is that what may seem prosaic to you might become essential information that colors her pitch to the media. Therefore, in creating your biography, spend a little time talking to friends and family to access long-forgotten events of possible interest to the media.

Martin Arnold of the *New York Times* wrote an article on author biographies and a tendency toward cuteness by mentioning the family pets, as in "he lives in Pennsylvania with his wife and two dogs." The lesson: Be aware of the impression you're creating in your author bio. (Do you really want to come off as cute?) Read how other authors describe themselves on their book jackets: Do their bios make them sound accessible and appealing? Use the exercise of writing the bio to get used to the way you will be talked about and perceived during your book's promotion.

Do not be daunted if writing the biography is difficult for you. After all, it's not often that you are called upon to summarize your life. If you've written a novel that's in any way autobiographical, then your author bio offers an opportunity to discuss the parts of the book that are based on your own experiences. Mary Gaitskill's short story collection, *Bad Behavior*, has a character who was a prostitute. Gaitskill's self-declared so-called bad behavior became the basis for the book's publicity campaign—a tricky position for the author to take. But Gaitskill's way of talking and writing about herself made her seem oddly vulnerable, and her personal appeal lay in the intersection of her bravado and her sensitivity.

Other writers feel that admitting to autobiographical elements in their novels diminishes the artistic merit of the work. The extent to which you share aspects of your life is entirely up to you, but if you reveal yourself, prepare yourself for what may seem like harsh public judgment and misunderstandings about you. Public opinion is even worse for memoirists, as critics judge not only their written words but also their lives and how they've lived them.

Although you may feel that your ethnicity is no one's business, certain marketing opportunities are available to you if, for example, you are Jewish or black or Irish-American. Many African-American bookstores and Black Expos (or fairs) offer good venues for writers to promote and sell their books. Jewish book fairs and newspapers are happy to promote Jewish writers.

Mention any languages that you speak other than English as well as your nationality. The information is helpful to the person in the subsidiary rights department who will sell foreign rights. Sufficient international interest might open the opportunity to promote the foreign editions of your book. Plus, the consulates and embassies of many countries in the United States have programs to support books of interest to their constituencies and will sometimes even help support book tours and book parties. (Of particular note are the French Cultural Services of the French Embassy and the German Book Office.)

BOOKS THAT COMPETE OR COMPARE WITH YOURS

What books are similar to yours, in terms of shared audience or similar literary quality or subject matter? In a sales call, the sales rep will mention comparative titles to the bookseller, who will then check their sales figures. The thinking is that if the comparative titles sold well to that customer base, then your book could sell well, too. Therefore, in your marketing plan, provide the title, author, publication date, publisher, and ISBN for books in your subject area. If the books on your list are well known in your field, then you should explain how your book differs. With the continual drive for newness among the media and consumers, many books on the same subject easily coexist in the book marketplace. What matters is that you convey to your publisher, and by extension to booksellers, that your book offers a particular point of view that will help it sell well in its category, despite the competition. Do not throw down every title that's been published in your field on your list of comparative titles. Other books that have sold poorly do not help your sales rep sell your book, unless the rep can convince the bookseller that yours is simply the best book on the subject.

When the sales reps were selling an important cookbook on the Hearst list, their use of comparative titles during the sales call was essential. The buyers naturally compared the book, *The Good Housekeeping Cookbook*, to its key competition—other name-brand cookbooks. The booksellers, while aware of the high sales figures for branded cookbooks, wanted to know that book offered something different and special to the consumer. Consequently, our marketing team prepared a detailed chart for the sales reps that compared the *Good Housekeeping* book to all its competition point by point, including page count, trim size, number of recipes, number of color photos, ability to lie flat, and so on. The evidence was overwhelming: The book clearly surpassed its competition in most categories, and the sales reps got the buys they were aiming for.

Comparative titles also help your publicist frame a pitch for the book. By telling a book reviewer that "Jane Doe's new detective will satisfy fans of Hercule Poirot," the publicist helps the book reviewer understand right away that the book is a mystery of a certain category and caliber. Of course your book is an original work. Nonetheless, an apt comparison to another successful book communicates a salable handle for your book.

You might also compare the book to a film or other form of entertainment. In my letters to reviewers, I once compared a first novel by Alexander Stuart called *The War Zone* to the film *Blue Velvet*, in that the apparently normal surface of the characters' lives cloaked a seamy emotional turmoil. The concept worked and the novel was widely reviewed.

Take your time coming up with comparison titles that will help your sales reps and publicist make the case for your book. This task is often left to the editor or the editorial assistant, but you know the literature in your field better than anyone else does.

PROFESSIONAL AND PERSONAL CONTACTS

Let your publisher know how your friends and associates will help make the book a success. They may throw you a party, arrange for you to speak at local organizations where they have their own contacts, monitor the presence of your book in stores once it's published, or give you a spare bed when you're in town on your publicity tour. Try to plumb these possibilities before you begin your marketing dialogue with your publisher. The more support you can establish in the early planning stage, the more likely you are to motivate your publisher to get excited about your book's potential.

If your contacts are sufficiently well known at least in their own field, then ask them for a "blurb," or a positive endorsement, for your book. This will appear on your book jacket or book flaps and in the publicity material. The names of the "blurbers" are meant to signal to the consumer that your book is worthy of buying and reading.

If you do not know any suitable blurbers, then simply write a list of names of appropriate potential candidates. Be imaginative. Though you've written a book on design, a novelist or even a filmmaker might give you a quote if your work resonates somehow with their own. Look for blurbers who will trigger positive recognition among your target audience. (The other day a friend told me that she bought a book only because a novelist she admires had endorsed it.) Your editor may approach some of the blurbers you've suggested through his or her own contacts.

Your contacts are also useful for you to create a mailing list database. When you create this list, do not stint yourself. Dig deep into your past friendships and business and academic relationships. People will be happy to hear what you're up to. Your list will likely be a hybrid of regular mailing addresses and email addresses, the latter being a much more efficient way of getting the news out. Beyond your own email contacts, tap into the email addresses of your friends and family: Ask them to kindly forward your announcements to anyone they know who might also take an interest in your work.

You will state in your marketing plan your intent to announce your book to your database just as the book arrives in bookstores, to motivate your core audience to buy your book early on. That way your book can start to build some sales momentum and reorders. Building the lists can be somewhat time-consuming, even dull, so it is a task best handled over a long period of time, perhaps for 15 to 30 minutes a day over several weeks or months. But take it seriously.

One author mastered the art of marketing among his existing relationships to create a grassroots groundswell of interest in his books. With the assistance of a supportive family, he assembled significant crowds at bookstore readings in 10 cities for his first novel. "Book signings are a way to say thank you," this author says, and acknowledges his friends and family as an essential part of his publishing process. He advises authors to concentrate on developing a core list of people who care about you and your books.

At your bookstore appearances, collect business cards from the audience to add to your mailing list. Likewise, when readers correspond with you, add them to your mailing list, too. You can also collect the names of interested readers from your website. You can do this by asking visitors to register at your site, but that's best done when they're on a page where you're offering something in exchange, such as the chance to win a prize. If you require a first time visitor to register upon arrival, chances are they'll skitter away. Over the years, bestselling novelist Debbie Macomber has built an active mailing list of 75,000 readers. "Every one of those readers has been in touch with me personally," Macomber said in an interview with the *Seattle Post-Intelligencer*. When she goes on a bookstore signing tour, she alerts readers in the appropriate destinations about her forthcoming apperances. Bottom line: Your mailing list will become a career-long tool to reach your readers.

PRIOR PUBLIC SPEAKING AND MEDIA EXPERIENCE

If the media has ever interviewed you, or if you regularly deliver speeches as part of your professional life, tell your publisher. Your level of experience and competence in public speaking and in media appearances will influence the size and scope of the publicity campaign that your publisher puts together. Be specific and name the groups you've spoken to and attach any significant press clips to the marketing plan. If you have videos of your interviews on television, state here that you can make those available upon request. They are essential for your publicist to be able to book you on national TV.

YOUR TOP 10 PUBLICITY GOALS

List your top 10 publicity goals in your marketing campaign. By defining what you want, you've given the publisher's publicity and marketing team something to react to and address. Your goals may very well change or evolve as your book progresses toward publication. That's okay. Just make them realistic to demonstrate that you understand the media market. For example, if you write commercial fiction, understand that the chance of a review in the more literary book review media is slim.

To know what's within reach, you have to do your homework. Read and watch the media to find out where your book could fit in. It takes practice to understand what the media thinks is a good story.

Often the most desired goal for a successful publishing launch is to get on *The Oprah Winfrey Show*, for two decades the single most influential media on book sales. Oprah Winfrey has democratized and demystified the act of reading, and so has encouraged reading—and book buying—among a broad swathe of the population. (As one book marketer says, all publishers should bow down daily in the direction of Chicago, where Oprah's show is taped, and thank her for what she has done for reading and for book sales.) However, no secret formula exists for appearing on *The Oprah Winfrey Show*. A persistent publicist can talk an author onto the show after months and even years of pitching a concept, or sheer fluke and luck of timing might lead to a speedy booking on the first try. And even then, the appearance does not guarantee bestsellerdom. While you should put time and thought into figuring out how your book might interest Oprah's producers (and more on that later), getting on *Oprah* shouldn't be the only focus of your book's campaign strategy. In any case, before you decide what show is right for your book you should familiarize yourself with that show by watching (or taping) and observing: what topics are discussed, what authors are interviewed, how is the interview conducted, and so on.

Beyond Oprah, the following media outlets have influenced book sales:

- Longer format shows like *Dateline NBC* or *60 Minutes*.

- The national evening news on one of the network stations—a supremely difficult placement to get but one that reaches many millions of people.

- *Today*, *Good Morning America*, *The Early Show*—ranked by audience size, the networks' morning television shows offer a great media launch for a book. In Canada, a spot on *Canada AM* is desirable.

- Television shows with on-air book clubs. When Oprah ended her book club in 2002—she started it up again a few years later—other TV shows jumped into the breach and launched book club segments including *Today*, which has a bestselling author choose a book and then invites a reading group on-air to talk about the title; and the monthly "Reading with Ripa" segment on *Live with Regis and Kelly*. Other influential TV shows include *The Daily Show with Jon Stewart* and *The Colbert Report*. Both comedy shows offer a surprisingly serious book discussion that influences book sales. (One of the more startling author appearances on *The Colbert Report* was Poet Laureate Robert Pinsky serving as moderator and judge in a dueling metaphor competition between Colbert and actor Sean Penn. The segment was hilarious and bravo to Colbert for introducing Pinsky to millions of people who may never have heard of him before.)

▪ National radio programming, like *All Things Considered*, *Fresh Air*, and the *Tavis Smiley* show as well as regional NPR shows help sell quality literary fiction and nonfiction. In Canada, the CBC's *Sounds Like Canada* has been ranked as the top radio show in terms of motivating listeners to buy books. Despite the radio show's raunchy content, *Howard Stern* can be surprisingly productive for authors who want to reach a male audience.

▪ A write-up in a nationally syndicated column can reach millions of readers. For example, columnists who sometimes mention books include William Safire (language, *New York Times Magazine*), Dave Barry (humor, based at the *Miami Herald*), and Liz Smith (celebrity gossip, *New York Post*). You can find the names of hundreds of syndicated columnists and sample columns online (Chapter 6 lists the appropriate links).

▪ CNN's *Larry King Live*

▪ PBS's *The Charlie Rose Show*

▪ A feature in the national wire service, the Associated Press

▪ A feature article in one of the nationally distributed newspapers like *USA Today*, the *New York Times*, the *Wall Street Journal*, and, in Canada, the *Globe and Mail*. Also effective is a feature article in a local newspaper—even a small community paper—which gets syndicated through one of the news syndicates like Gannett, Scripps Howard, Cox, or Knight Ridder.

SALES LEADS

Special sales—high volume and generally nonreturnable orders to non-bookstore customers—can be highly profitable. Finding viable leads is one of the most time-consuming parts of the special sales business. Most special sales outlets are unconcerned about the newness of a title and will reorder a book as long as it continues to sell. Unlike bookstores, which buy books based on catalogs, galleys, and sales reps presentations, most special sales channels will consider a book for purchase only after they've seen a finished copy. Even then, some special sales outlets may not commit to a book until they've test-marketed it or until the appropriate buying season.

Special sales accounts include mail-order catalog companies (Signals, Miles Kimball, Jessica's Biscuit); nonbook retailers (Renovation Hardware, T. J. Maxx, gift shops); display marketers (Scholastic, Books Are Fun, Publications International) who set up book displays in schools, hospitals, and businesses and collect bulk orders; gift wholesalers (Cogan Books); and others.

Special sales opportunities exist primarily for nonfiction books, and rarely for fiction. If your book has some connection to a type of product or service, then it is a candidate for special sales. Your book may in fact already include special sales leads in its resource section. For example, if your book is about candle making, then you've probably listed vendors of candle-making materials, which your publisher's special sales reps can approach to sell your book. Cookbooks benefit from many special sales opportunities, as nonbook retailers will frequently offer cookbooks as customer premiums. Books about health are candidates for premium sales to HMOs or to pharmaceutical companies.

THE AUTHOR PHOTO

In some instances, the author photo becomes a significant part of a marketing campaign. Certainly you've seen the pictures of celebrity authors and noted writers: Their images are an important part of their book launch. For unknown authors, an interesting or unconventional author photo can help create a media profile, as newspapers and magazines are more likely to reproduce the image adjacent to a review or interview. Susan Minot's debut novel was promoted alongside her striking author photo. Sebastian Junger's first book, *The Perfect Storm*, was released along with images of the handsome author hoisting logs, presumably shot during his stint as a climber for a tree company. Dennis Lehane's publisher had him photographed to capture a moody noir image just like the atmosphere of his novels. Publishers view the image of the author as a vital part of the marketing campaign, particularly for novels and memoirs.

Your publisher will eventually ask you to provide a photograph of yourself for use on your book jacket and in publicity materials. Ask your editor if the publishing house intends to pay to have you photographed. Publishers will sometimes pay for author photos (an item that may be addressed in your contract). Otherwise you will need to provide a decent jacket photograph on your own dime.

If you do not have a good recent photo of yourself, and if your publisher isn't planning on having one taken, then have an experienced, if not professional photographer take your picture. The photo should be shot in color, giving the publisher the option to print in either color or black and white. Or email your publisher a JPEG file of a photo taken with a digital camera, which can also be handy later for posting on your website or blog (if you have one) or for sending your image to publications or websites that might want a photo to accompany a review or an interview.

Some authors give their publishers blurry photos or family snapshots for their book jackets. Many people are ambivalent about their looks, and their anxiety often reveals itself in their choice of author photos. Remember that the consumer will often look at the picture of the author while considering buying a book. And a couple of book critics have told me that as they peruse the pile of books to decide which ones to assign for review, a good-looking author photo "doesn't hurt." One fellow, a book reviewer who was notorious for not returning publicist's phone calls, called me back moments after I left a message that the book I was calling about was written by an attractive blonde of Jewish and Italian descent. I played shamelessly on that critic's particular preferences, but he called me back to talk about the book. Even radio producers will respond to an author's good looks, though the author's appearance can clearly have no effect on listenership. I called one NPR producer to follow up on a pitch about a relatively unknown author. She booked him on the spot, telling me in a knowing voice, "Oh yes, we've all just been looking at his photograph." You have every reason to look your best or most interesting in your author photo.

Every now and then an article appears about the "new" trend of promoting the images of good-looking authors, and usually someone is quoted huffing and puffing about how terrible and debasing to the literary merits of the work this is. This may be true, but it is naïve to pretend that critics and producers do not make any judgments based on someone's appearance.

Again, do your homework. Go to the bookstore and browse the bookshelves for author photos that you think are successful and attention-getting. You will notice how family snapshots rarely make ideal author photos. For a comprehensive and engaging overview of a gallery of author photos, check out a book called *Author Photo—Portraits, 1983–2002* by Marion Ettlinger, one of the leading author portraitists.

BESTSELLER LISTS—HOW IMPORTANT ARE THEY?

Not all lists are created equal, but they can all help your book. The *New York Times* bestseller list used to be the only one that really counted, but its clout has diminished in recent years. The two largest chains, Barnes & Noble and Borders, no longer use the *Times* list, and instead use internal sales rankings to determine bestsellers and the candidates for up-front display and discounting. (Discounting is good, making the book more affordable for more people.) Although it is no longer the only game in town, a spot on the *New York Times* bestseller list gives the sales reps an opportunity to call on their customers and sell-in more copies. Success breeds success: Your appearance on the list gives your publicist another way to pitch your book to the media and earns you another credential.

Other national bestseller lists include the *Wall Street Journal* and *USA*

Today, perhaps the most purely democratic of the lists, as it mingles all formats and price points. Books sometimes become regional or local bestsellers before becoming national bestsellers. Many newspapers offer their own bestseller lists, with the data gathered from local bookstores, which means that effective publicity in those regional markets can help to drive books onto the local lists quickly. Others will run lists supplied by *Publishers Weekly* or the *New York Times*.

Some authors have attempted to manipulate the bestseller lists by asking friends and associates to buy multiple copies of their books within the same week. This tactic can work in a limited way only: It is expensive and some booksellers will not report bulk purchases to bestseller lists to eliminate the chances of list manipulation. Before you embark on this strategy, think of the economics. Say you purchase 50 copies of your hardcover book in one market, then you're probably investing about $1,300 just to get onto one local bestseller list for one week, a tactic that may or may not work. For the amount of cash you will have to spend, you may as well enlarge your publicity efforts to extend your reach further, create some real readers and word of mouth, and produce effects that last longer.

Amazon.com has taken bestseller lists to another level by ranking every single title's sales at any given moment. Infuriatingly or wonderfully, any author can find out how his or her book ranks at any time of day. A good television or radio appearance can stimulate immediate sales and send you zooming to the top of Amazon's list or sales ranking, only to plummet again by the next day. Remember that the ranking is no indication of sales volume—which can be a very low number—but rather a reflection of how your book's sales compare to every other book on this site in that hour. The Amazon rankings are a helpful measure of whether a media appearance or good review reached and motivated consumers, but try not to read anything more into the sales ranking than that. Also, don't fall for the idea of manipulating your bestseller rankings on Amazon by having friends purchase your book all at once in a given time period. And please don't fall for one of the paid services that offer to help you top the Amazon lists. Unless you really want the ego-rush from printing out and framing your high ranking, the cost of manipulating the rankings simply doesn't deliver a long-lasting effect in the marketplace. For an excellent and in-depth discussion of Amazon rankings, see Steve Weber's book about online marketing called *Plug Your Book*.

Stumped for Marketing Ideas?

For hundreds of great ideas about how to market your book, go to www .publicityhound.com. Joan Stewart, aka The Publicity Hound, shares information about how to pitch the media, where to find media resources online, how to prepare for your interviews, what not to say to reporters, and so on. Her tone is smart, friendly, and inspiring. You can subscribe to a free weekly e-newsletter, which offers tips on publicity and promotion. Not all of them will apply to your book, but you will come away with many good ideas. Print out the extensive archives for previous editions of this newsletter and you will find much of interest. You can also participate in her reasonably priced teleseminars on topics like how to get on TV and radio talk shows. If you can't participate, then you can buy the transcripts.

AN AUTHOR'S MARKETING PLAN IN ACTION

Beth Bruno's marketing plan for her self-published parenting book, *Wild Tulips*, is short and simple. (Actually, it is deceptively simple because it evolved over time, as the author discovered what marketing techniques work and what don't.) While the written plan does not elaborate on specific strategies, it does serve as a constant reminder to Bruno of her overall intent.

The plan is governed by Bruno's knowledge of her core audience, her experience in education, and her understanding of her own capabilities: Bruno is not trying to take on more than she can manage herself. Instead she started in a methodical, grassroots way and built from there.

Marketing Plan: *Wild Tulips*

Audience: mothers, fathers, teachers (pre-K through adult), special educators, mental health professionals, pediatricians and OB-GYN physicians, grandparents, child caregivers, writers, small business owners (which Bruno includes because she networks with local businesspeople at luncheons and other gatherings), homeschoolers, clergy, nonprofit family support organizations, storytellers, and the young at heart.

Media: newspapers, magazines, television, radio, the Internet.

Retail: bookstores (chains and independents), gift shops, other stores, wholesalers, libraries, and corporate and nontraditional markets.

General approaches in all markets: direct contact (in person or by telephone), email, regular mail (sales letters to friends, colleagues, and associates), advertising, book talks, book signings, conference seminars, and seeding (free copies of *Wild Tulips*).

Bruno has implemented her plan in an ongoing and effective campaign. Some of her marketing efforts included:

- Direct sales efforts to friends, relatives, and colleagues, which "started sales off with a bang," Bruno reports.

- A local librarian was featured in a newspaper article about a "gifts to newborns" program. Bruno contacted the librarian, who then bought 80 copies of the book.

- Appearances at local bookstores and libraries have had good crowds, good book sales, and generated invitations to speak at other events, including at writers' groups about self-publishing.

- A local hair salon agreed to display a poster and copies of the book, as part of a celebration of local artists and authors. The salon sold dozens of books and invited Bruno to return for a fund-raiser later in the year.

- Bruno booked herself into the annual Connecticut Storytelling Festival to present a workshop about the craft of writing stories. (There are local, statewide, and regional storytelling festivals that take place annually around the United States.) Jonesborough, Tennessee, is home to the National Storytelling Festival in October. Bruno contacted the Storytelling Store there and convinced them to offer *Wild Tulips*.

- Bruno is developing parenting workshops for preschools. She is also targeting relevant organizations with grant money to be possible sponsors of the workshops.

- Online initiatives included chats and free articles, though Bruno felt that for her, online promotions delivered less value relative to the amount of time invested.

Bruno's experience offers an encouraging example for writers undertaking their own promotions. While she initially felt shy calling bookstores, her confidence was bolstered after the first few positive responses. "After a few people said yes, it got easier," she says.

HOW TO WRITE A MARKETING PLAN—A SUMMARY

Tackle the marketing plan's individual components to come up with a complete, step-by-step plan for promoting your book. Once you've assessed your own goals for the book as well as your personal resources—such as your contacts—you will define your audiences and figure out how they can benefit from your book. Spend some thoughtful time figuring out your positioning statement and your audience. You can't come up with a meaningful marketing strategy until you know who you are trying to reach and why.

Then you will figure out how to reach your audiences through various strategies such as:

- Connecting to current news trends or creating a controversy

- Conducting a survey

- Creating a celebrity angle

- Joining forces with other authors to set up group events

- Planning for demonstrations or tastings

- Providing interesting visuals

- Public speaking

- Setting up an award

- Staging a fund-raiser, a panel discussion, a party, or a stunt

- Continuing to pay attention to the media to identify opportunities for your book

3

You've Submitted Your Manuscript. Now What?

To work effectively with your publishing house, you must understand the normal sequence of events leading to your book's publication. You need details about who does what and when they do it. For example, some houses require that the publicists make contact with all the authors at least once. Other houses do not. Their publicity staffs have no obligation to contact an author—particularly one whose book has no significant plans. So if you have not heard from your publicist within four months ahead of your book's publication, then ask your editor for his or her name and politely make contact. This way you can apprehend in good time what, if anything, the house has planned for your book. Then, at least, you have information early enough to self-market and self-promote your work.

THE NUTS AND BOLTS, PART ONE: WHO DOES WHAT?

The following job descriptions apply to a large publishing house. In a smaller house or an academic press, the job functions may be shared among a smaller staff. However, the nature of the work remains the same for any size house.

Publisher: The decision to acquire a book, how much to pay for it, and the approved marketing budget all fall under the publisher's purview. The publisher establishes the overall direction of the publishing house and is ultimately responsible for all the decisions that are made about the publishing list. Usually the editorial, sales, and marketing staffs all report to the publisher. In some houses, the sales team reports to another person, perhaps the president, which means that the publisher has less direct control over the sales force.

Editor in Chief/Editor: Your editor most likely reports to the editor in chief who would have endorsed the original acquisition. The editor in chief works in partnership with the publisher and brings in the books that the publisher is willing to publish. Your editor is the point person for all activities surrounding your book. He or she is responsible for conveying everything that the publishing staff needs to know about your book in order to position it in the marketplace and publish it well. The editor is your advocate and representative in-house.

Sales Director, National Account Reps, Field Force, Special Sales Reps, Telemarketing Sales Force, Canadian Rep Group: Everyone in the sales group sells your book in his or her sales territory. The reps take their direction from the publisher, who sets the house's agenda at sales conferences, and from the sales director, who pushes them to reach their sales targets. A few of the sales reps will work at the publisher's headquarters. These are likely to be the reps that sell the national bookstore chains and special sales reps. Other reps live throughout the United States and Canada and call on accounts in their assigned territories. Some reps are employed by the publishing house. Other reps work on a commission, probably for several publishing houses.

Subsidiary Rights Director: Book club, serial, foreign, audio, large print, and paperback reprint sales are handled in the subrights department. The director may have evaluated the book club and international sales potential of your book before its acquisition. Serial sales are excerpts of your book that appear in magazines or newspapers. First serial refers to excerpts that appear before publication date; second serials run after publication date.

Director of Production and the Production Staff: You may never meet the production manager assigned to your book. This person works with the printer to determine manufacturing costs based on the trim size and extent of your book. He or she buys the paper and other goods and services required to manufacture your book, and sets the press date. If you deliver your manuscript late, the production manager, in tandem with the managing editor, works with the printer to try to accommodate the tardiness and keep your book on schedule.

Art Director: This person may run the jacket design department, and depending on the publishing house, may also run the interior design department. A successful jacket or cover design is of utmost significance to a book's success.

Marketing Director: This person is often involved with acquisition decision-making, particularly during a competitive acquisition that requires the publishing house to produce a marketing plan. The director will set overall advertising and promotion budgets. The marketing staff assembles and distributes all the sales materials such as catalogs and copies of book jackets, handles the preparations for sales conferences, and sets up mailings and promotions to booksellers.

Publicity Director: The person who runs the publicity department formulates the overall strategy for the top titles on the list and supervises a staff of publicists. The directors generally meet with the major media several times a year to present the publishing list. Some directors, particularly in smaller publishing houses, will handle some book campaigns themselves. With a number of talented publicists rising to the top of the publicity department, a publishing house might have several directors, but only one of those runs the entire group. This person will also get involved with competitive acquisitions.

Your Publishing Team

You will work most closely with your editor, your publicist, the editor's assistant, and the publicist's assistant. Yes, everyone else is important, too, but these four people will be among your closest contacts and sources of information. From the moment your book is acquired, you will make friends with your editor's assistant. Underpaid and overworked, these assistants are the unnoticed heroes in any publishing house. Treat your editor's assistant well and you will have a valuable ally in your camp. The assistant can tell you why the editor isn't calling you back, remind the editor to call you, and help generate buzz in the house among all the assistants (who go to parties with assistants from other houses and start to spread the word about you and your book).

Similarly, the publicist's assistant, whom you will meet later, can keep you in the loop when the publicist is too busy to get back to you right away. This person is learning publicity and may set up a few of your bookings. He or she is probably also taking care of all your travel arrangements if you are touring. Be a friend to this person, too.

Many other people are involved in creating and publishing your book. The managing editor helps keep all the schedules on track, the copyeditor may be the unseen hand that made good suggestions to improve your book, and the sales and marketing administrative staffs put together your sales kit. Take the time to find out their names and drop them thank-you notes. (Never underestimate the power of the handwritten thank-you note, especially in these electronic days when receiving a personal letter has become a rare event. The recipients will remember you.)

NUTS AND BOLTS, PART TWO: THE SEQUENCE OF EVENTS THAT LEAD TO THE PUBLICATION OF YOUR BOOK

Understanding the flow of work that leads to your publication will help you get involved at key junctures to influence your book's success. This is a typical schedule at many publishing houses, but you should check with your editor about your own book's schedule. Here is the sequence:

- Acquisition
- Scheduling of a publication date
- Manuscript submission and editing

- In-house launch meeting where your editor formally presents your book to key sales, publicity, and marketing staffs. (Publishing houses have different names for the launch: It could be called publishing planning, the title meeting, or something else. But the substance of the meetings is the same.)

- Jacket planning and design

- Ongoing publishing planning leading up to the printing of the publisher's catalog and sales conference

- Sales reps make the first early calls on national bookstore chains

- Sales conference or the meeting where your editor (or other staff person) presents your book to the entire sales force. This generally occurs about three months after the launch meeting, and three to eight months preceding your publication date depending on how early or late your book is scheduled in the publishing season.

- Editor sends out bound galleys for advance endorsements (three to five months before publication). Publicist sends galleys to long lead magazines and book reviewers.

- The print run is set (two to three months before publication, longer for illustrated books)

- Publicist books the tour and sends the book to reviewers (four to six weeks before publication date)

- Early trade reviews begin to come in (*Publishers Weekly*, *Kirkus Reviews*, *Library Journal*, *Booklist*, and *The Horn Book* and *School Library Journal* if you've written a children's book)

- Books are shipped to bookstores about two to four weeks before publication date

- The in-store date is when your book is expected to be fully distributed and publicity can start to happen. The publication date itself is generally cosmetic unless there is a marketing reason to choose a specific date.

A Publishing Time Line From an Author's Point of View

Author Neil Gaiman published a blog (before they were called blogs) in the months leading up to and after the publication of his novel *American Gods*. Read it at www.americangods.com in the journal archives to get an excellent idea of the sort of planning and activities that can take place leading up to a book's publication. The site also offers a good example of how the author creates an ongoing and authentic conversation with his readers.

HELP YOUR EDITOR PREPARE FOR THE LAUNCH MEETING

The publisher, marketing, sales, subrights, art, and publicity directors and some of their staffs attend the editors' presentations for the books planned for publication in a particular season. In a large publishing house the launch meetings take place over several days. During the editor's presentation, the members of the publishing staff are making up their minds about the book's potential, whether it should get a tour or a significant promotion budget, the likely size of the first printing—all of which makes the editor's on-target positioning of the book essential. As an author, you can influence the meeting from afar. The primary task is to get the decision makers as excited and motivated as possible about your book. Truth is that most of them *want* to get excited about books. You just need to show them why they should like yours.

Begin by offering to help your editor prepare the tip sheet, the working document used at the launch meeting. Every publishing house has its own format, but it is usually one or two pages long and includes a book description, sales handles, your bio, and main competition. A good tip sheet helps equip everyone in the publishing house with persuasive information about the appeal of your book. Thus you can help your editor be an effective advocate for your book at that crucial meeting.

If a marketing reason exists to request a specific publication date, then now is the time to make that point. An obvious example is a book on love that might carry a Valentine's Day publication date. A book that addresses the workplace could be launched on Labor Day. A book on education might be published in August to coincide with the bookstores' back-to-school promotions. Black History Month takes place in February, around which bookstores will set up promotions. Gay Pride Month is in June, which is why some gay-theme titles are published then to afford maximum display exposure in bookstores. A book that ties into a historical anniversary could use that date as publication day. Again, check out *Chase's Calendar of Events* to find a date that might be appropriate.

Publication dates used to serve as concrete guidelines for reviewers for when a book review should run. While book review editors try to schedule a review to appear around the same time as the book's publication date, many book review sections are backlogged. Some reviews appear weeks after a book's publication. Unless the book's publication is highly anticipated—like the final installment of the Harry Potter series—reviews can trickle out over the course of several months. If you choose a publication date that is somehow tied to an event or anniversary, then you might be able encourage timely reviews.

If you think you should tour for your book, then prior to the launch meeting suggest to your editor that the house avoid publishing the book in television's sweeps months—February, May, and November. During sweeps, the ratings determine how much the stations can charge advertisers. Therefore, the programmers and producers schedule the most compelling and sensational shows and guests possible. If your book does not address a hot topic, and if you're not a celebrity, your chances for television bookings are slim. If your book's publication date occurs in a sweeps month, then work with your publicist to schedule your tour during the following month, rather than trying to book you on television during the months of greatest competition.

The launch meeting is an opportunity to distribute additional information about you and your book. This might include any significant press coverage for previous books or achievements, excerpts from past good reviews, a mini biographical essay that entertains and informs, and so on. Concentrate on providing only the most interesting and useful information for your publishing team.

Last, and this idea may sound kooky, but there's nothing better than food to perk up a room full of tired people who have been in a daylong meeting. It gives them a welcome, unanticipated break. And most important for your book, the sugar temporarily raises everyone's energy level. Arrange with your editor and editor's assistant to have cookies and milk (or some tasty something) delivered to the meeting just as your editor is presenting. The participants will remember you, even though you are not present, which is what you want. It doesn't matter if your book is a cookbook or not. This is just plain old bribery by food. But don't be discouraged if your editor objects to having food at the meeting. The approach might not fit his or her style. Go with the flow.

THE RIGHTS GUIDE

The rights guide is an annotated list of upcoming titles that the subrights department creates for foreign publishers and book clubs. Again, ask the editorial assistant whether she can use your help in producing the summary paragraph that's required for the guide, or show you what she plans to submit to the subrights department. Very often this task is done in haste and with limited knowledge of your work, so your involvement could make your book's description just that much better.

The subrights department might try to sell foreign rights to your book at the Frankfurt Book Fair. (Publishers from around the world assemble in Frankfurt every October to buy and sell publishing rights. A savvy subrights director can make an array of foreign sales for a book in the course of that one week.) Give your editor as much of the manuscript as possible by September for the rights director to take with her to Frankfurt.

BOOK JACKET DESIGN

Your publisher will schedule jacket design meetings around the time of the launch meetings—either shortly before or after. Help your editor and the jacket designer by outlining several cover concepts. Spend some time in bookstores to understand which jackets are effective and eye-catching. Educate yourself about the competition in your subject area. With many book-purchasing decisions made at the bookshelf (as opposed to predetermined by the customer before going into the store) your jacket's selling power is essential. Make a list of the visual elements in your book that could inspire an interesting book jacket design. Your art director will not have time to read every book on the list and will appreciate your notes.

Ask your editor if you can see early drafts of jacket designs. Note that if you do not have jacket consultation rights in your contract, then your publisher is not obliged to show it to you until it's finished. Some publishers are more willing than others to show jackets to the authors. If you do get to see the jacket while it is still a work in progress, allow yourself to be surprised by an art director's originality. Then listen to why your editor thinks the jacket is effective. If you're not sure if the jacket is right, show the jacket to your agent, your friends and associates, and then get back to your editor within a couple of days with your suggestions. In the end, if you don't like the jacket, do not accept a design that you really dislike. If your book is not a lead title, the publishing house may not give your jacket the same priority you do, so you and your agent might need to lobby hard for a new design.

Once a front cover design is approved, ask to see the spine and back of the jacket, too. Publishers often forget to embellish the spine of a jacket, which is often the only part of the book that's exposed to consumers in bookstores. If your cover has a graphic element, ask that it be repeated on the spine to help the book stand out. Or if the book has an all-type cover, then eye-catching colors and typeface should be used on the spine.

It is said that verbal people often lack a sense of design. If this is true, then it makes sense that both you and your editor might have trouble figuring out the direction to suggest to the jacket designer. Some editors do not know what they want but tell the designer that they will know it when they see it, which does not make the art director's task easy. Conversely, some designers are not sensitive to the appropriate use of fonts for a good reading experience, and make the type treatment on the book jacket subsidiary to the overall design. Be reassured. The jacket for your book will finally emerge despite—perhaps even because of—the tension inherent in these creative relationships. You can assist the process to your benefit. An easy way to provide input is to let your editor know which jackets (in the same category as your book) you find appealing. Having something to show the art director is very helpful.

A note of advice: Show respect to your jacket designer. His or her ego is on the line, too. Yes, the book is yours, but the design is not: The designer's creativity is on display, just as your own is. Be sensitive to your designer's feelings and you will more likely have a cooperative and willing design partner in creating the ideal jacket for your book.

If the jacket you hate is the one that ends up in the publisher's catalog, it may not be too late for the jacket to be redesigned. Most publishers will respond to an author who is truly unhappy with a book's jacket design. As soon as your new jacket design is ready, make sure that your editor follows up with the art department and the sales administrative staff to redistribute revised copies of the jacket to all the sales reps to share with their accounts. Check that your editor has alerted the sales force that the jacket has changed.

PUBLISHING PLANS TAKE SHAPE

The planning season following launch and leading up to sales conference is the most critical stage leading up to your book's publication. This is roughly a three- to four-month period during which you have a real chance to truly convince the publishing team that your book deserves time and money to reach its market.

Just after launch, talk to your editor about the ideal publicist for your book. Encourage your editor to lobby the director of publicity for the publicist of choice. The editor will not always get his or her request, but can sometimes influence the publicity director's decision. Whether the publicist assigned to your book is good, bad, or indifferent, you can make him or her an essential ally in your campaign. During this period you will also assess whether to hire your own publicist.

At the appropriate time—either shortly before or after launch—your editor should arrange for you to meet key people in the organization. If the editor doesn't mention this to you, then ask when he or she plans to introduce you to the others on your publishing team. The introduction might be informal—you meet the team in passing when you drop by your editor's office. Or your editor might set up a formal planning meeting with your publicist or with the larger publishing team. No matter the size or formality of the meeting, treat it like a sales call, as though you are informing the participants for the first time why they and the buying public should read your book. Do not take offense if no one in the room other than you and your editor has read your book. These people are *busy*. The editor may not have given them your manuscript yet, or they may not have had time to get to it. Do not add to their sense of guilt: Most people in publishing have a never-diminishing stack of manuscripts by their bedsides. Instead, view them as the public you will convince to read your book that very night.

Bring copies of your marketing plan for everyone attending the meeting. Do not assume they've seen your plan or have had a chance to read and focus on it. At the meeting, your job is to ingratiate yourself. You are so thrilled to be with these people right now in this room that they can feel your glow. And you will maintain this attitude throughout the campaign because it will motivate your publicist. (I worked with an author whom the short-story writer William Maxwell would have described as "a woman who never draws breath except to complain." Every time I called her, even when I had good news, she managed to turn the conversation to focus on what went wrong that day. Boy, was it hard to keep pitching that woman's novel and not turn my attention instead to the many other titles on our list. A publishing house has no shortage of interesting projects and or work to do. At the end of every working day, a publicist can always choose to make a few last phone calls to the media. You want your publicist to choose to make those calls for you, and not for another author. Remember that you are competing with other authors on your publicist's assignment list for the same resources—whether those resources are money or your publicist's time and interest.)

If you've ever appeared in the media before, whether on television, radio, or in print, bring copies of tapes and clippings to the meeting. (Do not assume your originals will be returned to you.) Your publicist needs videotapes to pitch television interviews, as producers must assess any guest's on-air abilities. Audiotapes of engaging radio interviews or readings are useful for the sales reps to get to know your work better and to share with their customers—the booksellers. The reps appreciate interesting tapes that they can listen to in the cars en route to the next sales call. Newspaper clippings of interviews provide leads to the publicist to pitch a follow-up story, and help the sales rep prove to booksellers that the media is interested in you. I once worked with a first-time author who at our very first meeting produced audiotapes, clippings, and reading schedules—in short, a full background on his active literary life. He was impressively savvy about the materials and information that would help me successfully pitch his book.

Talk about your book in a way that demonstrates your understanding of its market. Everyone in the room is evaluating your potential. They're thinking about whether you should tour, attend a sales conference to meet all the reps, or meet booksellers at specially arranged prepublication events.

Do not be alarmed if your publicist appears to be fresh out of college. Many of the media people that your publicist is talking to are the same age. If what your publicist lacks in experience he or she makes up for in genuine enthusiasm and a natural comfort with Internet technologies, then you're in a good situation that you can work to your advantage.

Do something memorable or eccentric in the meeting. Be charming, roguish, sensitive, and generous. Seduce them. Hand out chocolates. (The food trick again, but it works nearly every time.) An author with whom I worked brought dozens of red roses to our offices and passed out handfuls to our staff members. You can imagine how his favor increased. The moral of the story: Make them remember you.

Be forthright about your goals for the book and your expectations for its publication. Ask them what they hope to see happen for the book. Ask them to explain how they intend to achieve that goal. Once they've committed themselves to you verbally, then they will find it hard to go back on their word later. The commitment gives your agent leverage to prod your publisher to honor its promises, should that become necessary. At the same time, bear in mind that you should not come off as too aggressive in meetings like these. The manner will be off-putting to your publishing team and make them think that you'll be one of those authors who will never be satisfied.

Don't bother asking what the budget is for your book. The number will mean very little. If they tell you $15,000, then what does that mean? That they will spend it on a *New Yorker* ad and call it a day? That could be a mistake. Or that they will send you on a publicity tour? That would be potentially more remunerative. So the point is not what the publisher plans to spend, but rather what it plans to do for your book. If you live in New York or Washington, and the budget formally assigned to your book is $1,000, your publicist can still make your book into a media success. It doesn't take money to get on the national media. It does take time and commitment on your publicist's part to pitch you in the right way for the right shows.

You may have your agent present at the meeting, too, which has drawbacks as well as advantages. On the downside, the agent's presence will make the meeting more formal, and the participants may refrain from sharing fresh ideas, as the agent might try to hold them to anything that comes up during brainstorming. But if your agent is a particularly powerful one, senior management is more likely to attend the meeting. You will command a higher level of attention.

Don't drag the meeting out too long. These people have no time to spare. Instead start the meeting by thanking everyone for taking the time to meet with you and saying that you hope to keep the conversation short and happy. This will set your tone with everyone, and they will appreciate the fact that you're not someone who will waste their time.

Try to assess which of the people present could become your in-house allies. Don't assume that your editor will continue to be your biggest booster. The nature of an author's relationship with his or her editor ranges widely and may change over the course of the publishing experience. Your publicist could become your strongest supporter, and may come away from this meeting so wowed by your media potential that he or she argues for an aggressive campaign. Or the sales director might take up your book's cause and motivate the sales staff to sell in more books. After the meeting, the staff that supports your book will be happy to hear from you with any new marketing and publicity ideas and updates. Put your name and contact information on the plan and invite everyone at the meeting to get in touch if they have questions for you.

Some editors stay close to an author throughout the publishing process. Others recede into the background once the book has been put into production, leaving the author in the publicist's hands. That's a shame, as an editor can be a good source of publicity ideas. Ideally, the editor and publicist should have an active partnership in making sure all publicity opportunities are exploited and drawing the author into ongoing publishing planning.

If a book's sales figures are discouraging, your editor might become incommunicado. Don't be surprised if your publicist stops calling you back. Once your editor has dropped you then the publicist is less motivated to deal with you, as well. The best way to keep all these relationships on track is to state clearly the degree of communication you prefer during the course of the book's campaign. For example, do you want your editor or publicist to share bad reviews with you? Do you want them to share discouraging sales figures with you? Talk to your editor and publicist about these issues early in the planning stages: This way, you will eliminate the cringe factor that they might feel if they have bad news for you later on and you'll keep the channels of communication open.

A final word of advice about your introduction to your publishing team: If you haven't yet met your publicity director, try to arrange for the publicist or editor to introduce you briefly when you're next in the offices. The publicity director is generally the voice of the department, so if you're creating some good ideas for your book's promotion, then telling the director in person helps reinforce your book in her mind. And when a publicity director is asked to cut budgets, she will have a harder time cutting funds for your book when she recalls your pleasant personality, good ideas, and great potential.

Nine Common Mistakes That Authors Make (and How to Avoid Them)

1. **You get involved too late in marketing planning.** Every publishing house has a sense of where any book ranks on its list four to six months before publication. Find out what your publisher is thinking and get to work.

2. You are cordial to your editor, but you condescend to the editorial assistant. The assistant is the grease that keeps your wheels moving—never forget that.

3. You assume that what's printed in the catalog is the final marketing plan for the book. The campaign evolves dramatically as the publication date appears—for better or for worse. Stay involved to make sure it's for the better.

4. You wait too long to hear from the publicist. Don't wait. Publicists are so overloaded and you might never get the call. If you're not sure of the right time to get in touch, ask your editor.

5. You declare in your first meeting with your publishing team or publicist that you are planning to hire your own freelance publicist. Before you show your hand, explore the publisher's willingness to contribute toward paying a freelancer, particularly if it becomes clear that the house's plans don't meet your expectations, or your publicist is either incompetent or swamped with too many projects to do an effective job.

6. You forget to fill out the author questionnaire and lose the opportunity to position the book and present marketing ideas. If you're not writing a marketing plan, then fill out this questionnaire. If your editor forgets to give you one, then ask for a copy.

7 You don't have a decent author photo—a lost marketing opportunity.

8. You behave like a big pain in the butt. Complaining about your campaign, gossiping about the publishing staff, and other passive-aggressive behaviors will alienate you from the publishing team.

9. You forget to say thank you for every little thing that someone at your publishing house does for you.

FOLLOW UP AFTER THAT FIRST MEETING

You might leave your first publishing planning meeting with a number of assignments: to send in copies of past reviews, or provide the names of contacts at the television station where you were once interviewed, or write a short essay describing the inspiration behind the book. Produce the information promptly. You want to stay in the minds of these people.

The single worst thing that can happen is that the publishing staff simply does not talk about the book—no follow-up queries, no sales director wanting more information or clarification, no editor tugging on the coattails of a publicity director, no nothing.

The strategy here is plain and effective: Suck up to your publicist. Keep the relationship professional, but treat this person well. After your initial meeting or conversation in which the publicist will probably give you a fair amount of time, keep the follow-up conversations or correspondences short and to the point. The reason for the brevity: Your publicist's workload is an awesome thing. Depending on the publishing house, a publicist might handle the various stages of publicity campaigns for 10 to 12 books at any one time. Perhaps two or three of those books have concurrent book tours. So no matter which publicist you're assigned— whether the department star or the rookie starter—you have to ingratiate yourself to get your share of attention.

Currying your publicist's favor should not stop you from asking the right questions to evaluate his or her abilities and intent. Ask her what media angles she is thinking of pitching to which media. Remember: At this early stage the publicist may not have had the opportunity to read your book. So be conversational, rather than make your questions seem accusatory or overly aggressive. And share your own thinking about publicity angles. You can certainly ask about the kinds of campaigns the publicist has previously worked on and how those went. You will be showing an interest as well as learning how he approaches his job.

While some authors do not push hard enough for attention, others push too hard and alienate or anger the publicist and the rest of the publishing team. You will need to find the right balance. Express your confidence that your publicist can do a great job on your book. At the same time, ask how you can help. Your publicist will be relieved to be viewed as a partner, a fine motivating idea when extra efforts so often go unnoticed. Talk about your book with conviction and enthusiasm and your publicist will feel that he or she's backed a winner, who—a bonus!—makes the job easier. Frankly, this is but one of a series of motivational hustles that you should initiate. You have to. No one else will. Yes, now and again your agent can step in to broker relationships for you, but at the end of the day you have to be your own fixer.

You might wonder why a publicist's hard work sometimes goes unnoticed. This happens because publishers launch countless books that get good publicity but don't sell. Naturally, most publishing houses really pay attention only after the book starts to sell—which means that the publicist must be willing to keep on trying even after the first few publicity hits have no apparent effect on sales.

If this is the case, then why should the publicist take the extra step for your book? Adrenaline is one answer. This is how it works: When your publicist secures a hard-fought-for media booking, he or she gets the publicity equivalent of a runner's high. For any publicist, there's nothing quite like the rush of scoring a good media hit, especially when the publicist likes the book and the author. And when that effort leads to increased sales, your publicist feels even finer. Any publicist who takes the job seriously sees your book as an opportunity to do well—to shine and achieve a good reputation, and consequently, better assignments. One hand washes the other, which is why you must be convincing that you're worth supporting.

One of the items on your follow-up agenda is finding out from your editor when the sales reps will call on the national accounts—the booksellers that are responsible for the lion's share of bookstore sales. The chains command about a quarter of the book market. The rep's best chance to sell your book to the store buyer is on the first sales call. So a good first impression on the buyer is essential.

Surprisingly, at many publishing houses, the national reps are left scrambling at the last minute for information and jackets to show their buyers. The marketing and editorial departments should treat the national sales call as a top priority, yet the reps are often left short of the materials they need. Therefore, talk to your editor about your desire to give the reps the ammunition they need to make the best possible pitch for your book *before* they make their first sales calls. (While you may never meet the sales reps, your editor will give them any appropriate materials.) Depending on what your editor advises, you might assemble a small packet of information including any updates, anecdotes, or background data that the rep might find interesting or useful. Don't bombard them with a deluge of paperwork. In your brief cover letter, hone in on the points that you think will help the rep make a cogent pitch.

Some publishing houses discourage direct communication between authors and reps unless specifically sanctioned ahead of time. In fact, once the selling process starts, some houses discourage much communication between the editors and the sales reps, which means your editor may not be fully informed about the progress of the sales calls. This is particularly true of the larger houses where the reps are selling many lists from various imprints, and simply couldn't manage the onslaught of communications if the editors and authors were allowed free access. You will simply need to ask about the protocol at your house.

Ask your editor if he or she can follow up with the sales rep after the sales call to see how it went. Though your editor might be embarrassed to report back to you if the sales call went badly, insist on hearing about it. If the sales rep's sales pitch just didn't go over, then you and your editor have a chance to come up with a new spin, a new angle to help the book sell in better at the other accounts. The Barnes & Noble sales call will likely be the first. If the sales call went well, then have your editor ask the sales director to share the good news with the other reps. (Chances are, a good sales director will have already done that.) If the reps sell the book in well, ask your editor if you can drop the reps an email note to thank them for their efforts. You might simply email your editor a message to pass on to the reps.

Like the sales rep, when the director of publicity makes her first calls on the national media, she, too, needs all the pertinent promotional information in time to make a cogent pitch. Again, check with your editor or publicist to ensure that the publicity director has everything she needs to make that early pitch to the nationals. (He or she may not have been given all the information that you might have already provided your publicist.) So drop a note to the director to provide the necessary information. Snaring a national interview—such as *Today* or *Good Morning America* or *20/20*—before a sales conference increases excitement among the sales staff. The early bookings give the reps real ammunition for their sales calls. It's not just the celebrity authors that can get booked during these early publicity calls. If the publicity director knows how to pitch your book well, the topic may just grab the morning show producers enough for them to commit early to a booking.

Make the Most of Your Time to Market Your Book, Even If You Have Only 15 Minutes a Day

Perhaps you do not have much time to devote to marketing your book. Here are some ideas about how to use a little time to maximum effect. Only 15 minutes a day becomes nearly two full hours a week that you can use to market your book. First, resolve to do at least one marketing task a day. Then use your time to come up with sales and marketing angles in the following ways:

- Bookmark sites about publishing and marketing (referenced throughout this book) that you'll check frequently to get ideas and learn about the publishing business.
- Research the names of reporters who might cover your book by visiting online newspaper websites.
- When you read your daily newspaper, pay attention to any leads to companies and organizations that might offer a book marketing opportunity. Then follow up by making a call. Set a goal of finding and contacting one or two leads a week. For example, a local business leader is interviewed about a new product aimed at young mothers. Your book targets the same audience, so contact the company and suggest that they sponsor a conference or seminar with you and other panelists. The worst that can happen is that they tell you no.
- Identify the people in your circle of friends and associates who can help you. Ask them how they think you should pitch your book.
- Research websites and blogs relevant to your topic. See if the blogs include contributions from guest bloggers and then pitch an article. Participate on their site by sending them meaningful feedback and therefore building relationships with people in your field.

- Gradually build your personal database, the list of people to whom you'll send a press release or email about your book's publication.
- Join an online writers' group or site that has a forum for asking questions and exchanging information. (Search for writers' groups under Yahoo! or Google Groups. Also go to www.readerville.com, an active site for writers to exchange advice and lend support.) Ask the group for advice about marketing and you'll find that others in the group will be happy to help you. Take a moment to dispense good advice to others, where you can.
- To get ideas about how to pitch your own book to the media, go to the websites for television talk shows to look at the archives of previous show topics.

HOW TO TREAT YOUR PUBLICIST TO GET THE BEST RESULTS—A FEW POINTERS

It's an old joke among publicists that the best author is a dead author. It is sad but, in some cases, it is true: Some authors are nightmares to work with. The stories of badly behaved authors are legendary: From the former bombshell movie-star "author" who made her publicist hold the phone to her ear when she made calls, to the British politician-cum-novelist well known for verbally abusing his escorts, to the drunk and well-past-his-prime bestselling novelist who invited his publicist to his hotel room to do cocaine, to those who simply will not stop whining and complaining. No matter how experienced your publicist, he or she is wondering what you will be like to work with.

Publicists like authors who show up for interviews on time; who are helpful in coming up with good angles to promote the book; who get to the point fast and then get off the phone, or else who get to the point fast and then are willing to chat for a while (and you'll have to figure out the right approach); who empathize with a publicist's workload; who are realistic about a book's potential, and who remember to say thank you. Publicists can't stand nags and complainers; unrealistic second-guessers ("Haven't you pitched my book to *60 Minutes* yet?"); passive-aggressive types who whine to the agent or editor behind the publicist's back; spendthrifts who squander the publisher's money on tour and so challenge the publicist's ability to manage the budget; authors who show up late for interviews or go AWOL while on tour, which means that the publicist can't slide in that last-minute booking with the local newspaper; authors who email or call several times a day to report, obsessively, on the book's latest sales ranking on Amazon. (While Amazon's rankings provide an immediate gauge of publicity's effectiveness, the data represents only part of the book-buying market in a given hour and can't be extrapolated.)

Remember: With inconsiderate behavior, you diminish the level of attention the publicist might have been willing to give your book.

Ideally, the relationship to cultivate with your publicist is that of a colleague or partner. The best results will come from your teamwork, where you may contribute a significant amount of creative thinking and legwork. No matter how much or little your publicist does for you, creating an open and mutually supportive and respectful relationship that preserves your access is very important. If you believe that your publicist should do all the work, then you are in for disappointment. He or she may not have the time to mount the campaign that you think your book deserves. You must get involved in a productive rather than an adversarial way.

Many publicists do fabulous jobs despite their limited resources. Don't assume that your publicist is wrong just because he or she doesn't agree with some of your marketing ideas. Your publicist may in fact have a keen handle on what the media is interested in. So ask why your ideas will not fly and what might work instead. As long as you've got a good and thoughtful conversation flowing, you can work together to craft a campaign. Worry instead when there is no conversation at all.

THE WARNING SIGNS OF AN INCOMPETENT (OR DISINTERESTED OR OVERWORKED) PUBLICIST— AND WHAT TO DO ABOUT THEM

Be concerned if your publicist:

- Doesn't return your phone calls promptly and publication date is three to four months away.

- Doesn't seem to understand what your book is about.

- Is endlessly caught up in process, like tweaking press materials and researching press lists. But then doesn't seem to know anyone in the media or talk about ideas for any pitches.

- Speaks in publicity jargon and you don't know what she's talking about.

- Talks to you about other author campaigns that she's working on but not about yours.

- Dismisses any ideas that you come up with yet contributes none of her own.

- Pretends she knows more than she does.

- Wants to get you off the phone too quickly every time.

If you recognize these symptoms in your dealings with your publicist, you are absolutely entitled to complain to your editor. If things look bleak, your editor will likely talk to the director of publicity to reassign your book to another publicist, or at least pay particular attention to how your campaign unfolds. If your editor is unwilling to have this conversation, then call the director of publicity to have a pleasant but concerned conversation about the caliber of your publicist. You can also choose to get your agent involved. Bear in mind that reassignments seldom happen. On a very few occasions, the publicity director will agree to freelance the book. The bottom line: You're not going to let someone else's incompetence ruin your book's chances, so plan to shoulder a larger share of publicity work and expense than perhaps you had anticipated.

AN AUTHOR WHO TALKED HIS PUBLISHER
INTO A CAMPAIGN

Gavan Daws wrote a book about the Allied prisoners of the Japanese during World War II called *Prisoners of the Japanese*. Unfortunately, the book's publicist quit on the eve of publication. In addition, the book had no assigned budget, and the publishing house was going through some turmoil with a newly appointed publisher. A group of new people had just been hired, including me, and the book was not at the top of everyone's mind, especially as we were focusing on the next season. Instead of resigning himself to his fate, Daws presented a cohesive and persuasive argument about why the revelations in his book were newsworthy and why his book was important. I assigned the book to a new publicist, who was itching to make his mark in the business. Through the publicist's persistence, and the fact that Daws's book revealed a little known aspect of World War II, *Prisoners of the Japanese* got some good media attention, including a feature in the *Washington Post*. For a few weeks the book was the house's number one selling title. The key factor in starting this campaign was Daws's own manner—gently but persistently persuasive and deeply committed to his cause.

THE CATALOG

The sales department sends catalogs to booksellers so they can determine which books to buy. The publicity department sends catalogs to the print and electronic media to select the books and authors worthy of review or interviews. The subrights department sends catalogs to buyers in the rights markets.

Ultimately, a full-blown marketing plan is distilled into the tightest possible format—a full or half page in the publisher's catalog that includes a book description, an author bio, and marketing plans. Check with your editor to find out the catalog copy deadline. Ask your editor to see the catalog copy before it's turned over to the marketing department and make any changes that seem important to you, even if you're not invited to. If your suggestions improve the book's positioning, your editor will likely accept them. If your editor shows you poorly written catalog copy, take this as an indication that the house isn't fully prepared to market and sell your book. The good news is that catalog copy is written at a stage when you still have plenty of opportunities to help your publisher better understand your book. So rather than take offense at the poor copy, be glad that you've been given a chance to set things right.

The draft catalog copy may not include the marketing plans, as these are often dropped into the copy after the editorial copy deadlines. If you've not spoken to or met your publicist or publicity director at this point, then your publisher is probably not planning to send you on a book tour. Tour cities are always printed in the catalog and rarely does the publicity department determine the cities without consulting the author. If you are convinced that you should go on tour, you must address this with your editor and publicity director before the catalog (and marketing plans) are finalized. Yes, the plans can evolve to include a book tour even after the catalog is printed, but you are in a stronger position with booksellers when they read in the catalog that the publisher is sending you on the road.

When you read the printed catalog, you may be surprised to find that your book has been assigned a national print campaign or a national media campaign. Do not necessarily believe what you read. These are merely buzz phrases in the business. A "national print campaign" might simply refer to a review copy mailing to reviewers—standard treatment for any book on the list. "National media campaign" might indicate that a publicist will pitch a few media outlets. If you're lucky enough to find that a $50,000 advertising campaign has been assigned to your book, don't be lulled into a false sense of security. Many an ad budget evaporates by the time publication rolls around. Remember that the copy is designed to hype the book to the bookselling community to get the best possible advance orders. The key to decoding catalog copy is to stay in touch with your editor.

You hope that your editor tells you the truth about what is going on, rather than falsely raising your expectations about what's planned for your book. Publicists meeting authors for the first time are often stunned to hear the author's unrealistic expectations about publicity based on their editor's promises. The editor may have had good intentions, wanting to keep the author in a positive frame of mind while writing the book. Tell your editor that you'd rather know sooner than later what the house is *really* planning. If you know early on, you are in a better position to address the problem, whether that means hiring your own publicist or doing your own publicity.

SALES CONFERENCE

Prior to sales conference, the marketing department sends sales materials to the reps, including tip sheets and selections from some manuscripts. The reps then come to conference prepared to focus on marketing and sales ideas. At sales conference, your editor, or possibly another staffer, will present your book to the entire sales force. The conference is valuable for the serendipitous ideas that arise, for in-house staff to learn about what's going on in the marketplace, and for the editors and sales reps to get to know one another. The problem with the conference meetings is that they are long and dull, with only so much information that can sink in before everyone's gone glassy-eyed. However, sales conference is not necessarily the most important part of your book's launch. Chances are, your editor has already done all the work to position your book in-house—at launch meetings, those informal drop-by-the-sales-director's-office chats, and during impromptu conversations in the hallways.

After sales conference your publisher may seem to go into a withdrawn, scarily quiet state as though they've forgotten about your book. You might not hear from anyone for weeks. In fact, this deceptively calm period is a critical stage in the publishing of your book. Your publicist plans the details of your campaign, while the sales reps are on the road selling your book, sending information back to the publisher about how the sell-in is proceeding. Your editor may be only partially informed about how the sales calls are going: Many publishing houses limit the sales feedback in order to prevent an irate editorial staff from descending on the sales department. The fact of the matter is that the sales advances that are finally delivered are usually lower than the editor's expectations. That is the reality of the marketplace.

Around the time of sales conference, you may suspect that you will not get the resources your book needs. Tell your agent about your anxieties so that he or she can intercede effectively, but discuss together what your agent intends to ask your publisher. Your agent may counsel you about your unrealistic expectations. But make sure your agent is a realist, as well. Not all agents are practical marketers and an agent's request for print advertising is easily dismissed (due to expense), but a request for specific publicity efforts has a better chance of getting through. Because your editor depends on your agent for the next good submission and wants to preserve a comfortable business relationship, he or she may take your agent's request to the publisher or editor in chief. The agent can always employ the tactic of talking directly to the publisher, who may in fact accede to the agent's request for more spending.

Sitting back and doing nothing is about the worst thing to do in these circumstances. If you suspect that support is not there but hope that it might appear later because "after all, they're the professionals, they must know what they're doing," then you've lost out on getting the most resources possible for your book.

As frustrated or angry as you might feel, tread carefully when you try to push the publishing staff to work harder on your book. As soon as you nag or accuse the staff, whoever it is you've annoyed will make a quick call to your editor, who is obliged to tell you to back off. You need allies. Proceed with caution and respect to preserve your good relationships with the publishing staff. If you decide to hire a freelance publicist, that publicist should be able to coordinate efforts with your in-house publicist, with goodwill on both sides. You also want your publisher to jump on board once you've created some publicity that leads to sales. As wronged or underserved as you might feel, keep a cool head. The decisions your publisher makes about your book are not personal. Losing your temper will not convince your publisher to give your book a promotional campaign. Worse, if you behave badly, the staff will begin to dodge your calls and keep future contact with you to a minimum.

BOUND GALLEYS AND HOW THEY ARE USED

A limited number of copies of your book are paperbound and sent to book reviewers, some producers, and key bookstore buyers. These copies are called galleys and the text is generally a typeset, but not proofread, version of your book. For the most important books on the publishing list, your publisher will send a large quantity of more elegantly produced galleys called advance reading copies (ARCs) to a wider circle of booksellers and media to pique early interest. Your editor will also send galleys to people who might give your book a positive endorsement to feature on the jacket. Be sure to check with your editor regarding the house's schedule and deadlines for cover endorsements.

Ask your editor to order a few extra galleys to send to people who might help start some buzz about the book. They might include individuals with whom you're trying to book advance speaking engagements, someone you're trying to convince to endorse the book, or a contact at a magazine who might get you some coverage. With other contacts you are better served by sending a copy of the book later. Resist the temptation to send galleys to your friends and family. With galleys costing an average of $10 each to produce, that money is better spent on something else.

THE FIRST PRINTING

Your publisher or sales director will announce your book's first printing and sales goals at sales conference. After that, the reps begin their sales calls and orders begin to come in—either higher or lower than the sales targets. Booksellers buy more conservatively now than in the past and may take only a few copies of your book. If and when the book starts to sell, they will reorder more copies either from your publisher or from wholesalers.

A few months before publication and when enough sales orders are in hand, your publisher will set the print quantity for the book. The size of the print run is based on the advance orders and anticipated demand based on the marketing campaign and early publicity commitments. (The exceptions are children's books and illustrated books that are printed economically overseas. The publisher must set those print runs months before receiving any sell-in data.)

During the sell-in, your publicist and editor feed any additional marketing information to the reps to help boost the numbers. If you've started to work with your own freelance publicist, it is imperative that you or she informs the publisher of any arranged publicity bookings and interviews. This allows the reps to get the best possible sell-in for your book. Remember: The more copies that are sold in, the more money your publisher will be willing to spend to promote the book.

TRADE REVIEWS

Booksellers, librarians, paperback publishers, foreign publishers, and some media read *Publishers Weekly*, the leading trade publication, to help them decide which books to buy or review. *Kirkus Reviews*, *Shelf Awareness*, *Library Journal*, *School Library Journal* and *The Horn Book* (for children's books), and *Booklist* are also important trade review media. A positive review in one or all of these publications can help spur in-house enthusiasm for your book, or give the sales reps and publicist another sales and media angle. Some booksellers rely on these reviews almost exclusively to inform their buy decisions.

Good trade reviews can help stimulate what's known as "prepub buzz." The value of prepublication interest in your book is the possibility of getting a film option, foreign rights sales, and your publisher's commitment to a bigger campaign. Good reviews in the library media can trigger instant orders from the library wholesalers.

A bad review is not a crisis in terms of selling to booksellers because upon reading the review, booksellers will probably not cancel their pending orders. But the review will not stimulate additional orders. A bad review can also deflate the house's enthusiasm for a book. Bear in mind that many books that were panned in the trade publications went on to critical or commercial success.

Not all new hardcover books are reviewed in the trade publications, and even fewer original trade paperbacks are reviewed. Illustrated books including cookbooks and some reference books are not available in the right format in time to earn early trade reviews. Consequently, booksellers don't rely exclusively on the trade publications to make buying decisions in these categories. They pay attention also to your publisher's marketing plan, your track record as an author, and the sales rep's pitch.

AWARDS

Your publisher will be aware of the most important awards—such as the PEN awards, the National Book Critics Circle, the National Book Award—but they may not be aware of other smaller awards for which your book might qualify. Depending on the book you have written, you might research appropriate awards. For instance, the Commonwealth Writers' Prize is little known in the United States but in fact many U.S.-based authors who are citizens of other countries qualify. (Find out about this prize at www.commonwealthwriters.com.) There's also a good directory called *Grants and Awards Available to American Writers*, published by PEN (www.pen.org) and available through PEN or *Poets & Writers* (www.pw.org).

If you identify the awards for which you might qualify and procure the application forms, your publicist or editor (or their dauntless assistants) will take care of the submissions for you.

TRADE SHOWS

The BEA (BookExpo America) is the publishing industry's annual convention. The show takes place at the end of May or in early June and showcases the fall list. Throughout the three-day events, hundreds of publishers' booths display the upcoming season's wares. There are numerous book signings, press conferences, and breakfasts where star authors appear before a packed ballroom of booksellers.

Your publisher starts to plan for the BEA in December—the deadline to submit authors to be chosen for the breakfast programs. A few months later, in March or so, the publisher begins to focus in earnest on which authors they will bring. Some houses like to throw multiple events—parties and luncheons to introduce authors to booksellers and media. Others are conservative about bringing authors to the show, preferring to concentrate instead on bookseller meetings.

If your publisher does not formally invite you to the BEA and you live in the same city where it is taking place, tell your editor that you would like to drop by and ask if he or she can arrange for an entry badge. At your publisher's booth, the sales reps and marketing and publicity staff will introduce you to key booksellers and media. A tip: Do not stand around at the booth looking sulky because you think no one's paying attention to you. With back-to-back meetings throughout the course of the trade show, your publishing team has a lot of work to do. Expect to be on your own most of the time, and if you're good at initiating contact with people, you can get a lot done by wandering around the floor. Here are some ways to use the opportunity:

- If your publisher's booth is not busy, then find highly trafficked locations where conference attendees are crowding around a focal point and park yourself there. You will get into all kinds of conversations.

- Attend educational sessions that are related to your book topic. Introduce yourself to the panelists and ask questions during the Q&A period. In recent years, the sessions on the growth of electronic media have been particularly informative.

- Offer to help your publisher at the booth.

- Talk to your publisher's sales reps as much as you can without disrupting their other business. They will introduce you to booksellers who drop by the booth. Be charming without taking up all of their time.

- Ask booksellers and sales reps about the kinds of books that are selling these days. Use the occasion not only to push your own book, but also to find out about the marketplace. Ask them about some of their favorite book promotions.

- Attend any press conferences on topics of strong media interest. You will meet members of the press there.

- Go to the *Publishers Weekly* booth and strike up a conversation with staff there.

- Go to the *Publishers Lunch* booth and make yourself known. Its parent service, Publishers Marketplace (which is well worth your investment to sign up for) has an informative series of videos that it produced at the BEA. Log in and watch and you'll get an excellent idea of what the BEA offers and what it can do for you.

- Cadge invitations to parties from your publishing staff. They may give you their personal invitations to events that they are unable to attend. These parties are usually good networking opportunities for you, as well as just being fun.

■ Walk the floor to visit other publishers' booths to find out how other publishers are promoting their books. They might stimulate new ideas for your own book's promotion.

Thank everyone on the publishing team at the show for his or her help and support. Keep notes of the names of everyone you've met from the publisher and send follow-up notes. Remember: Keep yourself in their minds. Unless you happen to visit their territories on your tour, you won't see most of those salespeople again.

The Canadian equivalent of the BEA is the CBA or Canadian Booksellers Association that takes place in June (www.cbabook.org). Do not confuse the Canadian meeting with the Christian Booksellers Association, which has several expos a year as well as an annual international convention (www.cbaonline.org). The websites for both organizations will tell you when and where they meet.

Regional book trade shows take place throughout the United States in September. Of these the largest are the shows sponsored by NEIBA (New England Independent Booksellers Association, www.newenglandbooks.org) and SIBA (Southern Independent Booksellers Alliance, www. sibaweb.org). These shows are considerably smaller than BEA. Publishers set up booths and booksellers drop by to check out the wares and schmooze over the course of a weekend and there are parties and dinners to introduce authors to booksellers. Like the BEA, signings and readings provide a good way for an author to gain exposure among the bookseller fairgoers. Publishers will sometimes feature a prepublication tour of the regional trade shows as a part of an author's campaign. For a complete listing of the bookseller trade shows go to www.bookweb.org, the site of the American Booksellers Association.

GET TO KNOW YOUR SALES REPS

The reps have a lot of information to absorb about the list they are responsible for selling. Anything to help your book stand out from the rest is a plus, and with the help of your editor you can accomplish this. You might enclose a friendly letter that relates an anecdote or two about the writing of the book. Chances are that the reps will use your comments in their sales calls to add color to their presentation. Even if your editor has shared the same information in launch meetings and sales presentations, repeat any key points to reinforce them in the reps' minds. If you write personal notes to the reps, mention any information that is specific to a particular town or locale in a particular rep's sales territory. Your editor can supply the reps' names and territories and will forward your letter on to them.

If you're the author of a cookbook, then perhaps send some goodies to the reps at sales conference. Your care package will get them talking to one another about your food and, hence, your book.

Another way to contact the reps is by voicemail. Sales departments have programmed multiple voicemails so, with the blessing of your editor and sales director, record a brief informative greeting to the sales reps for instant transmission to their voicemail. Or your editor can forward your email greeting to the sales director, who will in turn disseminate the message to all the sales reps, as long as the message is short and useful or entertaining.

Near publication, if possible meet the telephone sales force. Often overlooked by the rest of the publishing team, the telephone reps are genuinely happy to meet authors. Spend a few minutes with each of them or arrange through your editor or publicist to have a brown-bag lunch with the group. Your meeting helps them shape their sales pitches for your book.

PREPUBLICATION BOOKSELLER TOUR

Your publisher may send you on a prepublication tour to meet bookstore buyers to build excitement and interest in your book, perhaps even leading to those booksellers talking up your book to their customers. The tour involves traveling to the key bookselling markets including New York City (home of the Barnes & Noble headquarters), Ann Arbor (where the Borders central buying office is located), and other cities that have a concentration of good independent booksellers. The tour might include

Boston and Washington, DC, where the local sales rep might organize lunches or dinners to introduce you to independent booksellers and local chain store managers. A West Coast–based publisher might concentrate on San Francisco or Los Angeles, instead. You might talk to your editor about other authors on the list to see if the house is willing to set up a couple of group author bookseller lunches or dinners in key markets or else some sort of group event at one of the trade shows.

If your book has a message that will interest booksellers, or if you've had a book published previously that was well received by booksellers, then bookseller meetings may be worthwhile. For instance, C. Britt Beemer's book *Predatory Marketing* reveals how to attract customers and to beat the competition. After early marketing meetings where it was decided to reach out to booksellers, Beemer, the chairman of a consumer behavior research and strategic marketing firm, conducted consumer surveys about book-buying preferences. The sales director then set up a meeting with executives at Barnes & Noble and Borders where Beemer presented the results of his surveys. Though his book was not a lead title on the list, Beemer's expertise gave his publisher a way to reach out to booksellers, to impress them about his book, and to elevate the book's initial buy-in from those accounts.

To introduce British writer Steven Hall to American booksellers for his novel, *The Raw Shark Texts*, his publisher set up a prepub tour. With a film deal and multiple foreign rights sales to the book's credit, the publisher decided to invest in the book's potential in the U.S. market. Did it work? The publisher claimed to have 100,000 copies in print and the prepub tour became the focus of a significant feature in the *New York Times*.

YOU'VE SUBMITTED YOUR MANUSCRIPT. NOW WHAT?– A SUMMARY

Find out the sequence of events at your publishing house so that you can understand when to step in and help. Your main tasks during the months leading up to your book's publication are to help your editor do a great job positioning your book to the publishing team and to develop a good, functioning relationship with your publicist. This is also the key period of assessment, when you will find out exactly what your publisher is planning to do to promote your book.

The key events during this period are:

- Launch meeting where your editor presents your book to the publishing team

- Catalog copy is written

- Meetings with the publishing staff

- The first sales calls and national media pitches

- Your ongoing assessment of your publisher's plans

4

HIRE YOUR OWN PUBLICIST

YOUR publishing house might show little interest in investing time and money to promote your book. Several reasons might explain this inertia, and most of them are beyond your control. It might be that the book falls short of expectations. Perhaps another book on a similar subject was recently published, which preempted the media and consumer market for your book. Maybe the lead titles on the list are crowding the publisher's time and attention. Or the sales force didn't advance as many copies into the field as the publisher had hoped and the publisher has become discouraged. Maybe your editor has little persuasive clout in-house, or has left the company.

Once you sense a lack of enthusiasm among the publishing team, you have a critical decision to make. Don't go on and on to your editor about how the publicity director doesn't "get it" or whatever your issue is. Your point may be valid but possibly beyond your editor's influence. The publishing house has its own system in place. Just because you've shown up doesn't mean the place is going to change, or even wants to change. Instead, become proactive on your own behalf. Try to make your editor and your agent your allies, instead of people who would rather avoid your phone calls. Your task is to work within the system when you can still help your book.

You are not alone. Sometimes even the big-name authors become frustrated with inadequate publicity efforts. Paul Theroux faxed a masterfully acidic letter of complaint to his publisher when his publicists fell down on the job. (The letter was intercepted before reaching the publisher's desk and was photocopied and circulated widely.) The point is that no author can take a publisher's support for granted.

A lack of internal support is the number one reason authors hire freelance publicists. But it's by no means the only reason. As one publicist puts it, what used to take 10 phone calls to make happen now takes 30: Savvy authors have realized that their in-house publicist can probably use the extra help in the form of a freelance publicist, especially when the book could appeal to multiple audiences and media. With so much competition for media and attention, it's simply more challenging than it used to be a few years ago for a publicist to set up interviews. A freelancer can cover a specific aspect of the campaign, like online marketing, or niche media like business trade publications. Other reasons to hire a publicist: Perhaps your publisher lacks experience in dealing with the national media and you think a freelancer could be useful to secure some national bookings; or perhaps your book has already been published and the first wave of publisher-sponsored publicity went well, suggesting that more media opportunities may exist. You may be able to get your publisher to pay for this if you are a significant author to the house. If not, you will probably have to foot the bill yourself. (Remember to track all expenses. Any money you spend on promoting your book is tax deductible against your income from royalties.)

Diane Mancher, who runs the book publicity firm One Potata, says that 50 percent of her business comes directly from authors, as compared to 10 percent some 10 years ago. Other freelance publicists confirm the trend. Authors have wised up.

Authors are hiring publicists earlier in the game than ever before. If you wait too close to the publication date to hire outside, you've lost valuable time to build marketing strategies leading up to publication. As Mark Fortier of Fortier Public Relations puts it, "Many publicists charge the same project fee or barely a higher fee if you start working with them early so there are almost no negatives for the author. The earlier a publicist signs a contract with an author, the earlier he or she can start contacting magazines, event venues, and network TV shows, which all start planning months ahead of publication date. The longer that a publicist spends with a book, the longer they have to read the book thoroughly and wrap their brains around it to strategize for a better quality campaign. Lastly, there is no right or wrong time to have bloggers start buzzing about your book, but the trend has been for that start date to keep getting earlier and earlier."

These authors are getting an even earlier lead on their publicity campaigns—as much as a year—if setting up a full schedule of speaking engagements is an important component to their campaign (see page 203 for some background on a publicity tour that focused on speaking gigs) or if they want to build a solid online presence and platform (see page 237 for an example of a successful online campaign with a very long lead time).

The ideal time to hire a publicist is five to six months ahead of publication date if you want your book to have a shot at long-lead magazine coverage and some speaking engagements. This means you should be interviewing publicists a month or so ahead of that. Make sure to keep the publicist on board for two to three months following publication date to continue booking media once your book is in the marketplace.

If your publication date is only a couple of months away and you've learned that your publicist is planning only a review copy mailing then you can still hire a publicist. Even though you're a bit late off the mark, the window of opportunity for making noise around your book launch hasn't closed yet. Do not squander the moment. This is not the time to learn how to set up your own publicity. If you cannot afford a freelancer for a full campaign, consider hiring one for some of the services you need, even if it's on a consulting basis to advise you on your own publicity efforts and provide you with mailing lists.

Once your book has been published, you may still hire a freelancer. If you have published a work of nonfiction in a subject area of perennial interest, then your book can potentially get media coverage well after your publication date. However, if you've written a novel, your prospects are slim. Unless your book has strong thematic elements that a publicist can peg to news events, your novel has limited potential for media coverage. Freelance publicists will often tell just-published novelists that they do not want their money, as they can't do much for them. Your best bet is to wait for the paperback edition, then hire a publicist well before that publication date.

BEFORE YOU HIRE A FREELANCER . . .

Carol Fass, who heads Carol Fass Publicity & Public Relations, gives prospective clients a list of questions to ask their publishers. The answers to these questions help her identify how she can create a constructive campaign for the author. All freelancers will ask you variations of the same questions. Follow her advice and find out as many of the answers as possible before you contact any freelancers.

- Will the publisher write any press material for your book? If so, what are they planning to write? What have they already written and may we see it?

- Will the publisher print galleys for your book?

- Will your publisher handle the trade reviewers such as *Library Journal*, *Publishers Weekly*, *Kirkus Reviews*, and *Booklist*?

- Will your publisher be approaching long-lead-time magazines with galleys? If no galleys are planned, how is your publisher planning to approach the long leads?

- What is the publisher's timetable for the book? When will books be ready and available at the warehouse? What is the planned publication date?

- Is there a formal publicity plan for the book that has been communicated to you, to booksellers, to your agent? What does it entail?

- If there is no formal publicity plan, what does the publisher intend to do to promote the book?

- Is there any advertising planned?

- Is your publisher sending the book out for endorsements or blurbs?

- Is there a jacket design and may we see it?

- Has flap copy or catalog copy been written and may we see it?

- What is the first printing for your book?

- Is there anything else we need to know?

- Is the publisher willing to pay anything toward the publicity? For example, will they handle the preparation of mailings (i.e., photocopying press releases, collating, stuffing Jiffies, postage)? Will they pay any part of a freelance publicist's fee? Will they contribute to other expenses incurred in doing the publicity?

Fass says that publishers will often contribute at least some monies or services to a freelance campaign, which can significantly reduce an author's expenses. You just need to know what to ask for and when to ask for it. For example, don't ask your publicist if the house will pay for $2,000 in photocopying and mailing expenses. Instead ask if the house is willing to have your press releases photocopied and mailed to the media.

WHAT DOES A FREELANCE PUBLICIST COST?

If you've determined that a tour is important, then take a deep breath: Expect to pay a publicist a fee anywhere between $500 and $3,000 per city, plus expenses (express mail, phone, messengers, photocopying), plus travel costs ($12,000 to $15,000 to cover hotel, travel, media escorts, and so on). There is also a fee for writing press materials. To lessen the financial burden, consider starting with a small tour. Visit two or three cities to test the media response and local sales. Then you can confidently invest in more tour cities, and may even earn some more support from your publisher. And for my money, each tour city should also include a speaking engagement to give you and your publicist a great local media angle and an opportunity to sell books.

There are other cost-effective ways to work with freelance publicists. You may focus on getting a few top-level national appearances. Your top 10 wish list might look like this: *The Oprah Winfrey Show*, *Today* or *Good Morning America*, *The Colbert Report*; a feature article or review in the *New York Times*, *Los Angeles Times*, *Washington Post*; a feature on the Associated Press newswire and *People* magazine; and a National Public Radio interview. By defining the publicity efforts, everyone's expectations are clear. The publicist is unlikely to take on the job if she thinks your media prospects are slim. This work might cost you anywhere from $3,500 to $7,500.

A radio phone-interview campaign might interest you. Several public relations companies offer radio satellite tours, where they line up 15 to 25 back-to-back interviews that take place in a studio or by phone. The cost ranges from $3,500 to $5,000. The advantage to this kind of radio campaign is that you reach a lot of top markets in one sitting. An alternative approach is contacting individual radio stations and scheduling interviews over the course of weeks or even months. You may reduce the fees for this service if you ask the freelance publicist to send the initial mailing, and then provide you with the contact lists to allow you to make the follow-up calls. Radio interviews are relatively easy to book, and if you plan to set up interviews on your own behalf on an ongoing basis, then radio offers an excellent arena to learn and hone your publicity skills.

If you're flush and if you think you can be an effective interview subject on television, then spring for the cost of a television satellite tour. Satellite tours run upward of $10,000 and comprise a series of back-to-back television interviews that are conducted in a television studio by satellite. You, the guest, sit in a chair with a single camera trained on you. One station after another links into the studio to conduct the remote interview. Some of these interviews are broadcast live; others are taped for later broadcast.

Another option is focussing on online media for interviews and reviews. PR firms are increasingly making blog tours part of their capabilities, where they arrange for you to contribute to relevant blogs.

Some public relations firms will create a campaign that works within your budget and publicity requirements. With a little research you will probably find the firm or publicist who will structure an affordable deal for you.

The book PR firm Planned Television Arts offers useful resources at www.plannedtvarts.com. Take advantage of the Tip Sheet section of the site, which includes interviews with members of the media about what they look for in a guest, dates for holidays that offer publicity tie-ins to your book, and sample media bookings for clients. The tips will help you understand how publicists do their job.

YOUR BUDGET

What follows is a range of expenses that you might incur in your freelanced publicity campaign. Prices vary widely depending on the freelancer you use and the extent of your campaign. You will need to shop around to find the most value for your money, and in some instances you will perform some of these tasks yourself and eliminate the cost.

Hiring a press release writer:	$200–$500 for one press release $500–$1,200 for a full press kit
Photographer for headshot:	$200–$1,000
Creating a website:	Free–$10,000
Fees for a freelance publicist:	$2,500–$7,500 for a national media campaign $5,000–$40,000 for a 10-city tour $3,000–$9,000 for a three-city tour $500–$5,000 for consulting
Throwing a publication party:	$250–$2,500
Mailing books to the press:	$2.00–$4.50 per book for postage and Jiffy bags
Photocopying press releases:	Free–$2,500 (depending on your resources and the extent of your press materials)
Television satellite tour:	$10,000–$22,000 (for 10–20 markets)

Radio satellite tour:	$3,500–$6,000
Tour travel expenses:	$1,200–$2,500 per city if you are flying, staying in hotels, and hiring escorts $2,500–$4,000 per city for cookbook tours including food prep expenses and food escorts

INTERVIEWING FREELANCE PUBLICISTS

Agencies are quite different from one another. Some focus on particular subject areas, like New Age subjects or serious political nonfiction. Some avoid literary fiction while others have special skill with literary projects. Some agencies will give you weekly updates and provide specific feedback from all pitches. Others will not devote as much energy to keep you informed. Some agencies comprise one principal; others are staffed with many publicists. Before talking with freelancers, make a list of your expectations and of what you want from the relationship.

Most freelance publicists offer these services: pitching national and local media, setting up bookstore signings, writing press materials, radio interview campaigns, online campaigns and blog tours, book review campaigns, events and parties, press conferences, and other press events. Some publicists offer services such as setting up speaking engagements and satellite tours.

No publicity agency or freelancer holds the secret formula for getting you the coverage you want. Some agencies will understand right away how to market your book. Others will not. A New York City–based agency may be physically closer to the national media based there, but its proximity alone does not guarantee superior results in placing media interviews.

When you start talking to freelancers, you will be asked about your goals for your book. Share your marketing plan, if you have one, and ask what media the freelancer thinks is achievable. Be prepared to talk about your budget, as this will naturally be a determining factor in the campaign. Freelance publicists who are good at client management will clearly explain the media possibilities. When Diane Mancher of One Potata talks to potential clients, she likens her work to that of a lawyer, who will try to get the best results for her client, but can't guarantee the outcome. Lynn Goldberg of Goldberg McDuffie Communications will ask about your long-range goals beyond the immediate attention for your book. She then determines how her services will help you achieve those goals.

You may expect to interview freelance publicists and then make your selection from among the group. Keep in mind that the freelancers are also interviewing you to see if you will be a good client and whether they think they can make some media happen for you. Client authors are more time-consuming to work with than client publishers are. Therefore the publicist will evaluate whether you're worth spending time on and will avoid an author who seems potentially high maintenance. Once you're signed on as a client, a publicist expects to spend some time educating you about the publicity and publishing process, but not at the expense of getting the job done. Some authors will badger their publicists, calling and emailing constantly, all of which can become disruptive to the publicist who is trying to get you some media. Don't become a pest—either to the freelancer or your in-house publicist. If you have a lot of information and enthusiasm and ideas to share, try to take care of them efficiently in one or two phone calls or emails.

That said, some freelance publicists themselves qualify as high-maintenance individuals. You might find their behavior high-handed or abrupt, even on the first meeting. They may respond to your questions with answers like "We don't do it like that" or "We don't really set up that kind of appearance." If this happens, it's your clear signal to get out of there! Do not tolerate a publicist who becomes annoyed with you at your very first meeting for coming up with new ideas about your book's promotion. There are plenty of other freelancers to choose from.

Essential Questions to Ask a Freelance Publicist

Among the freelance public relations firms specializing in books are some of the finest publicists in publishing. Because freelance firms are small entrepreneurial businesses, their success depends on excellent staffs to a greater extent than in-house publicity departments: Mediocrity survives longer in-house largely because of corporate inertia. That said, you should still check out a freelance agency's references to ensure that you're spending your money wisely. You can do this by asking the agency for the contact information for past clients who would be willing to talk to you. If an agency won't provide you with references, take that as a bad sign.

Before you enter into a contract with a freelancer, ask the following questions to protect your interests:

- What publicity opportunities do you think there are for my book?
- Have you worked on books like this in the past? What media did you get for them?
- Who do you think is the audience for my book? What do you think is the best way to reach that audience?
- Do you work directly with a lot of authors or is most of your work through publishing houses? Which authors have you worked with and what publicity did you get for them?
- Do you mind if I call every day with questions?
- Will you or a publicist on your staff work on my book? If it will be a staff publicist, then what experience does she have and can I meet her?
- How do you develop a campaign strategy for the books you're working on?
- What are your goals for my book? Do you think my book poses any particular challenges? What are they?
- What can I do to make the book a success? How can I help with publicity?
- Do you recommend a publicity tour for my book? How do you choose the tour cities?
- Do you set up bookstore appearances? Do you set up speaking engagements?

- **What happens when the campaign is finished and you receive calls from the media about my book?**
- **What are some of your favorite past projects and why?**
- **May I have three references to call about your work?**

GOING TO CONTRACT

Once you and the freelance publicist agree to work together, then you will sign a contract or letter of agreement. The contract will require that you pick up expenses and pay a fee in installments. Many a freelance publicist will protect his or her financial interests by collecting more money up front from client authors than from client publishers. This is because some authors have reneged on their final bills when the publicity results did not meet their expectations. Some freelancers go a step further and require that the author arrange for the publisher to pay the freelancer and the author then reimburses the publisher. Remember: If your publicity campaign and book sales disappoint you, then you still owe the freelancer the agreed-upon fee. (Refusing to pay is, plainly put, theft.) Keep in mind that the final payment should still be large enough to motivate the publicist to do a good job in the second half of the campaign.

You will negotiate the term of contract with the freelancer. The standard duration for a campaign is three to four months. If you believe that your book is going to take a long time to gain attention, you may want an extended period of publicity coverage.

Naturally, freelance publicists have different payment structures. Some offer a fee schedule based on a flat rate per city, per publicity kit, per phone interview campaign, or per national media campaign. Others base their fees on how long they will work on a campaign and charge a monthly retainer. Solo freelancers may be more flexible on negotiating a price as they have lower overheads than agencies with a staff. Negotiability will also depend on the freelancer or agency's workflow at any particular time. Their business fluctuates seasonally, with publishers' loaded fall schedules placing a heavier demand on freelancers in the last half of the year. In some years, a notable absence of big books diminishes the freelancers' workload and cash flow. Always negotiate. Creative pricing could work for you and your publicist. You might offer a flat fee for services with bonuses if certain media bookings are achieved. While a somewhat unorthodox approach in the book publicity business, the approach certainly builds in a good incentive for performance. Again, not everyone will be willing to try this, but there's no harm in asking.

What follows is a typical contract between a publicity agency and an author. This particular agreement is for a title to be published on Valentine's Day. The campaign commenced in September and concluded at the end of March. The author felt that long-lead magazine coverage was important, which is why the campaign started so far ahead of publication date.

Letter of Agreement

Date

Dear _____,

This will confirm our agreement concerning our role in publicizing your new book, [title], which [name of your publisher] will publish on February 14, [year].

Under the terms of this agreement, we shall use our best efforts to bring the book to wide public attention. Our specific responsibilities will include:

—Creating all press materials. This will include a press release, author biography, an author Q&A, and other pieces to be decided.

—Preparing a galley letter and a list of long-lead magazines and reviewers to receive galleys and following up to confirm coverage. Among the long-lead publications we will target for coverage are: *Vogue, Glamour, New York Times Magazine, Elle, Harper's Bazaar, Vanity Fair, Parade, USA Weekend, Civilization, People, O: The Oprah Magazine, Entertainment Weekly, The Nation, The New Republic, The New Yorker, The Atlantic,* and *Harper's.*

—Coordinating with your publisher to arrange bookstore appearances in the following cities: New York, Washington, Atlanta, Birmingham, and Chicago.

—Working in advance with the national electronic and print media to secure interviews. Among the national media we will approach are: *Today*, *Good Morning America*, *Weekend Today*, *CBS Sunday Morning*, *The Charlie Rose Show*, *The Oprah Winfrey Show*, *Open Book* C-SPAN, *Fresh Air*, *All Things Considered*, *The Diane Rehm Show*, *USA Today*, Associated Press, the *New York Times*, *Los Angeles Times*, the *Washington Post*, *Time*, and *Newsweek*.

—Working with feature and lifestyle editors at the top 40 metropolitan daily newspapers to secure coverage in Valentine's Day features.

—Arranging appropriate television, radio, and print interviews in the tour cities.

—Working with the book reviewers at the major metropolitan newspapers to secure timely reviews.

—Seeking online mentions on blogs and other websites.

—Coordinating all travel and escort arrangements in each city.

We will begin work on the project in September and will conclude our duties under this agreement on March 31, [year]. We will coordinate our efforts with you and your publisher and will update both parties periodically about our results.

Our fee for the project is $15,000.00, payable as follows: $8,000.00 upon signing the agreement, and $7,000.00 payable on February 1, [year].

In addition to the retainer fee, you agree to pay expenses incurred in connection with the campaign within 15 days after receiving a bill from [name of publicity agency]. Examples of these expenses include postage, Federal Express, telephone, messengers, Lexis-Nexis online research, photocopies, and printing. Any single item beyond $250.00 will be preapproved by you.

You understand and agree that payment for our services is based upon our efforts and is not contingent upon results or on specific responses from various media as these cannot be assured.

[Name of publicist] will be the account executive on the project.

If the terms of this agreement as stated herein are agreeable, please sign and return one copy of this letter to me for my records.

Author   Owner
                                          Publicity Firm

_____   _____

_____   _____

Date:_____   Date:_____

HIRING A FREELANCER—SUCCESS STORIES

Andrew Sobel, coauthor of *Clients for Life* (www.andrewsobel.com), started his publicity campaign early on. Though he was a neophyte to book publishing, he has a background in business consulting and marketing strategy and knew he needed to invest some time and money in promoting his book. When he interviewed freelance publicists, he found that they had more extensive promotional possibilities at their fingertips than in-house publicists. Most important, they would have the time to make follow-up calls that the in-house publicists would not.

The campaign he eventually devised with Meryl Moss of Meryl L. Moss Media Relations included a six-month intensive outreach to business trade publications that reached his core audience: Business professionals in the service industries such as accounting, advertising, banking, law, and so on. Moss and her staff researched and pitched all the related trade publications and placed interviews, features, and excerpts in many publications to appear upon his book's publication including *Advertising Age*, *Consulting to Management*, and *Consultants News*. The articles helped leverage appearances for Sobel on several national business shows on CNBC and CNNfn, as well as a review in *USA Today*—a powerful vehicle for business books, as business travelers rely on the publication.

Sobel's advice to authors is to ask yourself, "Who am I trying to reach for this book and what are all the ways I can get in touch with this audience?" Then decide whether you are willing to put the time in to help develop the right materials for the publicist to work with. He cautions that you can't do everything at once and you can't do it all. "I struggled with how to define the universe of available media," he says. "You have to focus on your target media, and reach them in phases during the course of your campaign." Of course, the good news about the large size of the media universe is that you have endless opportunities for coverage and, if you choose, you can continue to promote your book for years. Sobel acknowledges that he could not have achieved the level of exposure that he did without the help of the right freelance publicist, or without investing a significant amount of his time.

When Mariah Stewart was starting out as a romance novelist (www .mariahstewart.com,) she chose to concentrate on booksellers rather than media for her publicity campaign. For her first book, Stewart had sent bookmarks and personal letters to booksellers, who—many novels later—remain among the core of her most supportive stores. But with a day job and three children, Stewart knew that she wouldn't have the time for such ongoing labor-intensive efforts. She hired a freelancer, Judy Spagnola, to focus on getting the word out to bookstores. Spagnola called stores before the sales reps had called on the accounts, and then followed up to report on any new developments about the book—such as a good review or an award—to keep the book at the top of the booksellers' minds.

Judy Spagnola specializes in romance and mysteries. A former literature buyer for Walden, she is well known to booksellers and has enormous credibility on behalf of her author clients. Her campaigns can comprise single mailings to booksellers and reviewers or a staggered series of mailings that might include three of four pieces of correspondence including bookmarks and postcards. (Romance and mystery writers can contact Judy Spagnola at info@book-trends.com.) She encourages her authors to attend the romance conferences and introduce themselves to the booksellers who often attend. "Get to the booksellers," she says. "Introduce yourself, send them signed bookmarks, set up book signings. Don't forget to include your book's ISBN on all promotional material that you send to booksellers. The ISBN makes it very easy for the bookseller to look up information about buying your book."

Only a few freelancers specialize in bookstore outreach. If you want to take this task on yourself, you should start making your phone calls about two months before your publication date. (So you'll need to research your bookstore lists earlier than that.) Persistence is required: The bookstore buyer that you need to speak with will likely be in and out of the store and you'll need to call back until you make contact. Once you reach the buyer, explain who you are and what your book is about, as well as any positive news about the book, like favorable reviews. If you have a website, invite the bookseller to visit to get a better sense of your work. Ask if he or she wouldn't mind if you send follow-up information from time to time. What you will have accomplished in the call is the start of a relationship with the bookseller, who, once you follow up, will start to remember your name and your book.

MANAGE THE FREELANCE AND IN-HOUSE RELATIONSHIPS

Upon entering into a relationship with a freelancer, you will ask her to specify the services she will be responsible for. You will also ask your in-house publicist to describe the work that he or she will handle. All parties—you, your freelancer, your in-house publicist—must know who's doing what. A clearly communicated division of labor and an ongoing dialogue between the freelancer and in-house publicist will eliminate confusion later. When a freelance publicist pitches the media, the in-house publicist commonly manages the book review mailing, keeps the rest of the publishing house informed of your activities, and possibly writes the press materials. The in-house publicist might also agree to send out the media mailing to save your freelancer from charging postage expenses back to you, and, most important, can also let you know if sales are increasing in certain markets as a result of your appearances. If your media appearances generate sales, then you have a case to make that the publisher should help support your efforts in more markets.

Continue to manage the relationship between the in-house publicist and your freelancer. Perhaps you will arrange periodic conference calls. You should serve as a shuttle diplomat for a couple of reasons. First, so that the in-house publicist doesn't drop the ball because of relying exclusively on the efforts of the freelancer. (Your in-house publicist should view the freelancer as an extension of the team, not as a way to abdicate responsibility for your book.) Second, so that you help preserve your freelancer's access to the house's valuable resources.

Don't expect your freelance publicist to fight any of your battles with your publisher or to tell the publisher what to do. Freelancers do not serve the same function as your agent. Particularly for the New York–based publicists, their livelihood depends on preserving good relationships with publishers. "We are diplomats with the publishers," says one freelancer. "Our role is not to play bad cop, which many authors expect us to do." Resist bad-mouthing your publisher to your publicist, no matter what you think about the house. You may need your publisher's help later; and your gossip places the freelance publicist uncomfortably in the middle. Nor make the mistake, once you hire a publicist, of sitting back and expecting the publicist to do all the work. The most productive campaigns are those where the author and publicist act like partners in a project, whether that publicist is a freelancer or in-house.

Sometimes an in-house publicist will become offended that you've decided to freelance your book's campaign but may not communicate that. But then as you move toward publication and beyond, you find yourself losing the benefit of your publicist's attention and what's more, pick up on an uncomfortable vibe in your few conversations. Your best move is to bring the in-house publicist into your decision-making process up front to help you make a better decision about which freelance publicist to hire and how to best support the in-house campaign. Clarify that your desire to hire a freelancer has nothing to do with your perception of his or her talents, but was intended to expand the team working on the book. Be reassuring. You need your publicist in your corner for many months ahead.

HIRE YOUR OWN PUBLICIST—A SUMMARY

You'll find an annotated list of publicity firms that specialize in books in the resource section of this book (page 281). Before interviewing publicists:

- Find out what your publisher is planning for your book.

- Think about what you want to see a freelancer accomplish for you.

- Determine your budget.

- Shop around for the publicist that fits your goals and with whom you are comfortable.

If you're not sure what kind of campaign is appropriate for your book, talk to a few publicists about what they recommend. Enter into a detailed contract with the freelance publicist so that expectations are clear for both parties, and most of all, plan on becoming an active partner in the campaign.

5

PRESS MATERIALS

THE pitch letter and press release and other written materials should be created and presented in such a manner as to convince a producer, reporter, or book reviewer to cover your book. The materials should be well written, persuasive, concise, attentive to what the media is interested in, and free of spelling errors and typos. Producers and reporters receive giant stacks of mail, as well as hundreds of faxes and emails, every day. With such voluminous correspondence to deal with, they will spend little time—perhaps only a few seconds—reading your book's press release before making a decision to pass or to pursue further.

Your publicist will write your press materials based on your manuscript, your marketing plan, and any conversations you've had. He or she will probably offer to show you the press materials. If not, then ask to read them to verify that they properly represent you and your book. You can edit the press release, but be careful of the publicist's feelings. As you might know, most people are sensitive about their writing. (A publicist who is a poor writer may still have fantastic pitching skills, so do not despair if you see bad prose crossing your desk.) Remember: A good relationship with your publicist is of primary importance. A friend of mine recently rejected the entire press release that the publicist had written. Though grammatically written, the release missed the point of the book and made the book seem dull. His publicist accepted the rewrite because he positioned the new release as making the book more salable.

Various types of press materials are used for different kinds of media pitches. The press release announces news surrounding a book's publication, and is generally sent along with a copy of the book to reviewers, producers, and reporters. Or instead of a press release, your publicist might instead write a personal letter to book reviewers about your book. The letter might describe your book in a conversational manner, a softer sell than a conventional pitch letter and an approach used more typically for fiction. Pitch letters encapsulate your expertise and the topics that you will talk about in an interview. These are aimed principally at press who will conduct interviews with you about your book and are generally accompanied by the press release as well as a list of suggested interview questions, your bio, and excerpts from the book.

To announce an event—say, a press conference—your publicist might send out a media alert. This form of release, which is sometimes also called a media advisory, tells reporters very specific information about the event and the press opportunity it offers. (See the appendices starting on page 291 for samples of all of these formats of press material.) Every single page of any press material must include the publicist's contact information— or your contact information if you're the one doing the publicity outreach. All of the materials together comprise what's known as a press kit, which might also include any favorable articles or past reviews about you and your work.

THE PRESS RELEASE

The press release (also called a news release) describes in one or two pages the book's news value and content. The release is not a book report—a misconception held by many authors and publicists. The release has a standard format and should mirror the way most news stories are written with the most compelling information at the top of the release and further information provided in descending order of importance. Another common mistake made by neophyte press release writers is to "bury the lead"—placing the most important and interesting information about the book too far down in the press release. A reporter who scans only the first paragraph will miss the news you're trying to convey.

Quotes from you or the book enliven the body of the press release and demonstrate how your expertise could interest a reporter's audience or readership.

Your publicist will send one version of the press release to most media. In markets in which the book has a strong local angle, the headline and the first paragraph of the release should be customized for recipients in that market. Another way to tailor the release to a particular reporter is to attach a separate note that explains the local angle. For example, books that survey the best boarding schools, or the best companies to work for, or the best inns or flea markets all have built-in local angles for their various markets.

The 20 Rules of Writing an Effective Press Release

Whether you are writing the press release yourself or simply reviewing the release written by your publicist, you should know the rules of press release writing. You can also find sample press releases at www.press-release-writing.com, a press release writing service, or see page 291.

The Rules

1. The words FOR IMMEDIATE RELEASE appear on the top left of the page above the headline.

2. Your contact name, phone number, and email address are stacked in the upper right-hand corner of the first page.

3. Next comes the headline, in capital letters, usually in boldface, and centered on the top of the page to emulate an attention-getting newspaper headline. That headline summarizes why anyone would want to know more about you or your book and announces some item of news interest. This headline is not newsworthy: NEW BOOK ABOUT BICYCLES TO BE PUBLISHED IN SEPTEMBER. This one is newsworthy: NEW BOOK REVEALS THAT TWO HOURS OF BICYCLING A WEEK CAN REDUCE RISK OF HEART DISEASE.

4. A dateline appears at the start of the first paragraph and also includes the location of the news source, for example: (Charleston, SC, July 26, 2008).

5. Following the headline, the first paragraph of the release presents the most important information about your book. If you hide the salient information deep in the body of the release, then you've lost the opportunity to capture the reporter's interest. Present information in descending order of importance.

6. The release should be no longer than two pages. Use double-spacing or at least one-and-a-half-spacing. Do not try to cheat for more space by single-spacing your text, which makes the release hard to read. Use letter-size stationery.

7. Do not use sans-serif typefaces or others that are hard to read. Instead use easy-on-the-eye typefaces like Times New Roman or Garamond. Do not mix different typefaces in the same release. Avoid italics.

8. Customize your releases for the media you are pitching. It is better to send out 10 customized pitches to targeted reporters than 200 generic releases in a mass mailing. Mention any information of local interest in your lead paragraph. A debut book from an author from Cleveland is of greater interest in Cleveland than Minneapolis.

9. Spell every word correctly and pay particular attention to the proper spelling of names. A reviewer of the first edition of this book thought this was an obvious thing to point out. Well, you'd be surprised at the number of sloppy press releases that cross reporters' desks. Proofread the release several times, and verify that all information is accurate.

10. Include any relevant quotes from your book, from you or an expert in your field, that substantiate and reinforce the topic of the release. Think of the release as an encapsulated newspaper article, and write it as such. Many reporters will include parts of press re-

leases in the body of their articles. Familiarize yourself with the tone and style of newspaper articles to present your book in an informative and nonhyped way.

11. Don't use exclamation marks, which give the release an amateurish air.

12. Do not use hyperbole. Avoid hyped-up words and phrases like "destined for the bestseller lists," "unique," "best ever," and "fantastic." Write simply and concisely.

13. Keep sentences short.

14. Edit the press release ruthlessly to eliminate redundancies or unnecessary text.

15. In their book *Jump Start Your Book Sales*, Marilyn and Tom Ross offer this smart advice: Write all your promotional materials (including your press releases) from a benefit point of view. In other words, clearly convey what the reader or end consumer gets out of your book.

16. After the first mention of your title in the body of the release, include in parentheses the name of the publishing house and the publication date.

17. Book titles are conventionally written all in capital letters.

18. Names are written as Joe Smith the first time he is mentioned, and after that, he is simply referred to as Smith, or, formally, Mr. Smith.

19. At the bottom center of the release, after the body of the text, type —30— or ### or —end— to indicate closure.

20. At the end of the release, list the publication date, page count, price, format (hardcover or paperback), publishing house, and ISBN. Also include the website address for the book.

See the appendix for a sample press release on page 291.

A point worth repeating: Some terrific publicists can't express themselves well in writing but can orchestrate a media campaign like no one's business. If editing or rewriting a poorly written press release is slowing you down or making you anxious, be straightforward with your publicist about hiring a freelance writer to fix the release. Publicity departments hire copywriters all the time. If this is not an option for you, then hire a freelance writer yourself.

To find a freelance press release writer:

- Ask your publicist for the names of press release writers frequently hired by the publicity department.

- The site www.elance.com allows you to post your press release project for writers to bid on. The writer's credentials and rates and a feedback and rating system are displayed on the site. Prices are reasonable.

- Contact your local college or university to have your press release assignment posted where communications majors will see it.

- One source of writers is the American Society of Journalists and Authors website (www.asja.org). You can post your project free of charge. Potential writers will contact you directly.

- The site www.directcontact.com offers press release critiques, press release writing, sample press releases, as well as a press release distribution service. Fees are reasonable. A related site (www.trash proofnewsreleases.com) sells an excellent downloadable e-book called *Trash Proof News Releases: The Surefire Way to Get Publicity*, by Paul Krupin. The book is a full tutorial on writing effective press releases and press materials, with many samples accompanying the instruction. If you're writing your own press materials, then the instruction provided here will show you what reporters are looking for.

PITCH LETTERS

For a book that's slated for a publicity tour or radio interview mailing, your publicist will write a "Dear Producer," "Dear Editor," or "Dear

Interviewer" pitch letter, which offers you for interview and explains what you would talk about. In some cases, particularly for customized pitches for major national media like *Today*, your publicist will personalize the letter to a particular show and producer. (Not all pitch letters need to be customized. Local radio, television, and print press usually don't expect personalized correspondence, and it is time-consuming for publicists to do mail merges, or make the necessary refinements to truly personalize all correspondence.) A handwritten note that accompanies the pitch also goes a very long way with producers.

While the press release talks generally about the main points in your book, your pitch letter is more directly persuasive. However, it's not the letter alone that will secure the booking. Your publicist will most likely need to follow up with a phone call to reiterate the pitch, or to find another angle to get the show locked in.

When you're reviewing or writing pitch letters, or helping your publicist come up with pitch ideas, bear in mind the following advice from publicity expert Joan Stewart. (Joan Stewart is a professional speaker, trainer, and media relations consultant. Sign up for her free publicity tips of the week at www.publicityhound.com.) She says, "The biggest mistake authors make when trying to get onto major radio and television shows is pitching either themselves or their books. Don't pitch authors! Pitch issues. Don't pitch books! Pitch shows.

"Example: If you wrote a book about how children of divorced parents suffer long-term effects well into adulthood, don't try to entice television producers with the book. Entice them with an entire show around the topic of 'Children of divorced parents: Do they ever recover?' Then suggest two or three other guests who might also be interviewed in the same show, with at least one of them on the other side of the issue. Do that and you've just given the producer the guts for an entire show, and they're more likely to bite because you've done their work for them." The point is that pitch letters should convey what you and your book offer an audience or readership.

The format for a pitch letter is fairly straightforward. (See page 293 for an example.)

1. Use letter-size stationery and keep the pitch to one page.

2. Set the pitch up like you would any business letter, with the date in the upper-left corner. If you are personalizing the letter, then also include the name of the recipient and address in the upper left, followed by the body of the letter.

3. If you want to personalize the letter but don't know the recipient, use the salutation Dear Mr. or Ms. Otherwise an acceptable salutation is Dear Producer/Interviewer.

4. The lead paragraph gets right to the point: "I am writing to suggest a story about . . ." or "I am writing to suggest an interview with . . ." followed by a compelling reason why the recipient should be interested.

5. The following paragraph gets into the details of what you would talk about in an interview, possibly including some suggested interview topics.

6. Support the pitch with any statistics that bolster your position.

7. If appropriate, the next paragraph should mention any visuals that could support a television interview.

8. The last paragraph includes contact follow-up information.

9. The letter closes with your signature, like any other business letter.

SUGGESTED INTERVIEW QUESTIONS

While your pitch letter will suggest topics for discussion, a separate page with a list of about 10 or so suggested questions for interview is also valuable to producers and hosts. With several hours of programming to fill every day, radio and television producers and interviewers find the prompt questions very helpful.

Some publicists like to create an author Q&A, sometimes called a canned interview. Generally speaking, Q&As are too long and dense to be of much value to reporters or interviewers. The exception might be an extraordinarily provocative interview that has news value of its own. If your publicist wants to write a Q&A, explore her reasons and perhaps in your case it is a good idea. But do not push for one if it isn't in the plans. A simple list of questions will suffice.

TOP 10 LISTS AND TOPICAL PRESS RELEASES

In addition to the general press release about your book, your publicist might also write topical releases or articles with content that is easily reprinted by newspapers or read on air by broadcasters. These releases can be included with the first press packet or sent out separately as a follow up to stimulate more press coverage after the initial wave.

"The goal is to produce and package the color around the message," explains PR pro Jeanne Krier, who runs her own publicity business in New York City. By producing for her press packets what she has nicknamed "lift and sticks"—press material that is lifted from the book in a format that's appealing and easy for reporters to use—Krier has generated much press coverage for the books she has publicized. One example is a book called *The Scholarship Advisor*, by Christopher Vuturo, for which Krier's press materials included an article called "Mining for Money You Didn't Know You Were Entitled To" about 10 little known sources of scholarship money for college-bound students. She also produced a "lift and stick" for a book called *The Internship Bible*, by Mark Oldman and Samer Hamadeh, on "Famous Former Interns." The list of interns required some additional research on the part of the coauthors beyond what they had included in the book but their effort paid off: Many print media excerpted the list and credited the book in their coverage. In the next edition of the book, the publisher expanded the coverage of famous former interns.

For a book published by Hearst with *Esquire* magazine called *Things a Man Should Know About Sex*, the authors included top 10 lists in the book, knowing that the media loves to pick up quick one-liners and that these would appeal particularly to the morning-drive radio show hosts. The lists included things like "The Top 10 Worst Breakup Lines" and "The Top 10 Worst Pickup Lines," and press materials drew attention to the lists.

Can you use any of the following topical approaches to discuss your book in a press release?

- The 10 Easy Ways to Lose Weight

- The Three Myths About Doctors That You Need to Know

- Take This Quiz to Test Your Survival Skills

- The 10 Secrets to Getting Ahead (That Your Boss Won't Tell You About)

- 10 Great Ways to Save Money

- Shortcuts to Finding a New Job

If you can think of topical releases for your book, then tell your publicist. To get some ideas, simply head to your local newsstand and read the headlines for the monthly magazines. The words Secrets, Myths, Never Before Revealed, Top 10 Ways, Save Money, Tips to . . . , and Behind the Scenes are common attention-grabbing phrases. Use them in your own press releases. If your publicist is unwilling to write another press release, ask if he or she will edit a release that you write and then send it to the media lists.

ONLINE PRESS MATERIALS AND PRESS KITS

If you have a website, post your press materials, making it an easy matter for you or your publicist to include a link when pitching journalists. A good online press kit could include a press release, multiple story angles for reporters, as well as tips from your book that you will invite reporters to use verbatim. You might also include suggested interview questions, lists of other experts who are also available for interview (making the online press kits very useful to longer-format television talk show producers as well as print journalists), background on the subject matter, download-able photographs (and you should offer resolution downloads available that are suitable for print media), and your bio. Your online press kit should be an evergreen collection of press material: Make sure to edit or remove any elements that have gone out of date. Bottom line: Any reporter should be able to easily find the information that he or she needs to start to create a good and interesting story. While novelist James Patterson's site (www.jamespatterson.com) does not include a formal press room, his web pages are chock-full of newsy sound bites that sum up his achievements.

Actually, it surprises me to see how few authors have a press kit on their site. Certainly many author sites provide a wide range of information that is helpful to reporters, but it tends to be scattered around the site rather than concentrated on one page. Thriller writer Jeff Carlson offers a simple press kit at his site, www.jverse.com: The press center is prominent on the homepage and offers a range of background information, press releases, and author photos. For another example of a good press kit, see The American Cancer Society at www.cancer.org and click on press room: There you'll find a complete online media kit. Now *that's* one-stop shopping for the media.

AUTHOR BIO

Your publicist will distill the biography that you prepared for the marketing plan or author questionnaire into a few lines. The bio may appear at the bottom of the press release or as a separate item in the press materials. If your expertise is an important part of the interview pitch, your publicist might create a longer bio that emphasizes your credentials.

MEDIA ALERTS

You or your publicist may need to invite the media to cover an event that you are staging or sponsoring. It might be a book party at which you will present a check to charity, the launch of a program in your community that brings writers into schools to talk to students, an event at a bookstore, or a press conference. This press announcement is called a media alert or a media advisory and has a specific (and very simple) format that is different from a press release. Your publicist will send a media alert to the following media:

- News assignments desks at local television stations

- Assignment editors at the metro desk of newspapers

- News producers at radio stations

- The Daybook editor at the closest bureau of the Associated Press, who will list events on the local wire for reporters, producers, and assignment editors throughout the area to decide whether to attend. (If you're doing this yourself, go to www.ap.org to find the local AP bureau. Call the bureau and ask for the fax number to send your media alert clearly marked for the Daybook. Do this the day before your event. Follow up with a call to the Daybook editor to make sure your information has been received and whether it will go in the Daybook.)

- The photo assignment desk of local newspapers. If you are working solo and sending out the announcements yourself, you can find the media contacts with the help of the directories mentioned in Chapter 6.

The media alert is one-page long and states Who, What, Where, When, and Why, as well as whether the occasion offers interview or photo opportunities. The alert should be sent via fax or email to the appropriate stations and newspapers a few days before the event. (See the appendix on page 294 for a sample media alert.)

PHOTOGRAPHS AS PRESS MATERIALS

The press packet might include your photo, but only for the print media. If the book is sent out with the press packet and your photo is already pictured on the book jacket, then your publicist will not send a copy of the photo to television and radio producers.

If your book has a striking jacket, you might ask your publicist to send out a photo of the book jacket rather than your headshot. After all, it's your book's jacket that you want consumers to recognize in the bookstore. The exception is when your image is used as a way to market the book, as previously discussed.

Suggest that your publicist ask the art director for a JPEG of your book's jacket at the beginning of your campaign. These are simply electronic scans. That way she has it on hand for when a reporter on deadline might need it. She can also state at the end of the press materials that a JPEG cover is available upon request. If you're doing some publicity outreach, ask for a copy for yourself. Bear in mind, though, that publications have different requirements for electronic receipt of art. Also, if you or your publicist can't get hold of a JPEG, and a reporter on deadline needs a copy of your cover, send the reporter a link to your book's page on Amazon.com or bn.com or other online retailer, as the cover images are downloadable.

Publicists for illustrated books can make a selection of photos available to the press. While duplicating photographs is expensive, what seems to work best for many books is preselecting a range of images to have on hand as needed. These can be provided to the media in the form of slides, photos, or, best yet, downloadable electronic files. (Identify the photos that you think promotable even while you are doing the photo research for your book. Clear any photo permissions for promotional use at the same time that you clear the book rights. If you're not sure which images are suitable for promotion, then ask your editor or publicist to help you decide *before* your book goes into production. The images are harder to retrieve once they have been sent to the printer.)

TO PRESS KIT OR NOT TO PRESS KIT

Some publicists like to put all the press materials in a press kit—a fancy two-pocket folder that might have a copy of the book jacket pasted on the cover. They believe that the press kit helps to catch the eye of the producer or reporter. For my money (and more important, yours!—if you're underwriting some of the costs of your campaign), that window dressing is a total waste of money unless the kit is truly an unusual visual knockout. Press packets are more effective and cost-efficient: They are press materials without the expensive folder. Your publicist folds all the press materials together and places the packet inside the front cover of the book.

There are also imaginative ways to package press materials so that they get noticed. When she was publicizing a book called *The Tightwad Gazette*, by Amy Dacyczyn, publicist Grace McQuade came up with an inspired press packet. The book reveals hundreds of imaginative and simple ways for families to save money and became a *New York Times* bestseller. Consistent with the book's penny-pinching philosophy, she mailed out the press packet inside brown paper lunch bags with a sticker of the book's cover pasted on the front. The campaign received a lot of media attention. For a mystery novel by Barbara D'Amato called *Authorized Personnel Only*, the author suggested that her publicist wrap the press materials in yellow police tape, an effective way to catch the eyes of reviewers.

But be cautioned: Do not waste money on expensive giveaways. Unless the item is truly unusual, or very funny, the reporter will toss the package straight into the garbage.

POSTCARDS

Postcards, with a picture of the cover of your book on one side and advance praise and a description of the book on the back, can be effective and inexpensive press materials. (You can find many sources for printing postcards online.) Novelist Laura Van Wormer (www.lauravanwormer .com) has an instinctive feel for publicity, and has successfully publicized her many books. For *Riverside Drive*, her first novel, she got the publisher to print a couple of thousand postcards with her book jacket on the front and excerpts from her reviews on the back. As the title suggests, the book is set on Riverside Drive in New York City. During her spare moments, Van Wormer would pore through the New York City phone book and write a postcard to anyone with a Riverside Drive address. For those of you unfamiliar with New York, Riverside Drive is an affluent residential neighborhood—a concentrated book-buying community. Indeed, every time Van Wormer sent out a new batch of postcards, the book would sell out at the local bookstore. Of course, she alerted the bookstore about what she was doing so that she could measure the effectiveness of her efforts and so that the bookstore could order books in time for her next mailing.

If you don't want to get into the cost of mailing postcards, you could try an electronic postcard campaign, but unless your recipients have opted to receive mail from you, you're running the risk of seeming like a spammer.

PRESS MATERIALS—A SUMMARY

Writing effective press materials means that you or your publicist must convey the essence of your book in an appropriate format. There are different types of press materials that serve specific purposes:

- A press release is a general summary of your book with the most newsworthy or interesting points mentioned up front.

- Pitch letters offer you to interviewers as a guest or interview subject.

- Suggested interview questions make a reporter's job easier by laying out the salient discussion points about your book.

- A media alert informs the press of an event and what's interesting about it.

- A press kit contains all the elements that could interest the media in you, including a pitch letter with story angles, suggested interview questions, a press release, possibly also a topical press release, your bio, and perhaps your photo.

- An online press kit allows you to make your press materials accessible in a most efficient way.

6

THE PRINT PUBLICITY CAMPAIGN

MANY publishers send copies of every book to the major book reviewers at newspapers and magazines in the United States and Canada. Then some of those publishers call it a day. For most books, however, a review mailing alone is insufficient, especially these days when newspapers are cutting back on their book coverage. Some marketers estimate that a consumer is motivated to buy a book or product only after five to eight exposures to that product. Therefore, unless you're already a well-known writer with an audience anticipating your next book, one favorable review in one market will not drive book sales in significant numbers.

In addition, many books are of no interest to newspaper book reviewers who almost exclusively favor literary fiction or works of serious nonfiction. However, reporters in other sections of newspapers—such as lifestyle, business, health, the opinion columnists, etc.—should receive your book and be encouraged to write about it. This "off-the-book-page" coverage in feature and other editorial sections of newspapers and magazines can help to stimulate book sales and to generate other media interest in your work.

THE PRINT MEDIA MAILING LISTS

To conduct a review copy mailing, your publicist will create mailing lists from the publicity department's database and send your book to prospective reviewers in two phases: The first is a bound galley mailing to 50 to 100 long-lead publications (monthly magazines that have an editorial lead time of three to six months), as well as to some book editors at the top daily newspapers and weekly magazines. The second mailing takes place when your book comes off press. The publicist will then mail 150 to 300 copies of your book with press materials to newspaper and magazine book review editors.

If you've written a work of fiction or serious nonfiction, the publisher's reviewer mailing lists should be fairly comprehensive and up-to-date because the book review community has little turnover. On the other hand, less frequently used specialty mailing lists might need some work. For example, if you have written a cookbook and your publisher offers only two cookbooks a year, chances are that its food editors mailing list is not current. Or say your book would interest readers of military history, you're going to want to look at the publisher's mailing list in that category to see that it includes the right periodicals in your field. Your publicist may not have the time to devote to updating the list for your particular book's mailing.

This is where your expertise in your book's subject matter comes into play. Have a frank conversation with your publicist about the depth of the speciality mailing list in your subject area and how often it is used. Offer to spot-check the contacts on the list. Make it clear that your goal is to supplement his or her efforts to make sure that the galleys get into the right hands. (If controlling expenses is important to you and you live close to your publishing house, ask to use a spare desk for a day to make the spot-checking phone calls from the office.) Plan on doing this at about the same time that the publicist is writing press materials, or a little earlier. Start with the long-lead specialty publications in your field, because that's the first mailing. Look at copies of the publications to get familiar with the reporters' bylines. Call and verify the name and business mailing address of the person who handles book review coverage and of any feature reporters who seem appropriate. Try to get an email address, too. Research the book review contact information for your alumni magazine and any trade publications that might reach your target audience.

Think broadly about the publications that should be included on your mailing list. If you've written a cookbook, has your publicist got bridal magazines on the list, which could be appropriate targets? Suppose your book, whether fiction or nonfiction, has a legal theme. *The American Lawyer* should receive a copy. If your book is about graphic design, the many appropriate trade publications should be represented on the publicist's mailing list, and so on. Most of these publications will have book review editors, or an editor who oversees general book coverage.

Give your publicist the name and addresses of appropriate web reviewers and bloggers. Many sites review books and you will need to spend some time exploring the sites in your subject area to identify the ones that seem worthwhile. (For more on reaching bloggers, see page 232.)

Now turn your attention to the shorter-lead publications. To identify appropriate newspaper reporters, go to the sites of the top newspapers around the United States and in Canada. When you log onto a newspaper site, search for the word *book* to turn up all the stories that mention a book in that day's paper. Pay attention to how the reporters cover books: Is it in a general manner or with a local angle? If local, how can you tie your book into a local story? Does your book raise a potentially controversial or interesting issue for that community?

To find the names of appropriate publications and reporters:

- Use the published or online media directories found at your publishing house and then call to verify the contacts covering your field.

- Go to www.newspaperlinks.com, a terrific portal that links to 1,200 U.S. daily newspapers, 885 weekly papers, 1,100 Canadian and international papers, 90 newspaper groups, 64 associations, and 23 media organizations.

- Go to www.newpages.com, for alternative magazines and literary periodicals in the United States and Canada.

- Go to www.studyworld.com/college_newspapers_online.htm for links to college newspapers around the United States.

▪ Go to American Online Columnists at www.blueagle.com and Headline Spot at www.headlinespot.com/opinion/columnists, portals that link to the sites of syndicated columnists.

▪ Go to www.literarymarketplace.com. The advertising and marketing section offers publicity resources including lists of radio, television, and print media including producers' names, phone numbers, addresses, and email addresses. The lists are incomplete but they are a decent starting point. You need to register before you can access the site's free resources.

▪ Go to the "news" link on Google's homepage and then search for your subject to find relevant media coverage. For example, a quick search on the word "collectibles" turned up an article on the subject that had been nationally syndicated through the Universal Press Syndicate. If I were an author or publisher of a decorating book, I would track down the reporter to find out if they want to see other books on interior design.

If you're not touring, chances are that the publicist has not considered pitching feature reporters at newspapers outside your hometown about your book. Come up with a strong angle and it's then reasonable to ask your publicist if he or she will pitch feature editors in markets where you are not traveling. Reporters can always interview you by phone.

Your "Big Mouth" Mailing

As long as you're in a mailing list frame of mind, assemble a short list of "big mouths"—people who should get a free copy of your book at publication because they will talk it up. If you give these names to your editor's assistant, he or she will happily send out copies of the book, especially if you provide the names on labels. Do not send free copies to your friends and family, no matter how tempted you might be. They should *buy* copies of your book. (Well, of course, you should give one to your mother.)

Sometimes publicists will handle this mailing for you. Freelance publicist Jeanne Krier will send a press kit and book to the author's big-mouth list along with a note that says, "Dear So-and-So, This book is being sent to you with the compliments of the publisher and the author. We hope you recommend it to your friends and associates and that it will reach a broad audience. We welcome your comments."

Your big mouths might not even be people that you know—they are simply people who could spread the word about your book. For example, I once promoted a comic novel about hairdressing by sending complimentary copies to the top hairdressers in town along with a note asking that they put the book in their salons. I knew the campaign was working because, by coincidence, I found myself at dinner with a woman who'd had her hair done in one of the salons who started talking to me about the book. Author Philip Howard did a neat trick to get word of mouth going for his book *The Lost Art of Drawing the Line: How Fairness Went Too Far*, about our litigious culture. Through his agent, he arranged for the management of the Four Seasons restaurant in New York City to put a complimentary copy of his book on every table at lunchtime. The restaurant plays host to a daily power-lunch crowd in entertainment, law, media, and finance, and the book generated a lot of buzz.

Here are examples of off-the-book-page newspaper articles:

- The *New York Times* ran a piece about Michael Ledwidge, an Irish-American telephone cable splicer who works for Verizon. He had written a thriller called *Bad Connection* featuring, yes, you guessed it, an Irish-American telephone cable splicer.

- An article about a book called *Playful Parenting*, by Boston-based psychologist Lawrence Cohen, ran in the *Seattle Post-Intelligencer* and was syndicated to other papers including the *Chicago Tribune*. The book was positioned as an antidote to other parenting books that focus on drumming out children's obnoxious behaviors.

■ Like many newspaper sections, the Health section of the *Detroit News* runs "briefs" or brief news items that often mention books. A recent brief mentioned a book called *Self-Coaching: How to Heal Anxiety and Depression*, by Joseph Luciani.

■ The Living Smart section of the *Oregonian* interviewed James Mulholland, author of *Praying Like Jesus,* a book that promotes the forgiveness and sacrifice reflected in the Lord's Prayer as opposed to the popularized, self-centered prayer of Jabez.

■ The Workplace section of the *Los Angeles Times* ran an article on interviewing strategies based on a book by Dr. Mark Goulston called *Get Out of Your Own Way: Overcoming Self-Defeating Behaviors.*

Look for articles in your subject area and keep a record of the reporters' names. You should also peruse opinion columns. These writers cover any subject that interests them, and often reflect the mood of their communities. Also check out the metro section of the newspapers if your book covers topics of local news interest. Call the newspapers to confirm the name of the editor or reporter of the beat that concerns your book. You will notice that in certain sections of the newspaper, several reporters will cover the same subject area. Note the name of anyone who might take an interest in your book, as your publicist can pitch more than one reporter at a newspaper. Give the list—including names, addresses, and phone numbers—to your publicist to include in the press mailing and to make follow-up calls.

Special newspaper sections offer a great booking opportunity and are often overlooked by publicists, partly because they appear irregularly on topics that the publicists aren't pitching frequently. Local and national newspapers and magazines run special sections on topics like career, education, personal finance, and so on. Newspapers often run the sections on a Sunday, the day of the week with the highest circulation. Special section editors work with a two- to three-month lead time. You can get their names from the Bacon's Media Directory and you should call the contacts listed there to verify the up-to-date contact information. (You will find

Bacon's at your local library or you can buy it online at www.us.cision .com. Each media directory—Radio/TV/Cable, Newspaper/Magazine— costs about $500. If you are planning to book a lot of your own media on an ongoing basis, and you do not have access to media directories nor time to gather media leads, only then are the directories a worthwhile investment.) Another, less expensive way to find out what special sections are planned is locating the newspapers' websites and looking for the online editorial calendar. The calendar is generally posted in the advertising section of the site, as a way to prompt advertisers to buy space in the publication adjacent to specific editorial content. The site will also provide phone numbers so you can then call the editorial department to find out the name of the contact for the special section. If the editorial calendar is not posted then call the advertising department and ask them to send one to you.

Suppose you come across a special section on a subject about which you could be quoted as an expert or that's related to your book. Send the editor a press packet and a letter that explains your credentials. Include some of the issues in your field that you could address in an article. Follow up with a call. (Of course you can ask your publicist to do this, but if your campaign is over, then you can pitch the editors yourself.) Alternately you can send the editor a brief and succinct email. Make sure your subject line is tight and informative, which increases your chances that the email will be read. Do not send attachments with the email; instead, include links in the body of your email directing the editor to your website where they can look at your credentials.

If you have only a little time to devote to your publicity campaign, then a finite assignment that might contribute to your book's success is finding appropriate reporters who might cover your book. Set aside perhaps 30 minutes a day over the course of a few months. Use this time to research and read out-of-town newspaper sites to target the reporters that your publicist should go after. Most likely you will come up with a rich contact list of leads that your publicist can follow up on.

A Booking Tip for Your Publicist—Leads to Reporters Looking for Experts to Interview

Tell your publicist about ProfNet (www.profnet.com), a terrific service that notifies publicists of dozens of press leads twice daily by email. The leads are queries from reporters who are on deadline and looking for experts to interview on all kinds of topics. The subscription is expensive for an individual but certainly affordable for a publicity department or for several departments to share in a larger publishing house.

DEBUT SHORT STORY WRITER MANAGES HIS OWN BOOK REVIEW CAMPAIGN

David Lida is the author of a short story collection called *Travel Advisory*. Because he wanted the book to receive as much attention as possible, he knew that he would get heavily involved in the publicity planning for the book. "I thought I'd have to do a lot, but didn't know how much work it would really be," he says. He worked for a full six months, pretty much full-time, on generating publicity for his book. A freelance travel writer, he caught a lucky break and traveled to Cancún, Mexico, for a story. His visit coincided with a writers' conference that was held at the local Club Med. There he met some book review editors, who later assigned his book for review. However, having connections and sending out a galley or a copy of his book did not guarantee coverage. He says that every contact required several tactful follow-up calls to generate the coverage he was seeking. Ultimately, he garnered a number of good reviews from leading book review publications, but they took a lot of hard work to get on his part.

He also had some success setting up appearances at universities in the Latin American Studies departments. He counsels that setting up university appearances takes perseverance to catch a professor during office hours, and the booking may take several calls to firm up. Some universities offered him an honorarium. He also got himself invited to the Inter-American

Book Fair in San Antonio and to the *Los Angeles Times* Book Fair. The same perseverance paid off with interviews in several newspapers and websites.

For the next book, he says, he will look into hiring a publicist to make sure that the reviewers and independent booksellers are aware of his book. Bottom-line advice from Lida to writers who are planning to get involved in their publicity campaigns: "You have to be willing to do what it takes, to take responsibility to do things that shouldn't necessarily be the writer's responsibility."

CORRESPOND WITH BOOK REVIEWERS

Generally, with a few exceptions for the leading titles on the list, in-house publicists do not follow up with book reviewers after a review copy mailing. Some publicists are reluctant to place follow-up calls that might "bother" the book reviewers. At worst, book reviewers won't take the call or behave in a snappish manner on the phone. But without follow-up calls, many worthy books would never get noticed or reviewed. Even for the big books on the list, follow-ups are important to inform book reviewers of the publication date so they can schedule reviews accordingly. (Unlike in-house publicists, freelancers will call most of the book reviewers on the mailing list if they've been hired to handle the book review campaign.)

Before pursuing reviewers, be gut-honest with yourself. Does your book really belong on the book review pages? If you've written a self-help book, newspaper book reviewers are simply not going to take an interest. Don't expect your publicist to call reviewers about your diet book, your cookbook, your craft book, your 12-step recovery program book, and so on.

As a publicist, I found it sobering to visit newspaper book review editors in their offices, which were often cubbies surrounded by stacks of books and unopened packages from publishers. I learned in my follow-up phone calls to identify a book by saying something like, "It's the thick one with the yellow spine," and asking the editor to put it at the top of their pile to take a look at. With close to 300,000 titles published a year, by some estimates, your book is up against an enormous playing field. A newspaper might review 260 books a year in its daily pages and another 150 to 1,200 a year in its Sunday pages, depending on the size of the paper. To pique interest, your publicist's calls or correspondence to the book editor must be dead on target.

You can negotiate with a publicist who is reluctant to make follow-up calls. Perhaps he or she would be willing to email a few reviewers or follow up by phone with 10 of them. When I was a publicist, if I truly believed in the literary merits of a book then those phone calls were easy to make. So try to make your publicist believe in your book. Again, part of your job is to make your publicist a convinced and therefore convincing salesperson.

Finally, if you believe that your book is worth attention on the book review pages, and your publicist will not make any phone calls, bite the bullet and pick up the phone yourself. But before you even dream of contacting a book review editor, or any reporter for that matter, study his or her section of the paper, which you will find online. In any of your own publicity efforts, you will stand a better chance of success if you take the time and trouble to learn about the media you're pitching.

If you prefer not to cold-call the book reviewers, first drop them a short note or email about your book. If you have a website, include the link in your email and invite the book reviewer to read the first chapter, perhaps, that you have posted. The immediacy of the link may encourage the reviewer to check out your work. Invite the reviewer to email you for another copy of the book, if necessary. You may also follow up with a polite call to see if they need a copy of the book. Your publicist can give you the mailing addresses, phone numbers, and email addresses. If she won't share the contact information with you, you can easily search for the newspapers' websites.

When you tell your publicist about your plans to contact the reviewers you might be surprised at the reaction. He or she might suddenly seem motivated to make those calls after all. Due to fear of embarrassment, some publicists dread the thought of their authors calling the media. Everyone in the business has stories of authors harassing book review editors and bad-mouthing their publishing houses.

Coverage in other publications sometimes prompts a reviewer to take a second look at a book they passed over. So once any reviews appear, your publicist can send the good ones to other publications that have not yet covered your book. Even better, a quick email note with a link to the review you want them to see is an efficient way to alert other book editors.

If you get bad reviews that you believe are unwarranted or unjustified, then you have a small measure of recourse: Write a letter to the editor. Refrain from writing in anger because your letter will most likely sound foolish. Be specific, not personal, about your complaint. Once you've sent the letter, it may run with a response in the publication.

A Booking Tip for Your Publicist—Getting a Syndicated or Wire Service Feature Article

The websites of the large media companies list all the local papers that they own. If one of the papers is located near you, then, by using a strong local angle, you have a good shot at scoring an interview that could end up running nationally throughout the newspaper syndicate. Among them are Gannett (85 local papers and *USA Today*, www.gannett.com), Cox (17 local dailies, www.coxnews.com), Scripps Howard (19 dailies, www.scripps.com), and The McClatchy Company (31 dailies, www.mcclatchy.com). Their portfolios range from large urban papers like the *Atlanta Journal-Constitution* to small circulation town papers like the *Ocean County Observer* in Toms River, New Jersey. Here's how your publicist can try to influence the chances of a local interview turning into a national story.

Once the interview is secured and scheduled, your publicist should call the national office of the newspaper service and talk to the features editor. This is the person who assigns stories and selects articles from the local papers to run nationally. Your publicist should pitch that editor to run the local story in the other papers owned by the chain. Another approach is to ask the local reporter to offer the story for the national feed, which they don't do automatically for all stories. A prompt sometimes helps.

> Similar to the news syndicates, the Associated Press wire service can create an enormous amount of coverage from just one press hit. If your book has a strong local angle or a compelling story to tell, then pitch a feature story to your local Associated Press bureau. (See www.ap.org.)

GOSSIP COLUMNS

Gossip columns, many of which are nationally syndicated, afford a significant opportunity to launch a book. The columnists want celebrity news (is your novel under consideration for a film option?), sensational exposés, and, for instance, might take an interest in the real inspiration for the characters in your roman à clef. To get into the gossip columns:

- Read the column so you know what kind of items the reporter is interested in.

- Write an item in the style of the column.

- Fax it or email it to the reporter's office on an exclusive basis (meaning that you've given the item to no one else, and that you've stated on your fax or email "EXCLUSIVE TO [NAME OF REPORTER]").

Here's an example of the power of gossip columns. Some years ago I sent columnist Liz Smith an item about Wilt Chamberlain's autobiography, *A View from Above*. Through the instant exposure afforded by her piece about the book and the fact that the other media assiduously read her column, the notorious sound bite—Chamberlain's statement that he'd had sexual relationships with 20,000 women—became household knowledge overnight. The phone started ringing as reporters and producers called to set up interviews with Chamberlain and then to ask if Wilt was telling the truth and if so how did he arrive at that number because "we've just been figuring this out on the calculator and . . ."

THE OP-ED PAGES

Local and national newspapers offer another print publicity opportunity. Op-ed pieces range from the extremely serious to the tongue-in-cheek, but they always connect to current events or current trends.

Apart from timeliness, writing and placing op-eds depends on your authority on a subject. For example, an author of terrorist thrillers known for his scrupulous research might have legitimate comments on the increase in worldwide terrorist activities. Other examples:

■ When the American Academy of Pediatrics announced that television viewing was found to be detrimental to children, a children's book author or an educator might have written an op-ed piece about their own position on the issue.

■ The author of a book on interior design could have written a piece in connection with Senator Hillary Clinton's move to a fancy, new furnitureless house in Westchester, New York.

■ The author of a book on work and labor could have written a piece after George W. Bush departed for his monthlong vacation in his first year as president.

■ Barbara Ehrenreich, author of *Nickel and Dimed: On (Not) Getting By in America*, wrote an op-ed for the *New York Times* shortly after it was announced that Wal-Mart employees were suing the company for forcing them to work unpaid hours. In her book she wrote about working at Wal-Mart as part of her effort to understand how the working poor live.

Before you tackle an op-ed piece, read your target paper's op-ed section to get a feel for the tone of argument and the required length. Most run between 500 and 800 words. Submission guidelines may be mentioned on the op-ed page or perhaps on the newspaper's website. (See the *Washington Post*'s website for an example at www.washingtonpost.com.)

Clarify the point of your argument in your mind before setting to the task of writing the essay. If your essay is reacting to a news event, then turn it in within a day or two of that event. Otherwise the op-ed is out-of-date and irrelevant to a daily newspaper. Submit your op-ed essay to one newspaper at a time, not simultaneously to many papers.

Some op-eds may be of general topical interest rather than strictly time sensitive. Novelist Cameron Stracher wrote an op-ed for the *New York Times* about moving to the suburbs because his apartment in the city had become too small for his growing family. The essay's point was about regretting growing older and having to make the mature decision to leave Manhattan. The piece reflected a general trend in New York City and so was not pegged specifically to the news; it gave the author a chance to display his writing and have his novel mentioned in his byline.

A subject that sometimes crops up on op-ed pages is what it's like to go on a publicity tour. Newspapers seem to revisit this idea from time to time: Pitch the idea to your local newspaper's op-ed page.

WHAT HAPPENS WHEN A BOOK ON THE SAME SUBJECT AS YOURS IS COMING OUT AT THE SAME TIME?

This isn't always bad news because two books on the same subject coming out at the same time usually create a greater level of attention than either book would have received alone. That said, your publicist will need to work double time to convey the outstanding merits of your book and to make the media as aware of your book as the competition.

In your interviews, resist the urge to bad-mouth the competition. When you're asked point-blank how you think the two books are different, then honestly point out the distinctions without being derogatory. Otherwise you run the risk of starting a mudslinging match or looking graceless.

If you're aware of another writer working in your subject area, then try to reach the marketplace first, or at least simultaneously with your competition. With the first book to market probably preempting all media interest in the topic, publishing months later could be disastrous.

THE PRINT PUBLICITY CAMPAIGN—A SUMMARY

Print coverage for your book can take several forms:

- Book reviews

- Off-the-book-page coverage or feature coverage

- Item mentions in gossip columns or more thoughtful coverage from more serious-minded columnists

- Op-ed pieces

Go online to gather leads to appropriate columnists and reporters to supplement the publisher's media lists.

7

THE PUBLICITY TOUR

A PUBLICITY tour normally involves visiting between two and ten cities, over the course of one to three weeks. During a tour, you will go to local television and radio stations for live or taped interviews, meet print reporters at your hotel or other locales, and give readings or talks at bookstores and other venues. A media escort may meet you at the airport to take you to as many as six to eight appointments in one day—all pre-arranged by your publicist. In between, you will stop by bookstores to meet store managers and sign copies of your book.

Publishers have reduced the average number of cities for their tours, because many local television and radio talk shows have been displaced by national shows. Instead publishers are forced to depend on national media, confining many publicity tours to New York, Washington, DC, and Los Angeles—the three U.S. cities where most of the national television media is located—and to Toronto, the major national media market in Canada. In turn, greater competition makes a national media booking more difficult to secure than in the past. As novelist Jane Heller points out, celebrities have become more accessible to the media and have further depleted the airtime available to everyone else. If a television show has a choice between booking an author and booking a celebrity, then guess who gets the booking.

To improve your chances, you might get to know the national media and the kinds of author guests that they book on their shows. In other words, watch the shows to understand how you might fit on them. Check out the shows' archives on their websites. The site www.govspot.com/pulse/talkshows.htm includes links to some of the top national talk shows like *The Charlie Rose Show*, *Larry King Live*, and so on.

The limited media opportunities in local markets means that you and your publicist have to get creative about finding a strong local angle for each city. Local print, radio, and television news need a compelling hook. One way to accomplish this is to anchor your visit to a city with a speaking engagement at a local university, corporation, or other venue. (See page 200 for a discussion about setting up speaking appearances.)

A publicity tour offers an experience of extremes—your greatest highs, your lowest lows. You might have some terrific interviews with smart reporters who really seem to understand and like your book. Then your next interview could be an encounter with someone who misses the point of your book entirely. One day you might have a crowded bookstore appearance, an empty event the next. (But you can turn a disappointing event into something good. See the section on Book Signing on page 194 to find out what other resourceful authors have done in those circumstances.) Your goal for the tour is to help your publicist create as many positive bookselling opportunities as possible.

BOOKING THE TOUR

Your publicist will consult you about your schedule to set tour dates. He or she will arrange your local bookstore appearances six to twelve weeks ahead of your tour (and sometimes even earlier for competitive markets like New York City and Los Angeles) so that the bookstores can include your event in their promotional calendars. Then six to eight weeks in advance come the pitches to the top local television shows in your tour cities, which tend to make their commitments to author interviews earlier than other media. When your books come off press—about four weeks before the tour starts—books and press materials are sent to the rest of the media in the tour markets.

Try to stretch your tour dollars by researching cheaper fares. Technically your publicist is the one who should do this, but publicists often wait to book flights until about 30 days before the first tour city. Come up with some bargain fares and you might be able to convince your publisher to spring for some extra tour cities without straining its funds.

Some publishers schedule tours tighter than the four-week booking lead. In other words, in some instances the first books arrive at the publishing house only three weeks before a tour is due to start. This might be due to a production delay, or perhaps the need to promote the book beginning on a certain date. This chain of events means that by the time the producers and potential interviewers receive their review copies, the publicist has only two weeks to book the tour. By then many of the top media slots have been taken.

Remember, the publicist is competing not only with other publishers sending authors to the same tour cities, but also with local celebrities, spokespeople, doctors, and business leaders who also want to appear in the local media. A head start is crucial.

Some producers and interviewers will set up an interview without seeing the book. This allows the publicist to book interviews using only the press materials. However, many interviewers prefer to see the book before committing to an interview. Make smart use of your time. If you suspect that the tour is being booked too late to create an effective schedule, then suggest that the publicist postpone the tour by a couple of weeks. Unless you have prearranged book signings or other appearances that are not easily rescheduled, a delay is good strategy.

Get involved in the planning of the cities and the tour dates. If you think that a particular city should be included on your tour then say so and be prepared to explain why. Ask the publicist for the expected date of the book's arrival in-house. Unless there's a compelling reason to start publicity on a certain date, opt for the tour to start five to six weeks (rather than three to four weeks) after the bound book date. The extra time between bound book date and tour date will give your publicist the necessary cushion for booking a full media schedule, even if there are delays in the book's production or delivery. You can control the dates of your tour because without you, there is no tour. Of course, if there is a fixed date to which your book's promotion is connected, like Valentine's Day, then you will not have as much flexibility.

Even with an exceptionally short lead time, publicists can readily create media tours for at least three kinds of books: Books that are controversial; books by celebrities, for which producers will always make room on short notice; and sports books, because sports producers and writers are used to scheduling interviews on a tight deadline.

Your publicist selects your tour cities based on several criteria:

- Your subject matter's potential appeal to television and radio talk shows

- The subject matter of your book; for example, Atlanta is known as a good cookbook market because local television will book cookbook demo segments and local cooking schools will host author events

- Where your contacts are located—i.e., friends, family, or associates who can put you up and help deliver audiences for book signings

- Your personal or business travel plans to which you can add book promotion activities

- The location of booksellers that have a good track record at hosting successful author events for books on your subject

- The size and opportunities of the media market

Once the cities and dates have been locked in, your publicist will select the media lists and send 10 to 15 books in each market to the media contacts there. Follow up calls begin about a week later. Your publicist will probably experience what I think of as "booking karma." Some booking days go very well where producers and reporters jump to say yes to the publicity pitch. "When can we have your author in our studio?" they eagerly ask. Those are the great days that give a publicist a booking high that fuels creative pitching for the rest of the day.

But other days might begin with a series of no's and, boy, those are frustrating! When I ran into days like that, I'd stop altogether, retool my pitch, and then wait until the next day before picking up the phone again.

All good publicists have techniques by which they pump themselves up during pitching time. Still, when some pitches inevitably go bad and there are few bookings to show for the efforts, many publicists feel embarrassed. They may become incommunicado or evasive. However, because of the good relationship you will nurture with your publicist, you will be ensured of hearing the bad news along with the good. Once the booking process starts, contact your publicist frequently. If the bookings are not going well, offer to help rethink the approach. Being a partner in the process saves you from nasty surprises later, like flying to a city to do only one interview and one booksigning.

A Booking Tip for Your Publicist:
Use a Media Booking to Leverage More

Publicists routinely send booking alerts by email to in-house staff. When the booking is significant—like a major national television show—one publicist I know will blind copy other producers who haven't yet committed to doing an interview. Some producers object to receiving an obvious mass email. But usually, the emails prompt other producers to quickly book the author.

Despite your publicist's efforts, lack of media interest may force the cancellation of a tour city or two. If your tour schedule looks thin, suggest that the publicist try the top stations in a couple of other "replacement" cities to see if the pitch works better. Tour markets can be inconsistent, with jam-packed days, say, in Pittsburgh and little to do in Nashville. Be careful at this stage about how you involve your editor. If you tell your editor that the publicity bookings are going badly, clarify that you believe that your publicist is trying his or her best (if that's what you believe). That way the editor will not make the publicist feel defensive in any follow-up conversations between them. Authors who tattle behind a publicist's back are extremely annoying if not threatening, especially if the editor and the publicist are not on the best of terms, or if the publicist is relatively junior in the organization. You can't know those internal politics, so stay out of them. They can hurt your book.

Your publicist might show you the evolving tour schedule and will certainly show you a finished schedule a few days before you leave so that you can plan for any interview requirements and pack appropriate clothes. The schedule may even change after you've hit the road, with last-minute interviews falling into place or sudden cancellations. The tour schedule should itemize every detail about your tour days: the name, address, and location of your hotel; name and numbers of your escorts; home, cell and office phone numbers for your publicist and editor; arrival time and start time for your interviews; whether the interviews are live or taped and if taped, the anticipated airdates; any particular information to mention in your interviews such as the time and location of the book signing in town that same day so that listeners can attend; your publisher's 800 number for radio stations to mention on air so listeners can order the book; the time you will depart for the airport and, always helpful, a comment about how long it will take you to reach the airport from your last appearance. Your escorts will also receive a copy of the itinerary. (See page 295 for a sample tour schedule.)

A Booking Tip for Your Publicist—Work the Weekend Shift

"Make it big, make it loud, make it Saturday" is advice from one media professional. The idea is to announce your news on a weekend when fewer news events compete with yours. The tactic is particularly effective with softer news that might not get as much attention during the week when it faces more competition from hard news.

Here's how it works: The weekend assignment editor, in a slow news week, looks for ideas for coverage that the weekly assignment editor might not feel so hungry for. The weekenders also have fewer calls to field from publicists so the caller is more likely to get a hearing. One book publicist learned to time his press pitches for the weekends when the more receptive weekend assignment editors were on duty, and was successful in planting a number of stories that ended up on the front pages

of the local tabloids. During the week, those same stories might have
been buried inside the paper. Of course what he was pitching had genuine news value, but his method of handling the publicity gave the books
the best shot at maximum coverage. It also meant he was willing to work
over the weekend.

WHAT TO PACK FOR THE TOUR

Pack a minimum of clothes. Take clothes you like wearing so that you are
comfortable in them. Take lightweight clothes that don't wrinkle easily.
You will wear a jacket for your television interviews—the television stu-
dios are cold, and the jacket will give you a tailored, professional look. Don't
take outfits that are inappropriate to wear on television, i.e., no striped patterns or bright whites that will "vibrate" on camera. In the weeks leading up
to your tour, watch morning television and pay attention to what the hosts
wear: tailored jackets in solid colors for the women and men. Wear clothes
that can be hand-washed at night and line-dried for morning's wear, if
necessary. Avoid blouses or shirts with tight collars that make you look
like you're choking.

Dress appropriately for your book's subject to enhance your credibility as an expert and reinforce your message: Doing a cookbook demo?
Then have an apron stamped with the title of your book on the bib and
wear it on the set. Your topic falls in the category of light entertainment?
Then wear something informal (though not a T-shirt or sweatshirt!).
Need to persuade the audience about your side of a serious matter? Then
go with a jacket (and tie for men) to convey a professional look. You will
soon get a sense of what dress styles are effective from watching author
interviews.

If you're not appearing on television, then your radio and print interviews have no particular dress requirement. Still, remember that some
print reporters will describe the way you look in an article and may bring
a photographer. You don't want to look like a slob (or smell bad, like one
of my authors did. The way he smelled made me reluctant to book any
face-to-face interviews for him. No kidding!).

You will also want a good book for the plane ride. If you're like me, you will take five books for fear of running out of reading material. But really, take only one or two books if you are appearing at bookstores. Very often, a bookstore owner will thank you by offering you a complimentary book. You will have plenty of opportunity to pick up books along the tour—don't weigh yourself down.

THE TOUR

The tour is exhausting and exhilarating. You set off from home to arrive at your first destination, where you might arrive late evening at your hotel. Early the next morning, your media escort will meet you in the lobby to drive you to your appointments all day and get you to the airport at night. You will be the subject of a series of radio, television, and print interviews through the course of the day, where everyone will ask you the same questions about your book. You will meet some interviewers who seem genuinely enthusiastic about your work, and you will meet others who seem just plain bored. The occasional interviewers who ask you different questions from the others will strike you as geniuses. As the road show begins to become a blur, in some interviews you may forget if you've already mentioned one of your key points. (Stay focused!) After completing your evening bookstore reading, you may take a late evening flight heading to your next tour city. If you don't fly out that night, then you will likely go back to your hotel room alone with your adrenaline still pumping, feeling like you're all dressed up with no place to go. But you'd better get to sleep because you've got an early flight in the morning.

When you are on tour, get the full names and addresses of all the interviewers, producers, and booksellers. Travel with a pack of note cards to write thank-you notes while they are all fresh in your mind, and you in theirs. While many people have bemoaned the decline of the art of personal correspondence in the age of email, let's not kid ourselves. Personal letters were well on the decline before our correspondence became electronic. If anything, email has helped restore written personal dialogue. Still, your simple handwritten note to a reporter or bookseller will create a lasting impression and remind the recipient of you and your book.

Stay in touch with your editor and publicist while you're on the road. Report any good news right away—large turnouts at bookstores, a good guess (or real tally) at the number of copies sold at an event, or aspects of the book that seemed to particularly interest the media. If your schedule is too crammed to allow time for contact during the day, then leave an informative message on their voicemail after-hours so they hear it as soon as they arrive at work in the morning. Your publicist can feed this information to producers in upcoming cities or use it to set up more interviews. If the tour is going well, the editor and publicist can use that information to advocate for more advertising or more tour cities for your book. Your good news keeps the publishing staff focused on sales and inventory levels for your book.

Your publicist might call bookstores a couple of weeks before you arrive in town to ask if you can drop by the local bookstores to sign stock. Very often the stores will order more books. The books you sign are stickered as specially autographed by the author and are often moved into a more prominent display area. If you don't have a publicist working on your behalf, you certainly don't need one to set up informal drop-ins. Simply call the stores yourself and ask for the store manager. If you do not have the lead time to call the store ahead of your visit, drop into stores and ask to meet the manager. Politely introduce yourself and ask if you may sign copies of your book. The manager will be happy to oblige you. Then thank the store manager. This advice might seem obvious, but you'd be surprised. One bookseller praised a friend of mine, an author, for being so polite when he dropped by the store. The previous author who'd swung by had been rude, signing his books and moving them to the front of the store himself without asking first—kind of like rearranging the furniture in someone else's house. As soon as that author left the store, the bookseller moved the books right to the back. Remember, you're on the bookseller's turf, so don't act with impunity or entitlement.

A bestselling author advises, "Visit every bookstore that you can." When you arrive in a tour city, ask your escort to take you to bookstores in between your scheduled interviews and signings. Introduce yourself to store managers. Get to know them. Carry "Signed by the Author" stickers around with you. Some stores are too small to be regular stops on the author trail, and may not be prepared for authors who drop in to sign stock. The store managers will be grateful that you have stickers and will place your book up front. You can have the stickers made by a local printing store in your neighborhood, or you can find similar services online. Make sure the stickers are the kind that come off easily, as you don't want to spoil the book jacket. If the bookstore does not stock your book, take the occasion to pitch the store manager about the book—even giving him or her a free copy of your book and copies of your promotional postcard or press release. Take the situation as an opportunity to win over a bookseller.

AN AUTHOR DREAMS UP AN IDEA FOR A LOCAL TOUR THAT LEADS TO NATIONAL PRESS COVERAGE

Novelist Jane Heller was in a funk because *Publishers Weekly* had given her first novel, *Cha Cha Cha,* a bad review. "I took to my bed," she said, but then realized that she couldn't let one bad review knock her off her plan to become a full-time writer. Instead, she says, the review motivated her to create a real success. When *People* magazine called the novel the "Beach Book of the Week," Heller saw her chance at vindication and came up with a plan for the "first-ever beach tour." Her publisher agreed and Heller got to work. She lived in Connecticut at the time and called a number of the larger state beaches and parks in her area to get permits. Then she worked with local bookstores to have them sell books at her beach events. Then she took her folding table, display poster, and books to the beach, and set up shop. While the booksellers sold some books, she says that the tour's real value was the publicity it generated. At every beach she visited, the local media covered her event, including print, radio, and television. Ultimately, the beach tour was one of the hooks that grabbed *Today,* which interviewed Heller shortly afterward.

Heller says that writers need to understand that "the Cinderella story is not the way publishing works." In other words, the fantastic stories about writers who are swept into the limelight for their first novels and catapulted onto national bestseller lists are rare occurrences. "The biggest reality," says Heller, "is that marketing your book is a constant battle. Your publisher will turn down many of your ideas, but sometimes they will say yes." With more than a dozen novels behind her, Heller's book contracts now stipulate that she has marketing consultation on her books.

CREATE BROADCAST NEWS COVERAGE FOR A NOVEL

Publicist Justin Loeber threw himself heart and soul into the campaign for a debut novelist named Diane McKinney-Whetstone. *Tumbling* became a house favorite, because the publishing staff enjoyed the book and adored the author. Loeber not only secured widespread book review coverage for this literary novel, but he also managed to book the author on CBS's *This Morning* (the forerunner of the current CBS *The Early Show*) and *The Geraldo Rivera Show*. He got the CBS booking by pitching hard, politely, and persistently: He pitched the triumphant success story of a woman, who was a public affairs officer for the Department of Agriculture Forest Service and wrote fiction by night, all while raising a family. *The Geraldo Rivera Show* happened because he pitched the idea of "Dreams Can Come True," all of which demonstrates that the positioning or packaging of an author is everything when it comes to trying to book the media.

Loeber, who now runs Mouth Public Relations (www.mouthpublic relations.com), suggests that authors research their opportunities for appearing on a show by trying to visualize why a segment on your book would interest the show's audience. Very often, when a show turns him down, he will talk to the author to try to figure out another angle so he can pitch the book another way. "A publicist would be lying," Loeber says, "if he claimed to be an authority on every subject." When he starts out on a campaign, he asks the author for two or three reasons why producers and viewers should be interested in a segment on the book.

An author who is passionate and knowledgeable about his or her subject area and who is actively engaged with the marketing of the book is Loeber's idea of the perfect author to work with.

MEDIA ESCORTS

Nicknamed "author-haulers" by humorist and writer Calvin Trillin, media escorts can provide a valuable service to authors on tour. If you've got a jammed schedule, then your escort is your best friend and ally in a tour city. He or she will meet you at the airport or at your hotel and troubleshoot any glitches that come up during the day. Escorts keep your day running smoothly, get you to your interviews on time, and arrange last-minute drop-ins to bookstores that are carrying your book. One escort in Seattle meets her clients with a care basket in her backseat, filled with sundry items needed throughout the day, such as energy boosters and water and even dry socks on a rainy day. Some escorts are delightfully indiscreet and will tell you stories about other authors they have driven around. This, of course, is entertaining gossip, but should remind you to behave nicely unless you want to become a tour legend yourself.

Naturally, the escorts know the local media very well. Most of them keep an active, up-to-date media list for their city and the surrounding suburbs. Every time I booked a tour, my first calls were to the escorts in the tour cities to talk about any new media opportunities. This always gave me confidence in my knowledge of the local media market before I started booking. Talking to the escorts also alerted me to reschedule the tour dates to avoid any major local events—like a football game—that might siphon off bookstore event attendees. For authors who are setting up their own tours, the escorts are extremely helpful. When you reserve a day of media escorting, the escort will give you a media list to work with. Some escorts have recently started to book publicity in their markets. Ask your publicist for the contact information for the escorts in your tour cities.

The escorts can help identify opportunities for off-the-beaten-track author appearances. If you and your publicist lock into your tour cities early on, then ask your publicist to brainstorm with the escort about speaking venues such as universities, libraries, and local clubs. (Or ask if you can call the escort.) Because speaking events sometimes require a longer lead time to set up, you and your publicist will want to have this information as early in the booking process as possible.

Some escorts specialize in cookbook author tours. Called food escorts, they will buy the groceries for your demo segment, and will prepare any food that needs to be cooked in advance for the set. If necessary, they will also help you set up your demo on set before you are interviewed.

TROUBLESHOOTING ON TOUR

Your publicist sends you the itinerary the day before you're supposed to leave, and it's filled with mistakes and long empty stretches of time with few interviews scheduled.

If there are gaps in the schedule, then ask the local escort to take you to every bookstore possible in the region, to build recognition among store managers for you and your book. Next time, though, stay in frequent contact with your publicist while she's booking your tour to redirect the tour to other cities.

You've just appeared on the city's number one live radio talk show at noon. You stop off at the local bookstore on the way to your next interview. They do not have any copies of your book and in fact have never carried the book.

This is a common plight for author and bookstore alike. Sometimes books are delayed in shipping from the warehouse. Sometimes the bookstore didn't order the book on time or the order got lost. Sometimes the publicist didn't alert the sales department of the tour city appearance or the sales rep didn't get around to alerting their customers. There's not much you can do about the city you're in, but alert your publicist so that the sales reps can contact booksellers in later tour cities. The booksellers will stock up on extra copies of your book in anticipation of your media interviews in their town, especially if they hear anecdotal evidence about how your interviews are driving demand in other markets.

You show up at the bookstore for your evening reading to discover that the bookstore sold out of your book following your noon radio interview.

This is good news—proof that your publicity appearances are effective in generating sales. In this situation, a bookstore will take orders for customers who've arrived to see you and you will sign bookplates for them to insert in their books later. The bookstore will reorder copies of your book and, because of your sales success, is likely to put the book in the front of the store.

You show up at a television station for your appointed early-morning live interview and the producer tells you that you weren't expected until tomorrow. (Or tells you that you weren't expected at all.)

Ask nicely if there's any possibility that the show can tape a segment to air the next day. Ask your escort to quickly call the producers and reporters for any interviews left in the day to reconfirm your itinerary. A publicist usually reconfirms all publicity appearances a day or two before you show up, but some publicists forget and producers make mistakes, too. Call your publicist to check that interviews have been reconfirmed for the rest of the schedule.

You arrive late in a city, show up at the hotel, and find they have no record of your reservation. Or they have a reservation but the room charge won't be billed directly to the publishing house. The hotel clerk asks you for your credit card.

Hotels are legendary for screwing up reservations, and the mix-up is probably not your publicist's fault. Be calm but insistent at the check-in desk, and ask to talk to the manager. If the hotel still refuses to directly bill your publisher, then have the charge put on your credit card. Then leave a message for your publicist at the office number to instruct the travel agency to redirect the billing for future hotel stays. The travel agency can sometimes even straighten this out before checkout. If this happens after-hours, *don't* call your publicist or your editor at home. They can deal with the problem the next morning.

You have a major national media campaign all lined up. But then there's major breaking news and your interviews are canceled for the foreseeable future.

The publicist will have trouble rescheduling these interviews. Even though the television stations booked your interview in the belief that you will make an interesting guest, when the publicist tries to rebook you, the station may consider your book old news. Also, rescheduling you would require the producer to cancel or postpone other previously scheduled guests, which they are unwilling to do unless your story is particularly compelling. Some of your interviews will be salvaged, some may be taped for later airing, but many will be lost and there's little that you can do about it. The bigger the breaking news, the longer it takes for the media and the public to return to their normal daily interests.

While breaking news is a bane for some authors, it's a boon for others as their books come to the fore. For example, in the immediate aftermath of the World Trade Center attacks, the major media interviewed Tom Clancy because of his authority as a writer of techno-thrillers and Eric Darton about his recent book, *Divided We Stand: A Biography of New York City's World Trade Center*.

Your media escort fails to show up to take you to your interview.

This is an unlikely event, though within the realm of the possible—perhaps her car got towed, which happened to one of my authors. If you can't reach the escort on the cell phone, get in touch with your publicist. If you can't reach him or her, immediately arrange backup transit through your hotel. If the publisher is already underwriting your tour, then don't worry about the cost. Your goal is to get to your interviews promptly. Leave a message with your publicist and with the escort's voicemail as to your whereabouts. Your escort has a copy of your itinerary and will probably catch up to you at a later stop in your day.

Your tour schedule tells you that you should take a taxi to your next interview but a taxi will not stop for you and you're going to be late for your live interview downtown.

This happened to one of my authors. Taxis wouldn't stop for him and he finally managed to get to the radio station with a minute to spare. If this happens to you and you don't have time to call a car service, find a pay phone (or use your cell phone) in a quiet place and call the producer. A radio station can conduct the interview live by phone.

Any author might have trouble getting a taxi, but it can be a particular challenge for authors of color. Your publicist, who is likely white, may not realize or may forget that getting a cab could be a hassle for you, so politely insist on a car service or a media escort to get to your interviews. Similarly, in unfamiliar cities where you might feel uncomfortable trying to get a taxi, ask your publicist to schedule car services for you.

Your flight is canceled and you will miss the event scheduled in your next tour city tonight.

See if you can get on the next available flight or try to switch airlines. Let your publicist know. If you get stuck and can't get on a flight, call your publicist to rearrange your interviews and reschedule the flight. If this happens after hours, then *do* call your publicist at home. Or call the 24-hour emergency travel agency number that should be part of your itinerary. Call the media escort in the destination city about your delay. If that does not work, call the producer or bookseller who's expecting you so that they can make alternate arrangements and let customers know of the change in plans. Make sure to leave a message about your revised plans for your publicist.

Your publicist quits the publishing house at the beginning of your tour.

Get on the phone right away with your editor and the director of publicity. What is the contingency plan? If the plan seems inadequate, say so. You may need to get your agent involved and ask that your editor step in to advocate on your behalf.

If the publicity director plans to reassign the title to another publicist on staff, ask the director about the number of other titles that publicist is working on. Ask also if the director will instruct the new publicist that your tour is a priority. Ask if the publicity director would consider hiring a freelancer immediately to work on the tour. Ask how the new in-house publicist will handle the additional workload and suggest that a freelance publicist be hired for certain tour cities (if your tour is a big one) or for national media bookings. These are expenses that houses are often willing to assume when they're suddenly short-staffed.

You're in the middle of an interview and the reporter seems disconcertingly hostile toward you.

Even if your book is uncontroversial, you may encounter hostile reporters. Some reporters use an edgy approach to goad their interview subjects into letting their guard down. If the reporter's manner is making you uncomfortable and it's a print or taped broadcast interview, you might ask—unemotionally—why he or she is so angry with you. The reporter will be surprised to be confronted and may back down. But if you don't think you can persuade the reporter to see your point of view fairly, then you may end the interview politely.

A radio host's style may be normally aggressive and you may find yourself taking part in a live hostile interview. In other words, you've become part of an act. Keep your cool, and do not rise to the bait. Try to stick to your message and display your good manners and humor, and perhaps bemusement at the antics going on around you. And remember that this, too, shall pass.

You're in the middle of an interview and all seems to be going well when the reporter suddenly asks you about that embarrassing police incident in your past that you wish no one knew about.

The best way to handle tough questions about personal or controversial events in your life is to prepare for them. Chances are you will never hear the question you fear, but tell your publicist about your concerns, and work together to shape the appropriate response. Practice that response so that you're able to get your point across with ease.

TOUR WITH OTHER AUTHORS

Increase your exposure by traveling with another author, even if you have different publishers. Generally, authors who tour together already know one another, and are prepared to spend many hours on the road driving from store to store, from town to town. Sometimes their publishers foot the bill; sometimes they pay their own way. The advantages of a shared author tour are reduced expenses, companionship to embolden you to make yourselves noticed in a bookstore, and a two-for-one lineup that appeals to booksellers and audiences. For an effective road trip, plan well in advance, and allow for more time than you think you will need for road travel so that you arrive on time at your bookings.

Check out Nuns, Mothers and Others (www.nmomysteries.com), a group site for four mystery writers: Lee Harris, Jonnie Jacobs, Lora Roberts, and Valerie Wolzien, who have teamed up in their promotion efforts. They tour together, produce group ads and promotional material, and publish a newsletter. They offer an account on their site of how they set up their book tours and how on one tour, they visited 17 bookstores and libraries in nine days. They've discovered that they all benefit from one another's readers, by enlarging the size of the audiences and exposing their work to new readers. Because two of them live in the East and two in the West, they've also enlarged one another's geographical fan base.

"We've gone on the road six times in as many years," they report. "One person does the initial—and most difficult—job of contacting stores and mapping the itinerary. Ideally any day that doesn't involve long hours traveling contains at least two events. While mystery and independent bookstores are the backbone of our trips, we've spoken at libraries, luncheons, local conferences, and on radio shows. Groups such as these enjoy having a 'ready-made' panel of authors. And the local press feels it's getting more bang for its buck with four of us so we do well with publicity."

The Sisters in Crime newsletter reported on two other formalized groups of touring mystery authors: The Deadly Divas and The Red-Headed League. Touring with other authors works particularly well for genre writers, as they share the same target audience. If you write mystery, science fiction, fantasy, romance, or children's books, consider partnering with another writer in your field. If you don't know any other writers in your field, reach out to writers you think are appropriate to start building collegial and cooperative marketing friendships. Even if no formalized marketing program results from your outreach, you can learn from your colleagues.

THE AUTHOR OF A FIRST LADY BIOGRAPHY TAKES TO THE ROAD AND CREATES A NATIONAL MEDIA CAMPAIGN

Carl Sferrazza Anthony's biography *Florence Harding: The First Lady, the Jazz Age, and the Death of America's Most Scandalous President* was not of obvious interest for the talk shows. However, the author had spent many years working on the book—a true labor of love—and wanted to give it a fighting chance at success. "I felt that this was a great person who had been ignored unfairly," he says of Florence Harding. "I felt an odd obligation to honor her and her memory, to give her the right kind of PR [that she never had when she was alive]."

Undeniably, as you will see in the story that follows, Anthony had some breaks. But as the old saying goes, luck smiles on those who are prepared. And Anthony worked hard to create his own luck.

Anthony started planning a media tour that followed the same path as the Hardings' cross-country whistle-stop tour 75 years earlier. He intended to underwrite the travel costs, or to find sponsors, knowing that his publisher would be unlikely to finance a tour for a book about a first lady who had been dead for many decades. He arranged for a meeting with his publicist and director of publicity, where he promised that he would pay the expenses and devote himself to the book's promotion if they would back him up and help to book local media in the cities he planned to visit. They agreed to do so. Anthony then approached museums and historical societies along the route to set up speaking engagements. He created a video from old newsreel footage of the Hardings' trip and offered to customize his talks for each location. During his research into speaking venues, he was referred to the Alaska Railroad, for which President Harding had driven in the golden spike and which was now planning a 75 anniversary celebration. The railroad invited Anthony to participate and eventually sent him on a two-week tour of Alaska.

Then events in the news framed an even broader context for Anthony's book. Just around the time the book was published, the Monica Lewinsky scandal broke and the author, who has written other books on first ladies, found himself in demand by the media to talk about how a first lady might cope with an adulterous husband. *Time* magazine had already run a photo of Florence Harding, drawing a comparison between her and First Lady Hillary Clinton.

While the news climate was propitious for Anthony's book, and his idea for the media tour was very smart, and while he was fortunate enough to have an energetic publicist who was willing to book interviews in multiple cities, Anthony nevertheless dedicated two and a half months setting up his campaign. Later he spent eight weeks on the actual tour where he estimates that he visited 25 cities and towns. While he paid for air travel—unless he had found local sponsorship—the publisher kicked in monies toward local travel and accommodation. Once the book's sales started to take off, and the media interest became more intense, the publisher began to pay for larger expenses as well. Ultimately, Anthony appeared on NPR's *Fresh Air*, ABC's *World News Tonight*, NBC's *Weekend Today*, and CNN's *Inside Politics*, as well as countless local media outlets. Anthony's tour was capped by a lecture at the Palace Hotel in San Francisco on the 75th anniversary of the day President Harding died. A local historical society helped to promote the event.

Anthony's success points to a few lessons. First, if you plan to get involved in your campaign, then you will invest a significant amount of your time, if not money. Second, as Anthony comments now on his campaign, try to get a meeting with the director of publicity, even if your book has already been assigned to one of the publicists on the staff. Make that meeting worthwhile—one in which you convince the director of publicity of your dedication and intent—and you will have garnered important support from the top.

BOOK FAIRS AND BOOK AND AUTHOR LUNCHEONS

Book fairs take place annually in many cities. You might appear at one or more of these as part of your book tour, or as separate trips during the year. (My favorite fairs are the Miami Book Fair International in November and the *Los Angeles Times* Book Fair in April, which are among the highest attended fairs and offer a wide variety of author talks and readings.) The fairs are wonderful venues for all kinds of authors, with panels, readings, and signings throughout the day. Well supported by local media, the fairs guarantee a level of exposure for all the authors who attend. Publishers sponsor booths at some of the fairs, which give authors a home base manned by sales reps.

Your publicist usually books events at the larger fairs. However, if you are a self-published author, or if your publisher does not plan to send you to the fairs, there is nothing to stop you from pitching yourself to the fair organizers at any of the book fairs and festivals. Just be prepared to pay your own transport and accommodations if you are working independently of your publisher. (Your publisher may agree to pay your way once you snag the booking—ask your publicist or editor.) Bear in mind that the fairs are interested in hosting authors whose books have been published recently in hardcover or paperback.

Another terrific venue is the Harbourfront festival in Toronto, which takes place in October. A friend of mine calls Harbourfront "hog's heaven for writers" because of the large book-buying audiences, the extent of media coverage, and the generous array of planned activities and dinners for the authors. Harbourfront sponsors author readings throughout the year, but the annual festival is a gathering of topflight authors, with a skew toward literary writers. Publicists will pitch their authors to the director of the festival, but in truth, some publicists are unaware of the Harbourfront opportunity. Check out the website (www.readings.org) to see if you think your book would be a good fit at the festival. Then ask your publicist to pitch you.

Besides providing a promotional opportunity for your book, book fairs are great fun to attend. The larger fairs offer many author events to choose from, and some offer a "green room" or meeting place for authors. There the author has the chance to meet and hang out with many other writers, creating a great community over the course of the few days of the book fair, with useful contacts made for the future. (See page 267 for a listing of fairs.)

Jewish book fairs take place throughout the United States and in Toronto in November. They take place in close sequence so that an author can make the rounds of the book fairs, with each fair paying a one-way transportation for the author to get to the next fair until the round trip among cities like Atlanta, Baltimore, Columbus, Detroit, Houston, Kansas City, Los Angeles, Miami, Orlando, St. Louis, Toronto, and Washington, DC, is completed. Administered by local Jewish Community Centers (JCCs), which you can locate online, the fairs showcase a wide range of books, which are sold to customers. These annual fairs welcome authors whose books have been published within the year preceding the fair. Again, a publicist usually sets up these events for authors, starting with a speed-dating type of audition for the fairs' organizers held in New York City. If you get into the tour circuit, each fair will allow enough time in each city for you to do bookstore appearances and media interviews. You should also reach out to the Jewish Book Council, whose mission is to promote Judaica and which will sponsor book tours for select authors. Ask your publicist to send a galley to the director of the council, which is based in New York City.

In addition to the book fairs, annual book and author luncheons take place throughout the United States and Canada and are sponsored by local newspapers and charities. The luncheons invite five or six authors to appear before an audience that buys tickets in advance to attend. Each author speaks for about 10 minutes, answers questions from the audience, and then signs books. Several of the luncheons are listed in the resource section. You can find others by searching online for "Book and Author Luncheon."

CORPORATE SPONSORSHIP FOR THE PUBLICITY TOUR

In some instances, corporations use authors as spokespeople. If your book topic helps promote the corporation's own interests, then you are a natural vehicle for it to gain publicity. This happens fairly frequently with cookbooks, where the author of, say, an Italian cookbook can help promote a particular brand of olive oil: The olive oil company underwrites the tour. The USA Rice Council is another organization that has promoted books as part of its campaign to promote rice consumption. The council underwrote some of the publisher's book tour costs for *The Healthy Firehouse Cookbook*, by Joe Bonanno. In exchange, Bonanno prepared rice recipes in his television demos.

EIGHT GREAT THINGS THAT CAN HAPPEN ON TOUR

- Your book sells out and the publisher goes back to press.

- You meet friends from the past who surprise you by showing up to readings.

- You have some really smart conversations with hosts/reporters who've read and genuinely like your book.

- Strangers show up at your reading because they heard you on the radio or read your book or read a good review.

- You give a talk or reading and know that you've got a happy audience in the palm of your hand.

- Someone who hears you interviewed invites you to speak at his or her organization.

- You get the idea for your next book from your encounters on the road.

- Your publisher extends your tour.

THE PUBLICITY TOUR—A SUMMARY

Your tour might include print, radio, and television interviews, as well as appearances at bookstores, book fairs, and other venues. Stay in close partnership with your publicist during the crucial stage of booking the tour. You can become productively involved in several ways:

- If your book does not offer a natural or obvious subject for touring, and if you can come up with a plan to make it so, share the idea with your publisher several months before your book is published so that a tour can be organized in a timely fashion.

- Alert your publicist of the cities where you have contacts to help create successful media stops.

- Research fares to stretch your tour dollars.

- Help brainstorm pitch ideas so that your publicist is well equipped to get you the bookings you want.

- Look into ways to create a hook for your tour, like touring with other authors and linking to events in the news.

Once you're on the road, stay in close contact with your publicist and editor to keep them informed of your progress.

8

GET ON *THE OPRAH WINFREY SHOW*

NOTWITHSTANDING the infamous exception of one novelist who disdained the idea of going on the show, the dream of most authors is to be invited to appear on *The Oprah Winfrey Show*. Exposure on this television show often propels a book onto bestseller lists. However, few authors really understand the show's requirements. *Oprah*'s format is one-hour long and generally speaking she's concerned with uplifting and positive messages for women. Few authors—unless they are celebrities or high-profile, colorful experts with the gift of the gab—appear for the full hour. With some exceptions, noncelebrity authors appear on *Oprah* as a small part of a larger theme show. Nor do many authors realize how difficult it is to secure a booking on *Oprah*. Let's look at the numbers: *Oprah*'s producers are creating some 200 hours of television a year. With multiple guests on many shows, then a fair estimate of annual bookings is around 500 guests.

The stark reality is this: With close to 300,000 books published a year, and with many thousands of individuals from other fields competing for those same spots, the chances of getting on Oprah's show are very slim. But to give yourself a fighting chance, be prepared with a strong pitch and the ability to prove that you will be a strong guest.

IMPROVE THE ODDS: STUDY THE SHOW TO COME UP WITH SHOW IDEAS FOR YOUR BOOK

The Oprah Winfrey Show has a variety of formats. Sometimes a single guest appears, usually a celebrity or one of a number of regular guests, such as Dr. Mehmet Oz or Nate Berkus. The show may comprise a string of pretaped segments about a particular theme, or center on one guest expert who discusses the problems of a panel of guests who have firsthand experience of the topic at hand. Then there's the periodic book club: Oprah's book club selections come to an author like a sudden strike of lightning as the selection process is not made public.

As reported on the *Wall Street Journal*'s website, author Jan Yager campaigned for a couple of years to get on *Oprah* (and finally did) for a book called *Friendshifts: The Power of Friendship and How It Shapes Our Lives*. She got on because she understood that her job as a guest on *The Oprah Winfrey Show* was *not* to sell her book. She knew that the producers would be looking for a guest to create an interesting and entertaining show on a topic that the audience can identify and empathize with.

Justin Loeber, as director of publicity for HarperCollins, pitched Anthony Bourdain, author of *Kitchen Confidential*, in many different ways. He placed one of his follow-up calls when the producers happened to be working on a show called "Profession Confessions" about behind-the-scenes trade secrets of various jobs. Loeber pushed for the producer to watch a videotape of the author and, believing that the author would make an effective guest, persuaded her to conduct a preinterview. This tape and the phone interview clinched the deal. The author appeared on the show to talk about what really goes on in restaurants, when not to order fish, what sort of restaurants to avoid, how the bread on the table is recycled, and so on. The other guests on the show included four other authors: Marcy Blum (*Weddings for Dummies*), Peter Greenburg (*The Travel Detective*), Teri Agins (*The End of Fashion*), and Ellen Phillips (*Shocked, Appalled, and Dismayed*, which is about writing complaint letters).

Lynn Goldberg of Goldberg McDuffie Communications says that when her publicists pitch *Oprah*, they offer a range of story ideas surrounding the author's expertise. They frame their pitches as concepts for television programming rather than as straight book interviews. Then of course, Goldberg says, the onus is on the guest to follow through with a passionate and energetic presentation that also manages to convey the book's message.

Improve your chances of getting on *Oprah* by watching the show and coming up with several pitches that will help your publicist position your expertise with the show's producers. The only way to do this is to watch and study *Oprah*. If you work during the day, tape the show, or watch the evening reruns. If you don't have time to tape and watch *Oprah* every day, check out www.oprah.com, which lists past show topics. For example, the show has covered "Overweight Children," "Wives Who Don't Want Sex," "How to Set Personal Boundaries," "Understanding Your Emotional Style," "I Was an Abandoned Child," and so on. To get on *The Oprah Winfrey Show*, you *must* understand what the producers are looking for: dramatic stories that offer viewers hope, paths to recovery, life-affirming values, entertainment. Unless your topic is extremely compelling, and your personality energetic and engaging, chances are that you could not sustain a full hour on *Oprah*. Therefore, think about show topics that can incorporate other guests. For example, a show called "Make Your Dreams Come True" featured a Hearst book called *The Business of Bliss: How to Profit from Doing What You Love*, which is about women entrepreneurs. It took a full six months for the publicist to get one of the entrepreneurs on the show, after relentless pitching and follow-up calls.

Some shows are based entirely on books. A show called "Messy Home Makeovers" offered ideas for removing clutter from your life. The guest was Julie Morgenstern, an "organizing expert" and author of two books called *Time Management from the Inside Out* and *Organizing from the Inside Out*. "The Marriage Sabbatical" featured women who had taken a sabbatical from their families to pursue their personal quests. They discussed how their time off improved their marriages and family lives. The main guest was author Cheryl Jarvis, author of, that's right, a book called *The Marriage Sabbatical*. Another example: The producers used a book called *Ordinary People, Extraordinary Wealth*, by Ric Edelman, to create a show by the same name to discuss the secrets of ordinary people who have achieved great wealth. Of course, the ideal scenario is having a show title named for your book—another important reason to come up with a punchy title for your book that conveys its core message.

All these shows have short, to-the-point titles and introduce the show's theme in a sound bite. As you develop show ideas, try to present the message of your book in the form of one punchy line, a sound bite, one that you can imagine Oprah using for her next show's preview announcement. Underlying many *Oprah* shows is the idea of the American Dream—some variation on how you can improve your life. It might be how to find happiness and personal satisfaction, triumph over adversity, mend a marriage or other relationship, find meaning in life, or achieve your dreams.

Getting on *Oprah* does not guarantee you a bestseller. But it sure improves your chances. On hearing the news of an *Oprah* booking, the sales force can leverage more copies into bookstores in anticipation of the show. The size of the reorders will depend on what the publisher tells the booksellers about the known extent of your appearance. Therefore, as the planning of your show takes shape and you find out from the producer that you are playing a larger part in the show than originally thought, then inform your publicist, who will alert the sales reps, who in turn will tell the booksellers. Because Oprah and her producers might even change the lineup mid-show, you never really know how much time you will end up getting until the show is taped.

Oprah has a staff of many producers, all working on different stories at once. This allows for publicists to develop a variety of approaches when pitching the show. Some have found that it pays to send the book and pitch to several producers at once. To prevent two producers from showing up to an *Oprah* pitch meeting with the same idea, the publicists state in the cover letter the names of the other producers to whom they have also sent the book. Other publicists prefer to cultivate a relationship with one producer. This person should be a mid- to senior-level producer, who will refer the idea to other production teams at the show.

Lynn Goldberg notes that a successful print campaign can favorably influence *Oprah*'s producers. A big plus is high-profile feature coverage in national print media like the glossy monthly magazines or leading newspapers. If you've been lucky enough to score such coverage in the national print media, then those articles should accompany your pitch to *The Oprah Winfrey Show*. Charles Cook, a former producer for the show, says, "Any good producer spends weekends reading through stacks of magazines. Producers are voracious readers of what's topical, looking for what their audience is interested in, always looking for new ideas."

There may come that amazing day when your publicist calls to set up a "preinterview" with one of *Oprah*'s producers. Many potential guests are screened by telephone and flunk the phone call. In other words, the preinterview is actually an audition. Therefore, get ready for this call—it's your big moment. Refresh yourself about your book's salient points. Prepare vivid analogies and anecdotes to illustrate those points. Talk about the show idea with your publicist so that you're fluent in elaborating on it. During the preinterview—and many national television shows other than *Oprah* conduct preinterviews—the producer will decide whether you have the potential to be an interesting guest. The producer will also assess the size of your role in the show—whether you should have, say, a five-minute spot, or whether you could command the attention to take the stage for the full hour.

If your publicist is no longer pitching *Oprah*, then you can take up the cause and pitch the show yourself. Ask your publicist for a copy of the correspondence with the show. Get the name and number of the producer. If the publicist won't share the contact information (this information is sometimes jealously guarded) or you're starting from scratch without a producer's name, you might choose producers who have worked on shows with themes compatible with your own book. Find out their names by watching the credits at the end of the show. You won't get the name of the appropriate producer by calling the show's switchboard. You will simply be told to send in your idea for a show, and that the show will contact you if there is any interest. (It's a little like trying to find a publisher by sending your manuscript in blind. Once in a while it can work, but very rarely.)

After you get turned down by the producer, which is more likely to happen than not, keep your cool. Be polite and ask if you might call again with a new show idea. As evident from what a former producer for the show has to say, you can pitch the show again and again until you finally give up or get on.

INSIGHT FROM A VETERAN TALK SHOW PRODUCER AND FORMER *OPRAH* PRODUCER

Charles Cook worked at *The Oprah Winfrey Show* for two years. He has also worked at other daytime talk shows, and offers the following suggestions to authors. His advice is equally applicable to other talk shows, particularly the longer-format "magazine" shows. First, Cook says that the show will accept pitch ideas directly from authors. The producers believe that good ideas can come from anywhere, and they are not always predisposed to deal only with a book's publicist. The constant hunt for good show ideas means that yours are welcome, especially if you present them cogently and with an understanding for what's current in the culture. The more ideas you have, the better. If you gain access to a producer, Cook recommends that you use your time on the phone well. From the phone conversation alone the producer can tell if you have guest potential.

Producers look for someone who can give concise answers that will appeal to the audience and who relates to the women at home who watch the show. Cook states that the worst guest is a professional expert who talks down to viewers. The best guest is someone who comes across as warm and accessible. During the preinterview, just pretend you're talking to your friends. That way you create an intimate but informative impression. The other thing the producer is looking for, says Cook, is the "take-home advice. What I want to know is what are the top three things that this author is going to tell me, what advice will I be able to use." In other words, the ability to be prescriptive is an important quality.

So remember: If you don't get on the show on the first attempt, don't give up. According to Cook, as long as you can come up with new ideas about positioning your book, then keep pitching. The show's production moves fast. New shows go into development all the time. Whether you are an author or a publicist, try to get a dialogue going with one producer to improve your access and to get noticed. Send handwritten notes to the producer. Fax clippings related to your pitch. Call periodically to touch base and float an idea. Do anything you can to cultivate that relationship, says Cook.

Also keep in mind that your package has a better chance of being opened first if it stands out. The show's producers receive carton-loads of books—most packaged in brown Jiffy bags, most looking the same. "You get so much stuff that you can't see straight," Cook says. So whatever else you do, if you want to get on *The Oprah Winfrey Show*, "Get on the phone! Pitch a producer!"

GET ON *THE OPRAH WINFREY SHOW*—A SUMMARY

Like any show that you want to appear on, *The Oprah Winfrey Show* has specific formats and requirements of its guests. Watch the show and study it to learn how to shape a pitch based on your book. Review the show's archives on its website to see what book segments have run in the past. Keep in mind that producers will take an interest in you if you reveal a strong potential to be an interesting, lively, and entertaining guest. The producers must create good television, and they are not deeply concerned about selling your book. Your challenge, and your publicist's challenge, is to offer viable television programming themed around your book's topic or else your expertise.

9

MEDIA TRAINING: HOW TO GIVE A GREAT INTERVIEW

IF television interviews could be an important part of your book promotion and yet you have seldom or never appeared on television, then urge your publisher to send you for media training to teach you interviewing skills, help you hone your message, and build your confidence. In the normal sequence of things, media training is the first step up to preparing for giving great interviews; next comes local television interviews where you hone your message. Then comes national television whose producers insist on seeing a tape of a previous interview before booking an author. Airtime is valuable and not to be squandered on a guest who can't hold the viewers attention.

At a training session, a media trainer, who has read your book, will simulate an interview with you—sometimes in a real television studio—by taking the role of the television host. The mock interview is videotaped and then replayed so that the trainer can give you pointers on how to improve your interview techniques. The trainer will cover everything from how you should sit (slightly forward on the seat so that you appear alert) to the color of your clothing to steering the interview in the direction you choose.

Businesspeople and politicians often hire media trainers to refine their presentation of complicated or controversial messages. Similarly, to ensure good appearances, publishers often hire them for important authors preparing for national television interviews. Authors with television interview experience might need a "touch-up"—a short session that refreshes their skills just before their new book comes out.

During a real interview, you may find that the talk show host has not read your book. This is not unusual, considering the demands of the job. A host may interview five authors or more a week. They don't have time to read the books, watch the movies, or listen to the music of every guest. Hosts have different styles. Some are terrific at keeping a conversation flowing, while others are not. Hosts may be warm and friendly, or sharply interrogative, or goofy. Media training helps you become adept at handling any type of interviewer that you might encounter.

Many authors want to know if they can media train themselves. You can, but you must take your self-training seriously and take every opportunity to understand what the media is looking for. For critical evaluation, you should practice with others and invest serious time to ensure that you know what to do once you're on air. Help yourself by studying the media. Pay attention to the manner and content of interview questions. Identify and practice the techniques employed by the most impressive guests.

Even if you have appeared on the media before, practice for your upcoming interviews. Do not think that you can get away without honing your message. I once worked on a book by a famous political consultant who works with presidential candidates to hone their media messages. We both assumed, wrongly as it turned out, that his appearance on *Today* would be a cinch. Instead, he got sidetracked on unrelated issues and failed to convey the points of interest in his book. The main problem was that the book was not fresh in his mind. He probably hadn't looked at it since he'd handed in the manuscript 10 months earlier. He was simply not prepared.

If your publisher is unwilling to underwrite the costs of media training, then you may choose to hire a media trainer yourself. Media training for television may cost from $2,000 to $4,000 for a full day, or $1,500 to $2,500 for a half day. You can find media trainers through an online search and I have listed several of them in the resource section of this book.

WHAT IS MEDIA TRAINING AND WHAT
WILL IT ACCOMPLISH?

According to Bill Parkhurst, who runs a media training company called Parkhurst Communications in New York City, authors have some misconceptions about interviews. The main one is that they need a string of prepackaged sound bites to sell books. Parkhurst believes that appearing on a television talk show is about creating a connection with the audience through the host. Only indirectly is it about selling. He explains that the audience remembers an overall impression of a television guest, not his or her words. These are soon forgotten. He advises, therefore, to concentrate on conveying your passion rather than a core set of sound bites. During a training session, Parkhurst first seeks the author's core passion—what stirred that person to spend such time and effort writing a book.

Parkhurst says that successful interviewing requires a set of taught skills, and that interviews on local cable or radio provide the opportunity to practice those skills. "No interview is too small to do, at least not at the beginning of your career as a writer," he says. "They give you that valuable chance to practice in a real interview situation and to boost your confidence and competence." Learning to give good interviews requires you to spend time watching the media or listening to radio shows. "If all you listen to is National Public Radio," says Parkhurst, "then you need to listen to other radio interview shows to understand what is really going on in this media. Once you understand the media, you know where you fit in.

"I put the author through every kind of interview that they're going to get to teach them that an interview is a proactive experience," says Parkhurst. For interviews where the host fails to address a book's core subject, he teaches "bridging" techniques that allow you to steer the interview in the direction you prefer. For example, you might respond to a question that leads you away from your book's message by saying, "Good question, and what I've always thought is . . ." or "What I think is important is . . ."

He teaches that you should refer to your book indirectly. Instead of responding to a question with, "In my book . . . ," you might say, "As I was doing research on my book I found that . . ." or "I have a chapter on such a subject that explains . . ." The idea is to sound natural and conversational rather than like a pitchman. Parkhurst spends a lot of time with authors working on the "topper"—the answer to that usual first question, which is always some form of "Why did you write this book?" During his training sessions, he has authors answer that question in a variety of ways, and in several different styles of interviews. Thus, the authors become comfortable conveying the book's key message in any situation.

Eight Ways to Mention Your Book Naturally During an Interview

"What I learned while I was researching my book was . . ."

"It was so interesting when I was working on my book to discover that . . ."

"When I sat down to write the book, I learned that . . ."

"People told me when I was working on my book that . . ."

"When I started the book I thought that . . . But instead I found that . . ."

"What I think people will really learn from my book is that . . ."

"It was important for me to write this book because . . ."

"Many people that I interviewed for my book said that . . ."

Just don't use all eight in one interview or you'll sound like a huckster. Generally one reference to your book should suffice, as the show's host will mention it during your introduction and possibly also at the conclusion of the segment.

I saw a good example of bridging in an interview with former President Jimmy Carter about one of his books. The show was *The Diane Rehm Show*, an NPR program in Washington, DC, that often interviews authors. This radio show is sometimes taped by C-SPAN. Carter had discussed his racially integrated childhood and Rehm followed up with an oddly redundant question. Carter, with great warmth, acknowledged her question and went on to talk about something else entirely. He saved her face, talked about what he wanted, and handled the transition gracefully.

During an interview, you may feel contempt at a host's dumb questions. However, whatever else you do, *never* condescend or try to "best" the host to show the audience how smart you are. Remember: The audience is loyal to that host. You are there for mere minutes. Your task as a guest is to redirect the interview, gently. Take it where you want it to go.

WHEN THE INTERVIEW IS A DEMO

Some interviews take the form of demos, in other words, demonstrations of, say, a cooking or gardening technique. For my own book *Reckless Appetites: A Culinary Romance*, I had to demonstrate how to make a recipe for champagne punch on *Today*. I had never performed a demo on television before, and so I spent the full two months leading up to the interview practicing the demo anywhere and everywhere. I did it in the back of taxis. I did it alone in elevators—holding imaginary equipment and ingredients while I spoke about the recipe and my book. At home, of course, I practiced with the real ingredients. It came to a point I could do it in my sleep. The results: My perfecting every word and motion helped my appearance run smoothly. The physical logistics of mixing and pouring ingredients never got in the way of my message.

Publicist Caitlin Friedman often coaches cookbook authors for their television demos and interviews. First she asks the author to name the three most important talking points about the book. "Sometimes what the authors think are the key message points are not, in fact, what would appeal to journalists," she says. By keeping to three points, she believes that authors can carry the book's main message effectively. She finds that too many message points can lead to an interview that goes "off message."

She also works with the author to identify dishes that are appropriate for demonstration on air. These recipes should be seasonal, colorful (to show up nicely on camera), and nonwilting (as the food will often sit under hot studio lights for several hours). "You need to pick a recipe that's easily broken down into stages," she says, "because you want to show some of the process, but you don't want to create the entire recipe. This would take too long for a television segment." It is enough that the author presents the dish in different stages of preparation, and then shows a finished dish. Friedman insists that the author reread and practice the recipe before any interviews. She wants the process and ingredients to be fresh in the author's mind.

Another consideration of recipe choice is the host's preference. Try to find out if the host has any allergies or a favorite food. If your host has a jones for chocolate, then cater to that taste. You are more likely to get that host excited about your food. Find out how the set will be decorated. Some shows have set stylists, many do not. If the studio is not providing set decorations, then bring along flowers, pretty serving dishes, a tablecloth. Remember to iron it first. Brand-new cloths have creases that look bad on camera.

Plan on preparing other complementary dishes to display with the recipe you are demonstrating: As well as dressing the set, the array of dishes provides a chance to mention other recipes in your book.

ACE YOUR TELEVISION OR RADIO INTERVIEWS— THE RULES

Here are the rules for your successful broadcast interviews. They apply to both television and radio, unless otherwise indicated.

- Reread or skim your book before your first interview so it is fresh in your mind. Reread the pitch letter and press materials that your publicist sent to the media, as interviewers may use the press packet for all their questions.

- Research your interviewer's background, and understand who the audience is. (Or ask your publicist to get this information for you.) Your knowledge will help you shape your responses to appeal to his or her interests.

- Know the several points you have to get across no matter what questions you are asked. Remember that the audience has probably never heard about your book.

- Be alert to the host's mentioning of the book's title. In short television and radio interviews you don't need to mention the title again, and doing so will alienate the audience. In longer format radio interviews, pay attention to the host's introductions after each commercial break. Chances are that he or she will say something like, "With me today is So-and-So, author of a new book called *Such-and-Such*." When you hear this cue, you can relax and not worry about mentioning the title. If the host doesn't mention the book title, then mention it once every segment, so that new listeners know what you are talking about.

- Be prepared to complete an interview in two to three minutes. In that time you must convey what your book is about and why the audience will find the book appealing or useful. You might get more time but be prepared for the short form.

- Make a list of all the questions that you might be asked in an interview. Then come up with punchy answers to all of them. Before any interviews, practice answering the questions out loud and refine your message points so that they are interesting and succinct.

- If you have reason to anticipate challenging questions, then practice the responses that will diffuse any controversy (which of course you've discussed with your publicist).

- Use vivid anecdotes and examples to illustrate your points, particularly on radio.

- Reveal facts and figures that support your book's message. (If I were marketing this book on television, I might lead with the fact that close to 300,000 books are published every year, so an author needs to know how to stand out in the crowd.)

- Practice your segues or bridges. In other words, if the interviewer gets stuck on one topic too long, then shift the conversation, perhaps by saying, "That's only one aspect of my book that can help people. The other thing I've found is that . . ." Another good segue is, "The most important thing to remember here is . . ." or "What your listeners will really want to know is . . ." or "Sometimes people ask me . . ." and then go on to ask yourself the question you wish the interviewer had asked.

▪ One of the worst answers to the host's question about the book's content is a coy, "Well, you'll have to read it in the book." While an intriguing answer might stimulate the audience to buy the book, your refusal to answer the question is an audience turnoff.

▪ Do not talk too fast, even though you may be tempted because television moves so quickly and you have a very short time to deliver your message.

▪ Be energetic and upbeat. Listen to the high-wattage on-air performance styles of interviewers. They like to hear the same level of energy in their guests. Guests who project low energy seem bored or indifferent.

▪ Before you start your radio or cable television interview, mention to the producer and to the host that you'd like to share an 800 number where listeners can buy your book or find out further information. The producer will put the number on the TelePrompTer for the host to read aloud at some point in the interview. On cable television, the producer may run the 800 number at the bottom of the screen. (Network television generally will not do this, but they will take your 800 number to give to any callers to the switchboard who want to get in touch with you.)

▪ Similarly, tell the producer that you'd like to mention your website on-air to share with listeners.

▪ Show up early for the interview and always bring a copy of your book with you. The studio copy sometimes gets misplaced, and the host may need to refer to the book or the television crew may shoot the jacket for an opening shot.

▪ Use the host's name to personalize the interview. (Check with the producer before the interview to find out what the host likes to be called on-air.) Remember that the listening audience is loyal to that host, so buddying up with that host helps the audience identify with you.

■ If the show takes call-ins and you get a hostile caller, maintain an even tone. Your politeness will present you as a professional; the caller will merely seem crazy. By ignoring the caller's anger, you also increase the chance that the producer will cut them off faster to move on to the next call. Once you engage with a caller's anger, you've created explosive entertainment, and depending on the show's style, the producer and host might prolong the call.

■ In television interviews, sit perched on the edge of your chair, which will keep you upright and make you seem energetic. If you sit toward the back of the chair seat then you will look slumped. Funnily enough, the same advice applies to your radio interviews. By sitting alert, you will sound alert. Slouching can induce a slower-paced interview, even though the audience can't see you.

■ Don't fidget during any interview, or swing your chair, or tap your foot. All of those tics distract the viewer, as well as the host.

■ After the interview, send a thank-you note to the interviewer and the producer. You might get a callback for a follow-up interview on the subject, which you can even suggest in your note.

For Television Interviews Only

■ If your book has photographs or other visuals that support your story, then ask your publicist to offer them to the television producer, and bring them along if needed. The producer may shoot them just before your interview to include as still frames throughout the segment.

■ Get over nervousness by following this very good advice from Clarence Jones's book, *How to Speak TV*. During your interview, think of your audience as one or two people in a living room, and direct your conversation toward them to create a feeling of intimacy.

■ Accept makeup if it is offered. The makeup artists will blot the shine on your nose and forehead. If you have a light skin color, then they will probably also use a darker tone of blush and foundation than you are used to so that you don't appear washed out on camera.

■ If you are wearing a tailored jacket, tug the hem underneath you and sit on it to keep the jacket uncreased and in place as you talk.

■ Unless you are an experienced guest, you may not know for certain when the camera starts rolling. Assume that you're on-air as soon as you are in place, and keep a bright, engaged look on your face. When you answer the questions, look at the host and never at the camera.

■ Wear solid colors but avoid all white or all black, or loud patterns. No heavy jewelry (unless this is the subject of your book).

■ Wear your glasses if you wear them every day. Changing routine for the television interview will add another unfamiliar element to your experience.

The Exception to the Rules

The two television stations on which you must abandon all restraint are HSN (Home Shopping Network) and QVC. If you are booked onto one of these, your job is to be as aggressive and hyped up in your on-air performance as possible. The segments are all about selling as much product as possible, whether it is a book or a piece of jewelry. Off camera, the station is measuring the dollars-per-minute for the segment. The shows on these stations are more akin to advertising than they are to programming. Your main job is to sell and to sell hard.

For Radio Interviews Taking Place by Phone, Rather Than in the Studio

- Avoid using a cell phone for the call. They are unreliable. Turn off any cell phones or second phone lines in proximity during the interview.

- Turn off the radio because leaving it on will produce feedback.

- Eliminate all possible distractions: Lock your pets well out of earshot, have your young kids well looked after out of earshot, and de-activate call-waiting. If you live near a busy street, then sirens or other traffic noise can spoil your interview: Take your phone into a quiet closet if you have to, or arrange to go to a friend's quieter home or office. If you're doing radio phone interviews in your hotel room, alert the hotel operator to hold any other calls when you're on the line.

- Sight unseen, you can refer to your notes. Keep a short list of your key points in front of you. Have a pen and paper handy to jot down any points to cover later in the interview. Have your book and press materials nearby to remind yourself of your book's content during commercial breaks.

- As soon as you've connected with the radio station, unless the host tells you otherwise assume that you are on-air. You will not necessarily know when you go live.

- Have a glass of water at hand, but do not sip and swallow with your mouth adjacent to the mouthpiece or at the moment you're expected to answer a question.

SOME TIPS ON PRINT INTERVIEWS

Interviews in the print media are quite different from radio or television interviews and might take place by phone, in person, or even via email. The pressure of time is lifted—you do not have to squeeze your message into a few minutes—and the reporter is likely to have read your book. You may have a thoughtful discussion, which can be most gratifying if the reporter likes your work. Whatever the situation, keep your answers on point and engaging.

First ask what the article is about. The piece might not be about your book alone, but rather part of a larger theme piece in which your book will get a small mention. Spell your name and title of your book for the reporter. Find out the reporter's deadline and contact information. This allows you to send any relevant follow-up information after the interview has concluded.

During the interview, do not fall for flattery. The reporter is softening you up to get a relaxed interview. Get too relaxed and you may say something you will regret later after it shows up in print. Good reporters can lull you into a sense of ease where you let your guard down. I know one writer who fell for a reporter's apparent interest in his work. He gave a frank and forthcoming interview, and was later stunned by the reporter's negative article. Another reporter's tactic is asking a provocative question intended to make you angry and reactive. Try to recognize when a reporter is trying to goad you and keep your cool while making your point.

Look out for reporters who have an agenda, who have already decided what to say about you. In an interview for my book *Reckless Appetites*, a reporter from a major metropolitan newspaper wanted me to come out with a theory about the relationship between food and sex. He wanted an explicit answer and finally told me that if I said something really provocative, then he'd run the article "above the fold," meaning on the top half of the page. I refused to oblige him: I felt railroaded and found his manner sleazy. In the end, the article never ran, but I didn't mind because I didn't compromise myself. In another situation, one author who had written about recovering from bulimia found herself under attack by a reporter who thought her a spoiled rich girl. The reporter was rude enough to go into her kitchen and open the refrigerator to see what food she had in the house. Unless the reporter is someone whose reputation has been vetted for you by a publicist you trust, or who is known personally, don't allow him or her into your home.

These cautionary tales are not meant to put you on the defensive during interviews. Rather they are intended to prepare you to handle reporters. The reporter's job is not to be your friend or to be on your side.

Their job is to get a good story for their readers. They are looking for angles in everything you say and do.

Remember that unless you have a long-standing relationship with the reporter and can trust them, there really is no such thing as "off the record." Why tell the reporter a confidence? If you do not want to see your words in print, then do not utter them.

At the end of the interview, reiterate your most important points. Ask the reporter, "Do you have everything you need?" or "Before you go, shall I go over anything for you?" Then ask the reporter the deadline for the story, and for his or her best contact information in case you come up with more information to share.

After the article runs, drop a friendly note of thanks. If you don't like what the reporter has written, then try to put it out of mind: You gain little by sending a note of complaint. If you really believe that you've been wronged, then write a letter to the editor to point out the factual errors or misleading statements in the piece.

The first few interviews that you do in any format—whether print or broadcast—may be challenging and nerve-wracking. Once you've put a few behind you, you will have a sudden burst of confidence and may take great pleasure in giving interviews. Hit your stride and you will find that the nerves and jitters will be vastly diminished or disappear altogether.

MEDIA TRAINING: HOW TO GIVE A GREAT INTERVIEW—A SUMMARY

Whether you undergo formal media training or prepare for interviews on your own, you must practice your interview skills so that you can deliver an effective, selling interview about your book. There are many rules about giving a good interview, but with repetition you can master them until they become second nature. The major elements of good interviewing to keep in mind are:

- Know your book's content—reread the book if you need to.

- Know the top three messages that you want to convey.

- Practice your bridging techniques so that you can redirect an interview that goes astray.

- Prepare anecdotes and facts that illustrate your points.

- Rehearse your interview responses until they feel natural and comfortable.

10

BOOKSTORE APPEARANCES AND SPEAKING ENGAGEMENTS

SETTING up local bookstore appearances and other speaking engagements can be a productive way to get involved in your campaign. Even if you have a publicist who is active on your behalf, you can track down more opportunities for speaking gigs.

Bookstore events are an important part of building your readership. Even if the events are not heavily attended—they average as few as 10 to 15 people—the book still enjoys visibility through displays and store promotions leading up to the event. Your book also benefits from increased awareness among store managers, which can lead to hand-selling. And you've begun to develop an audience as the people who attend the event talk about your book. In fact, for children's authors, who find access to the media more limited than for authors of topical adult books, bookstore tours done in combination with school visits are the essential way to build readership. Admittedly this type of grassroots effort is time-consuming, but if you are an unknown writer, here's where you can start to build your readership.

Speaking engagements at nonbookstore venues can also deliver larger audiences for you. Host organizations might include universities, corporations, libraries, museums, YMCAs, garden clubs, fraternal groups, and so on. Usually, these require a longer booking lead time than bookstores, so start your research and outreach five to six months (or even longer) before you expect to visit a particular market. Of course, some speaking engagements can be set up with a shorter lead time, but if you have the luxury of time, then use it to your advantage.

A word of advice if you are setting up your own bookstore and other appearances: Make sure to schedule them to take place *after* your book has been published so that books can be sold at the events.

HOW TO SET UP BOOKSTORE SIGNINGS

According to *Publishers Weekly*, publicists work through the home offices of Barnes & Noble and Borders to set up six thousand chain bookstore events a year. In addition, independent booksellers and the chains' local store managers set up thousands more.

Your publicist will probably set up some bookstore appearances for you. But you can continue to appear at bookstores after your official campaign is over by setting up the events yourself. Be aware that bookstore chains do not pay for travel or serve as a publicist.

Once you obtain a list of stores to contact—see the box about bookstore directories on page 190 to identify bookstores—send the information to your publicist to find out if your choices are appropriate. After checking with the sales reps, the publicist will give you her assessment whether the stores are capable of mounting good events. Give your publicist at least a week to get back to you with this information. If you hear nothing even after following up, then proceed in setting up your own events. Also ask your publicist to provide you with electronic copies of the press release and JPEGs of the book jacket and your author photo, as bookstores will need those to help promote the events in their communities.

When you're ready to set up the events, contact the local stores directly. (Don't bother contacting the home offices of the major chains, as the events planners prefer to work directly with the publishers.) Ask the store's events coordinator if you can schedule an event at the store. Describe the appearance you envision for your book, whether a reading, a lecture, a question-and-answer session, a slide show, or a how-to cooking or crafts demonstration. Avoid bookstore events where all you do is sign books. Unless you create some kind of talk or event surrounding your appearance, you're unlikely to draw many people. Say how long you are prepared to talk. It's best to plan for a 20-minute presentation followed by questions and answers. Let the events manager know if you have a local mailing list, which makes you a more attractive candidate.

Once you've booked an event, follow up promptly with an email confirming the arrangements, accompanied by a press release, a photograph of yourself, a book jacket, and any other information that the bookstore can use in displays or mailings and other promotions. Tell your publicist about the forthcoming event

Set up the bookstore events six weeks to three months before your appearance. This allows the events coordinator sufficient time to list your event in the store's newsletter and calendar. The events coordinator may ask you if co-op money is available to promote the event. (Co-op monies are matching promotional funds paid by publishers to booksellers. The amount of co-op funds that a bookstore is entitled to depends on how much business they transacted with your publisher during the previous year.) Because you cannot know what co-op is available, ask the events coordinator to get in touch with the publisher's sales rep. Your publisher may allow a small amount of money to be spent on co-op programs, which might include a newsletter mailing to store customers (costing as little as $50), a small store-produced ad in the local paper or on the radio, or refreshments at the signing. As you might expect, publishers are less liberal about co-op spending during times of economic recession. If the funds are not available, the store might not cancel the event if it's already made a commitment to you, though it will not have as many resources for promotion. If the store asks you to pay the co-op charge, politely decline the opportunity. Co-op marketing is a way for booksellers to get money out of publishers: Authors shouldn't have to foot this bill.

If you're planning to appear in all the local bookstores in your proximity, schedule your events far apart so that you're not appearing at a chain store a couple of days before you appear at the independent bookseller down the street, or vice versa. Because booksellers are competitive, timing events too closely will only anger them and that will not help your book. Separate your appearances by weeks or months.

Bookstore Directories

You have several options to locate addresses and phone numbers for bookstores.

- Talk to your publicist to get a list of appropriate stores.
- Go to www.bookweb.org, which has a directory of bookstore members of
  the trade group the American Booksellers Association. The site includes
  addresses and bookstore websites.
- Go to www.booksense.com, the site of independent booksellers, and use
  the ZIP code locator there to find stores. The list will include independents
  only, not chains.
- Go to the store-finders sections at the sites of the national chains, www.bn
  .com, www.booksamillion.com, and www.borders.com, to locate stores.
  The sites include maps as well as store contact information.
- For stores in Canada, go to the site of the Canadian Booksellers Association (www.cbabook.org) and go to the Find a Bookstore tab.

Let us suppose that you set up a hometown bookstore appearance.
You probably know many people in your area and can provide the store
with a good-sized mailing list. Give the store a copy of the list on labels to
send out notices about your appearance, or else a list of email addresses. If
the store is not prepared to take care of the mailing, make up a simple
flyer and send it out yourself or notify your contacts by email. You can use
your mailing list more than once. Some authors will list all of their appearances in one flyer. Others will send sequential mailings.

Ask the bookstore's events coordinator if he or she plans to contact
the local newspapers and other publications to get the event mentioned in
the listings section. If not, ask for a copy of the store's media list and
make the calls yourself. Getting listed is a pretty straightforward procedure. Call the local papers and ask for the calendar or listings editor. Then
fax, mail, or email the information as the editor specifies. Ask if the paper
can use a photo, and if so send one.

Go to the professional development area of www.bookweb.org. Under Education, click on "bookstore sales and marketing" and you will find a Bookstore Publicity kit with information about promoting bookstore events, sample media and calendar listing alerts, press releases, and pitch letter templates. Then check out www.netread.com. The site emails a free calendar of author events in any ZIP code you desire. Even if you have a good and active publicist, take the time to list your own events in the EventCaster section. Trusting the bookstores to properly market the event to calendar listings, publicists tend to concentrate instead on securing feature interviews.

Setting Up a Bookstore Event—a Checklist

- Prepare your mailing lists to invite attendees. Work with your personal acquaintances in your tour cities to see if they can provide contacts of their own.
- Plan the format of your appearance and remember, if you're not a well-known writer then a topical discussion is more marketable than a straight reading.
- Contact the bookstore and ask for the events coordinator.
- Describe the proposed format of your appearance and the size of your mailing list.
- Suggest any local organizations that might be approached to attend your talk. The bookstore may already have ties with them, and if not, contact them yourself.
- Ask the events coordinator if he or she will need a press release, book jacket, and photo to promote the event.
- Let your publicist know about the event.
- Ask if the store will order books directly from the publisher or a wholesaler, and provide them with the phone and fax numbers for your publisher's order department.
- Ten days (approximately) before the event, call the events coordinator and reconfirm. Ask if the store has received its order of books for the event. If the order is late, ask when it is expected and follow up again then. If books

> still do not arrive, then notify your publicist to help get books shipped to
> your event in time.
> - Ask the events coordinator if he or she is planning to pitch your appear-
>   ance to the calendar listings of the local media. If not, ask for a copy of the
>   store's media list and send out a media alert.

Bookstores often have ties to community groups. Ask the events coordinator for the names of local groups or associations that the store will
notify about your appearance. If you have ideas about specific groups in the
area that might be drawn to your event, then contact them directly. Ask if
they are willing to notify their members about your event. Pitch them the
idea of cosponsoring the event (at no charge). If they go for it, ask for a
copy of their mailing list (on labels), which you will give to the store to send
invitations. The invitations should, of course, mention the name of the
cosponsoring organization. In this instance, everyone gains an audience.

MAKE YOUR APPEARANCE A SUCCESS

Your principle obligation as a speaker is to engage your audience. You
want to inform and entertain—and ultimately motivate listeners to buy
a copy of your book. Use humor or eloquence, surprise or pathos—
anything that will capture your audience's attention. Whatever you do, do
not bore.

Unless you are a brilliant spontaneous speaker, you should practice
what you are going to say before you appear at a lecture or reading. Some
authors speak for too long. Some deliver lengthy passages in a monotone,
dulling the audience. Instead, consider your audience's interests. If your
book is a novel, read short segments of your text and, in between, discuss
various aspects of your book's development. If your book is nonfiction,
then create a short talk based on the key themes of your work: A straight
reading of nonfiction almost never works. These approaches will help you
connect with the audience. No matter the content you select for your
appearances, remember to look up and make eye contact. Raise your voice
so that the person farthest away from you will be able to hear you. Re-

member that the carpeting and surrounding books can absorb or mute your voice.

Prior to your events, you might listen to tapes of writers whose readings of their work you admire. Practice your own presentation style until it sounds as smooth, natural, and entertaining. Another sensible tactic is to attend bookstore readings and evaluate what you find effective in others authors' presentations.

The novelist Edna O'Brien has a gorgeous resonant voice and an Irish accent. She is a dramatic and mesmerizing reader. So is Toni Morrison, who creates a charged atmosphere at her readings. Nikki Giovanni is an impassioned reader of her poetry. Frank McCourt and T. C. Boyle are successful and engaging speakers. For utmost effect and beauty, first prize goes to Dylan Thomas. Listen to an audiotape of his captivating and resonant voice presenting his poetry. This sort of private education is essential if you are planning an extended reading tour and have little experience in giving readings.

Relax about the prospect of bookstore appearances. Even if you are unpracticed at public speaking, you will eventually hit your stride with audiences. The old saying is true: No two audiences are alike. Each has a distinct, individual personality. The trick to managing them is to be yourself. Then there will come that magnificent moment when, as you stand in front of a room of strangers—whether a handful of people or a crowd—and as you speak about your book, you will feel their pulse of avid interest in what you are saying. Their engagement will be palpable. They will be putty in your hands—and made to laugh or cry or sigh in empathy with your characters or with you. When this magical moment arrives, show restraint. Don't be tempted to speak for too long. It is best to cut your talk a little short. Leave the audience wanting a little more, which is, of course, the art of the seducer—as well as the art of a successful author on tour.

Apart from giving a straight talk and discussion about your book, create other types of appealing bookstore events, such as:

- A presentation that includes other writers in your genre—say, an evening of mysteries or horror stories.

■ A singles' night, where you talk to the crowd about your book of any topic that singles might take an interest in from health and cooking to relationships and wine tasting.

■ A networking breakfast where local businesspeople are invited to the bookstore to hear about your business book.

■ An evening of spooky stories where you invite parents to bring their kids in pajamas for a story hour.

■ A crafts-making session.

■ A subject of perennial interest to bookstore audiences is "How to Get Published." Tailor a talk around that theme that also works in appropriate mentions of your own book.

■ Would visual aids enliven your talk? Whitney Otto, bestselling author of *How to Make an American Quilt,* produced a slide show for *The Passion Dream Book,* a novel that drew inspiration from the work of great painters. The slide show and the art theme gave Whitney the opportunity to speak in art schools as well as bookstores.

■ Anne Rice's tour for *The Vampire Armand* doubled as a blood donation drive at her bookstore appearances, a smart way to draw attention to the book as well as to a good cause.

THE BOOK SIGNING

You will arrive 15 minutes or so before the event is scheduled to begin. The store manager will greet you and show you where you will be reading. Bookstores are well practiced at running these events. They provide all the necessities: podium, microphone, or perhaps a table and chair if you are only signing books. If your appearance takes place in a city where your sales rep lives or is visiting, then the rep will probably attend the event.

If you are an unknown author, the crowd could range anywhere from a disappointing handful to a happy group of 15 or more. For authors who have written topical works of nonfiction, the crowd can become significantly larger. For example, Susanna Kaysen's appearances for her memoir about mental illness, *Girl, Interrupted*, attracted many people who identified with her experiences. At the time, Kaysen was an unknown writer, but favorable review coverage and the subject matter made her bookstore events a hit. Similarly, Mary Karr, author of a memoir called *The Liars' Club*, attracted large audiences based on the terrific review coverage and her feisty and appealing perspective on her dysfunctional family.

This should go without saying, but during the question-and-answer period, you should treat the audience with the greatest respect. Always. Even someone who asks a loopy and long-winded question. Remember: You need them so much more than they need you. I once witnessed a famous literary writer answer a member of the audience member with contempt, telling the poor man that he had obviously missed the entire point of the presentation. No one deserves that treatment. Such a bully was that author that the audience immediately wilted and no one asked any more questions. To my mind, the author got his just reward. His nasty behavior certainly did not motivate me to read or buy his books.

Your greatest fear about your public appearances might be that no one will show up. Sometimes appearances fail to attract an audience because of competition from a local event or bad weather. Keep your chin up, keep smiling. Perhaps do what one resourceful friend of mine did. He became a volunteer bookstore clerk and helped customers. Whatever you do, do not complain to the bookstore staff. You will only alienate and embarrass them. An essential part of your job is to keep the bookseller motivated and interested in you. After all, they invited you to appear in their store because they thought your book would appeal to customers. Take this opportunity to get to know the store staff. They might become your allies in a hand-selling campaign long after your event is over.

Let's say you tour five or six cities, and only about 12 people show up at each reading. You may come away wondering whether all your effort was worthwhile. As you see it, you're selling only a handful of books at a time. But, behind the obvious, what you are accomplishing is building an audience. With the handful of people that showed up and bought and read your book, you have created a baseline audience upon which to build for your next book. Finding an audience can be a slow growth process. Sometimes this requires long, hard work. But with persistence, you can reach the payoff.

On one occasion, a friend of mine showed up at his own reading and found that the bookstore had made little effort to promote the occasion. The store was located in a mall in Atlanta. Making the best of a bad situation, this author stood outside the store and started to drum up attention, noisily, for his book. He called people over and invited them to come inside to hear his reading. Big on personality, he soon gathered 20 or so people for the reading, and even convinced two strangers to buy copies of the book, though they never set foot in the store. He knew that if he didn't get busy to try to make some success out of the event, then his time and effort on tour would have been wasted.

You will decide for yourself if you are comfortable with showmanship when it comes to building an audience. Remember that shyness does not sell books—unless you're able to create a Salinger-esque mystique. To thwart shyness, remind yourself that you're not promoting you. Rather, you are promoting your book and the wisdom, service, or entertainment that it offers. If it helps, you can even think of yourself as promoting reading, not just your book.

THE 13 RULES FOR AN EFFECTIVE BOOK SIGNING

1. If you are appearing on interviews that will air before your bookstore event, remember to mention the signing's date, place, and time. Alternately, before you start your interview, ask the host to mention the event.

2. Engage passing customers by talking about your book or just being friendly.

3. Most bookstores will display posters about your appearance around the store but not necessarily at the table where you're sitting. A simple blowup of your book jacket mounted on an easel board will help create a point of interest at your table. If your publisher doesn't make one of these for you, make one yourself. A color photocopy or printout enlarged roughly to the size of a legal sheet of paper works just fine and is easily portable.

4. Make lasting contacts of the bookstore staff by being memorable and polite. Make them into effective hand-sellers of your book by talking to them about the book and by taking an interest in them.

5. Practice your reading or talk ahead of time. Keep it short. Remember, your job is to entertain and interest people in your book: A long speech will tire them and squelch any yearning to read the book, let alone spend money on it.

6. Cue your audience twice during your presentation that you will be happy to answer their questions at the end. Prearrange for a shill to ask a question if no one steps forward to ask the first question. Or break the ice by telling the audience that "people often ask me . . ." and asking the first question yourself. Another way of engaging with the audience is to plant your talk with some tantalizing points of interest that you don't explain in detail. Inevitably someone in the audience will ask you to elaborate. For example, you might say that it was essential that you publish this book before you turned 40, and then leave the somewhat mysterious comment hanging unexplained. You will most certainly be asked about why you had to publish with such urgency. You've led your audience into dialogue with you.

7. Be gracious to all customers who approach you, even if they only want directions to the bathroom.

8. Collect the business cards of members of the audience for your database. If you have a seated audience, circulate a sign-up sheet, or else place a collection bowl for the cards at your table.

9. Thank the staff and the audience. Or take pictures of yourself with the bookstore clerks and email them along with thank-you notes.

10. With a smile on your face and a relaxed attitude, you will make the audience feel comfortable. If you show your anxiety, you will make the audience anxious.

11. Play to your audience's mood. If you sense restlessness, keep your talk engaging, lively, and short.

12. As people approach you to sign your book, engage them. Ask how they'd like the book personalized, or what else they like to read, or how they heard about the event (to learn what publicity is working). Creating a memorable event is one way to keep people talking about you. Keep the conversations brief if you happen to have a long line of people waiting for signed copies.

13. Ask the staff if you can sign any unsold copies, which will be stickered and displayed up front.

BOOKSTORE EVENTS (WITHOUT AN AUTHOR)

"Authorless" bookstore events are an alternative to bookstore appearances. These are common in children's book publishing, but less so with adult books. While children's books can be promoted with storytelling sessions (where the store's staff read to children) or with character's costumes (in which a store clerk dresses up in a costume loaned to the bookstore by the publishing house), authorless promotions for adult books are less obvious. The beauty of these events is that because they are tied to your book, the bookstores order your book for the event.

Some examples of authorless events:

■ Promote a popular history book with a trivia contest. Some booksellers turn events like this into singles nights, seizing on the chance to create an interactive social event. Provide the store with a quiz with the answers on a separate sheet for the store manager to hand out.

■ Booksellers will promote self-help or how-to books by working with local experts. For example, a local financial planner might talk about this year's tax changes. The bookseller sells books related to tax planning. The expert gets to promote his or her business. Propose events to booksellers that identify an expert that the bookseller could call on for an event. Offer handouts such as bookmarks or postcards—anything that reinforces the event's connection to your book. Even though the bookseller will present an array of books on the subject, your materials will help your book stand out. Another example: A staffer from a local fabrics or craft store can demonstrate easy-to-make Halloween costumes for kids, with the costume design coming from your crafts book. The kit materials that you might offer for the event are instructions, a supplies list, and an illustration or photograph of the suggested costume. Any activity-based book can be promoted in this way.

▪ Create attention and display for your book by creating a gift basket that a bookstore can raffle off. The basket might contain gourmet goodies and a copy of your cookbook. On a practical level, the number of stores that you can offer this promotion to is limited because the baskets will be expensive to put together. But choose your bookstores right (ask your publicist to talk to the sales reps about identifying the top upscale independent booksellers in their territories) and run the promotion during peak traffic times (holidays, Mother's Day, Father's Day) and the promotion might pay off in increased sales at those accounts. If so, then your publisher might offer the promotion in other markets.

Assembling the event kits that the bookstores will need in order to stage the event can be somewhat time-consuming and therefore a strain on an already overworked marketing or publicity group. However, if your publisher thinks the idea is a good one and will pitch your concept to booksellers, then you can offer to assemble the event kits yourself.

Your publisher's cooperation in pitching the chain booksellers is important. The two major chains prefer to send materials to their store managers directly from the home office, and prefer to work through publishers rather than authors. If your publisher doesn't think your idea is strong enough to pitch, then your alternative is to set up events store by store. With this latter approach, you can start small and experiment with a limited number of stores. The local store managers of the chains as well as independent booksellers can set up events. When those events go well and help the booksellers sell your book, then report your success to your publisher and ask if the sales reps will now pitch the chains with your idea.

Prepare a kit, including the materials that a bookseller requires to host an authorless event:

- Press release and a JPEG of your book jacket and author photo for the bookseller to create a promotional poster for the event

- Newsletter copy for the store newsletter

- A script for the store manager or other person who will be hosting the event

- Any other materials that are specific to your book's event such as a handout that the bookseller can photocopy

- Last, enclose a "Dear Bookseller" cover letter that describes how the kit contents can promote your book.

Take a look at the newsletters and advice for booksellers on www .bookweb.org. If your authorless event is a good idea, then you or your publicist could pitch the editor of the newsletter to share the idea with other booksellers.

SPEAKING ENGAGEMENTS AND OTHER
NON-BOOKSTORE APPEARANCES

Talk to your publicist about setting up speaking engagements in your tour cities. Speaking engagements are usually sponsored by a local organization with a membership base to invite to the event. The events deliver another audience and an excellent way to anchor your visit to a local market and to appeal to local media.

For example, literary fiction writers or writers of serious nonfiction can enhance their tour schedule by contacting the heads of the applicable university departments—English or African-American studies or women's studies and so on—to set up readings and invite the relevant classes to attend. In some cases, the universities will offer a small honorarium of, say, $250 to $500. They will often agree to display posters promoting the event, but you or your publicist may have to provide them. These are simply made from the book jacket image, an author photo, and information about the event pasted onto easel-backed foam core or cardboard. Meanwhile, let the university bookstore know about the talk on campus so they can order the book. Arranging university appearances can take longer than setting up bookstore events, requiring several conversations with professors, who are available only during their infrequent office hours.

Not all in-house publicists can or will book local speaking engagements. (Not all freelance publicists will book speaking engagements, either, so if this type of promotion is important to you, then clarify that before you hire someone.) Anyone can research and book his or her own speaking engagements, which should coincide with the publication date or later. Because you've tied the theme of your talk to your book, you've created a ready theme for bookstores as well.

You might also speak at libraries. Throughout the United States and Canada, many libraries have active speakers programs that range from grand and formal, such as the main branch of the New York Public Library and the Cambridge Public Library, to informal though well-attended programs at local branch libraries. The booking lead time for branch libraries is four to eight weeks, longer for some of the larger library programs. You also benefit from being listed in the events' brochures or newsletters. It's all exposure for you and your book.

Some librarians will let you sell your book at the event, but ask first. While library appearances, like university talks, do not deliver significant book sales, they do deliver audiences—sometimes very large ones. These audiences can help build favorable word of mouth for your book. To find libraries in your region or in areas where you will travel, log onto www .publiclibraries.com, a portal to libraries throughout the United States, and to www.nlc-bnc.ca/canlib/epublic.htm for Canadian branch library websites. As previously mentioned, to get a feel for the library market, read *Library Journal* or, if you're the author of a children's book, read *School Library Journal*.

Other possible speaking venues include the Smithsonian Institution in Washington, DC, which has a terrific year-round program called the Resident Associate Program and offers lectures on a full range of topics, and The National Archives in Washington, DC, which also has a varied speakers program. So does your local YMCA or YMHA, the chamber of commerce, the Junior League, garden clubs, museums and historical societies, design centers, botanic gardens, and grade schools, which are particularly important for authors of children's books. Cafés and restaurants sometimes look to attract a certain kind of literary clientele and may sponsor readings. Local church groups and synagogues often welcome speakers to speak on spiritual and secular topics, and so on. Another source of ideas for places to speak is www .booktv.org. This is C-SPAN 2's site for its Book TV programming.

Unless you have a large mailing list and can easily pull a crowd of people to hear you, I would not recommend that you book a venue to speak that is not affiliated with an organization. Otherwise the burden of marketing the event will fall entirely to you. Far better to set up an event with an established group that routinely brings in an audience.

Speak at Libraries—One Author's Success Story

"You cannot speak at enough libraries," says novelist Laura Van Wormer. Most libraries have brown-bag lunch programs for speakers. Appearing at these events leads to an increase in demand for copies ordered at that branch and to librarians talking to colleagues at other branches, which in turn leads to increased sales and a growing readership for your work. Libraries have websites and are relatively easy to research and contact. "You can also create bookmarks," Van Wormer says. "The circulating staff is happy to leave them at the circulation desk as patrons check out their books."

She advises, as well, that authors get involved with their local Friends of the Library programs. Her own involvement with the restoration of the old library building in her hometown of Meriden, Connecticut, led to an invitation to give the keynote address at the annual Arizona Library Association/Mountain Plains Library Association Conference. "They wanted me to speak not because I'm an author," she says, "but because I know what they do and what they are interested in."

She knew because she made it her business to educate herself about the library marketplace. Her books appear regularly on library reading lists and account for a nice portion of sales for each new novel.

Pay particular attention to Van Wormer's last piece of advice: "Always be nice to librarians," she says. "You never know if one of them is a buyer." Meaning that the librarian may be the person selecting how many copies of your book to buy for the library system.

Still stumped for venues? To find more, just type in "author lecture" and "friends of the library" and "junior league" into your search engine and you will start to unearth hundreds of opportunities for authors, along with contact information for the organizers of the events.

Perhaps one of the most accessible organizations for authors to enter the speakers market, as well as perhaps to make a little money is the Learning Annex. With programs in Los Angeles, New York, San Diego, San Francisco, and Toronto, the Learning Annex offers 800 inexpensive adult-education classes every month on a wide range of practical and in-spirational topics. These include the arts, business, money and careers, personal growth, relationships, spirituality, sports and fitness, technology, and much more. Authors can earn a percentage of the class fee and if the course registration is more than 100 people, then the Learning Annex will sell books at the classes. (If the registration is smaller, then you are re-sponsible for book sales.) Classes are promoted through catalogs distrib-uted in street stands, in stores, and through direct mail. The average class length is three hours, and classes are held in hotel and conference rooms arranged by the Learning Annex.

Here are examples of some other interesting speaking forums for au-thors on tour:

- Frank Rich, the former theater critic for the *New York Times*, spoke at regional theaters to promote the paperback edition of *Ghost Light*.

- Bill Nye the Science Guy appeared at aquariums to promote his book, *Big Blue Ocean*.

- The American Museum of Natural History scheduled a lecture with Simon Winchester, author of *The Map That Changed the World* about the founder of modern geology.

- The Junior League of Richmond sponsors an annual Book and Au-thor Dinner. Go to the website to see if you think your book qualifies for the event. (See www.jlrichmond.org under the tab Book & Author Dinner.)

■ The Friends of the Farmers' Market in Santa Fe sponsors many local events, including cooking and crafts demonstrations, childrens' storytelling, chef visits, and book talks (www.farmersmarketsnm.org).

■ The author of *The Spirit of Butterflies*, Maraleen Manos-Jones, was invited to appear at The National Zoo to talk and to sign books.

Your speaking appearance at a local institution gives you or your publicist an additional angle to pitch in that market. Your publicist may set up a radio and newspaper interview in advance of your departure. That way the media can mention your event in advance so that interested readers can attend. The sponsor for your appearance may have its own publicity department, which can collaborate on promotions.

Start the Campaign Early for a Speaking Tour

"For an event-oriented book tour, starting early is the key," says PR pro Meryl Moss. Her approach on behalf of her clients is to anchor their publicity appearance in any one city with an event affiliated with a local organization. "That way you have a built-in audience and a promotional partner in that market," she says. For a book called *On My Own Two Feet: A Modern Girl's Guide to Personal Finance*, by Manisha Thakor and Sharon Kedar, Moss's agency had the great luxury of being able to start work on the campaign in October, well in advance of the book's June publication date. The resulting tour schedule included 20 cities, which the authors divided between them, with appearances concentrated in June and September. Each market features an appearance at a local organization, including universities (Bryn Mawr, Wellesley, University of Texas) clubs (Commonwealth Club of California) women's groups (Atlanta Women's Network, Financial Women's Association) financial organizations (Drexel, 85 Broads, Dallas Credit Union,) and others (Teach for America, Dress for Success). The long lead time allowed Moss's agency to pinpoint groups that would take a natural interest in the book's message and to set up speaking engagements to coincide with the book's publication.

BOOK SALES AT EVENTS

You have options when selling books at events. At small local events that you, rather than your publisher, have arranged, you can buy books from your publisher (at your author discount rate) and sell copies at the back of the room. Better yet, the organizers of the event where you are appearing might agree to buy and sell your books. If they agree to do this, refer them to your publisher's special sales department. For much larger events, publishers will sometimes arrange for a bookseller to sell books. You are also free to contact local booksellers directly to arrange back-of-the-room sales. Remember: Keep your editor informed periodically about what you are doing so that he or she can remind the publisher of your ongoing activities to keep your book in print.

If you plan to buy upward of one thousand books for yourself—either for resale or to give away—then you might have your agent negotiate a more favorable discount in the contract. If the contract is long since executed, you might still try to negotiate a discount based on the large number of books that you intend to buy. The standard author discount is generally 40 to 50 percent. This sale is nonreturnable. Standard bookstore discounts range from 46 to 49 percent on a returnable basis. This means that the publisher's terms of sale to you are favorable to the publisher because it runs no risk of getting the books back. If the publisher refuses to give you a higher flat discount, propose a sliding scale based on the number of books you buy.

AN AUTHOR SETS UP SPEAKING ENGAGEMENTS
TO PROMOTE HER BOOKS

Katherine Wyse Goldman has written a number of books, including *Working Mothers 101*, *My Mother Worked and I Turned Out Okay*, and *If You Can Raise Kids You Can Get a Good Job*. She is a marketer by profession and finds the "hunt" for promotional opportunities exhilarating.

To publicize one of her books, Goldman called the Greater Philadelphia Chamber of Commerce and proposed that the organization sponsor a panel discussion targeting the area's working women. The chamber agreed and found a local bank to underwrite the event—a breakfast talk called "The Distinguished Woman: Taking Charge." Joining Goldman on the panel were the president of the local United Way, the district attorney, and the general manager of a local cable channel. The chamber used the breakfast panel as a way to promote a convention it was sponsoring called The International Women's Show: The ticket to the breakfast talk included admission to the convention and more than 500 women attended. Books were available at a 30 percent discount. To publicize the event, the chamber sent brochures to its members and ran a full-page ad in the *Philadelphia Inquirer*.

When calling a company with a book promotion idea, Goldman identifies the name of the right contact from the newspaper or magazine article where she read about their organization, or else from research online. Failing those leads, Goldman simply approaches the head of corporate communications. "That person usually reports to the CEO, and so is a good doorway into the company," she says. Other successful events that Goldman has set up for herself include:

■ The Women Incorporated annual conference called "Uncommon Women on Common Ground" aimed at women entrepreneurs: After reading about the forthcoming conference in a magazine, she cold-called the organizers to ask if she could participate. Before her call, they hadn't considered including a session on work/life balance issues. They sold books, paid half of her expenses to California, and Goldman convinced her publisher to pay the balance.

■ *MetroKids*, the parenting newspaper in Philadelphia: Goldman simply called the editor of the paper and asked if it ever sponsored any conferences. When the editor later had an idea for a conference, she called Goldman to participate as the keynote speaker on the subject "Family Focus: Resources for Today's Families."

■ Delaware County Community College: Goldman called the college after reading an article about its program for older women who want to get a college degree. She interviewed the head of the program for her book, who later invited Goldman to be the graduation speaker.

■ Goldman also set up and participated in The Nordstrom's Grandmother Club breakfast, the Child Abuse Council annual fund-raising breakfast, the Lakeshore Health System's Annual Women's Symposium, and the Women's Division of the Jewish Welfare Fund for a fund-raising dinner where she spoke on "Working Women as Role Models for the Family and the Community." She also successfully pitched the Cleveland Bar Association's program on "Making Mentoring Part of Law Firms" and Case Western Reserve University's "Women's Voices Lecture." In her appearances, Goldman often delivered the keynote address to audiences ranging from 50 to 800 people. At all events, the sponsors sold copies of her books, which is her prerequisite for appearing at an event. She also suggests that instead of selling the book to attendees, the host organizations buy copies of the books to give away as table gifts.

Another idea that Goldman had that did not pan out, but is nonetheless a good example of how to think like a marketer, involves Ford Motors. When Goldman read that an all-woman team designed the Ford Windstar, she figured why not ask the company to offer her book as an incentive for potential customers to test-drive the vehicle. After all, their customers and her customers are the same people. Though the idea fell through, it was a good one: Car companies sometimes use books as test-drive incentives.

Goldman advises that when you talk to companies you should pitch to their goals. Corporations have deeper pockets for promotion than book publishers do. But they will support your book only if the program you pitch furthers the marketing goals for their own products or services.

A SELF-PUBLISHED AUTHOR CREATES HER OWN GRASSROOTS PUBLICITY CAMPAIGN

Nelvia Brady is a self-published author who planned all her own promotions and publicity for her book, *This Mother's Daughter*. Through interviews with women about their mothers, the book addresses the nature of the mother-daughter bond. The author's promotional efforts resulted in good publicity and sales, enough so that St. Martin's Press later bought the paperback rights.

To promote her book, Brady appeared at churches and private parties, set up by friends in many cities. She says, "The events where I can speak to the substance of the book are more successful than just a book signing." She planned the events carefully. Her approach was to begin with interactive games that drew the audience into her subject matter and made them feel comfortable. Then she addressed the serious aspects of relationships between mothers and daughters. An educator by training, Brady drew on her expertise to engage her audience. She also shared stories about her own mother, and so created an atmosphere in which people felt free to open up. At her events, she sold copies to most people in the room.

To tap into her network of friends, Brady simply called them and asked for help in their community. Some friends belonged to professional organizations or clubs that sponsored events. Others hosted events for their friends in their homes or at bookstores. At every event, attendees were impressed about meeting a genuine author. This took Brady by surprise: She had hardly begun to see herself in such terms.

Having her friends set up and host bookstore signings worked particularly well. Her contacts called bookstores to offer to host events in the store. They'd send postcard invitations, supplied by Brady, to friends and associates. They even supplied refreshments.

"Bookstores like it because it ensures a turnout," says Brady. "It also takes the pressure off a hostess because she doesn't have to worry about using her home or finding a site. There is always parking and the locations are usually pretty convenient. I have also had organizations host their events in the bookstore. Most recently I did a book-signing event for a suburban YWCA that was held in a Borders bookstore." For Today's Black Woman Expo in Chicago she set up a game show, based loosely on television's old show *The Newlywed Game*, staged, instead, with mothers and daughters.

Brady says that setting up promotions and publicity requires total commitment, which gave her the impetus to accomplish as much as she did.

JOIN THE SPEAKING CIRCUIT—
BECOMING A PROFESSIONAL SPEAKER

If you are an effective speaker and your subject matter is topical, consider building up your credentials and signing up with a speaker's bureau, an agency that will set up paid speaking engagements on your behalf. The agency's desire to sign you will depend on several factors:

- How well you deliver a speech

- How well your speech is put together (there is an art to this, and you may need to work with a speech coach on both delivery and content)

- The extent to which your speech is marketable to potential audiences

Speaker's bureaus will want to see a videotape of you giving a speech, as well as a complete press kit about you and your book. You will need to market yourself to them much in the same way that you might have done when you were first looking for a literary agent. (For hundreds of tips on giving effective speeches, basic presentation skills, understanding your audience, getting over stage fright, and other advice related to public speaking, check out www.antion.com.) If you manage to get signed on with a speaker's bureau to set up regular speaking engagements, you will benefit from supplemental income as well as exposure for your book. Your hosts will arrange to sell the book at the back of the room. Speaker's bureaus take a commission of 15 to 30 percent of your fees.

If you're not proficient enough to command a speaker's bureau interest, start small and work your way up. This could mean taking speaking engagements for little or no fee, but you get to polish your skills and keep your book's audience growing. To find a list of speaker's bureaus (or lecture agents), go to www.literarymarketplace.com. You will need to register, and then you will have free access to several useful publishing databases, including lecture agents and publicity firms.

When starting out on the speaker's circuit, it will be difficult, at first, to get paid for your appearances. In the beginning, however, generating an income should not be your goal. More important is improving your credentials by starting with local chapters of national organizations. Increase your exposure. Ask your hosts to recommend you to the groups' national chapters. Gradually you will sharpen your speaking skills, create exposure for your book, and possibly attract interest from speaker's bureaus.

How do you find these organizations? You will need to invest some time to research and contact leads. You will need to create a professional-looking packet of information about yourself: A one-sheeter about your proposed topic; a press release about your book; a biography of yourself; a photocopy of the cover of your book; and a copy of the page from your publisher's catalog. A website is essential to display appropriate information to the people you are pitching.

If you are at all serious about speaking, take the time to prepare a professional-looking presentation kit. The speaker's market is a competitive one. You will market yourself to speaker's bureaus and to organizations with the same assiduousness and smart thinking that you will bring to the marketing of your book to your various target audiences.

BOOKSTORE APPEARANCES AND SPEAKING ENGAGEMENTS— A SUMMARY

Like your media appearances, your bookstore and speaking appearances should entertain your audience to motivate them to buy your book. The opportunities for public appearances are limitless, if you can come up with an interesting and effective presentation and are willing to pitch yourself. To do this:

- Create a talk about your book and practice it before you unleash it on the public.

- Research venues to speak in your community by paying attention to events and businesses that might take an interest in your book. You can pitch yourself to speak to the organization, or for the company to cosponsor your bookstore events so that you can attract a larger, targeted audience.

▪ Be bold and cold-call individuals at organizations that might host you—the payoff could be big.

▪ Have your press materials at the ready so that you can respond quickly to a potential host's interest.

▪ Set yourself a reasonable goal for continual exposure—perhaps one appearance a month.

11

ONLINE MARKETING

SELLING your book successfully is an impressive achievement—for you and your publisher. Competition in the marketplace is fierce. Consumers enjoy so many choices of entertainment and news media, your product has to stand out in order to survive. According to Seth Godin's book *Permission Marketing*, consumers see an estimated 3,000 marketing messages every day. Your challenge is to raise your book above the media clutter.

The good news is the Internet, with its bounty of promotional opportunities, online retailers, and its amazingly fast and efficient research capability. Through readily available online resources you can find out about competing titles and the names and addresses of reporters who have written articles on similar topics to your book, as well as locate freelance publicists, writers' groups, and other communities that might be interested in inviting you to speak, and so on. But most important, you can reach your readers directly and engage them in an ongoing conversation about your book. That is the essential value of this medium to authors, one that is only just starting to be tapped.

Your publisher's sales reps call on the larger online book retailers like Amazon and bn.com, but the reps do not have time to scout out all online bookselling opportunities. Likewise, your publicist will have time to reach out only to a limited group of bloggers and websites. If you want to exploit all that the Internet has to offer, you should build relationships yourself with the many sites and individuals that might care. This is well worth your time. With the link between a successful online promotion and a purchase being only a click away, your efforts could pay off big.

It might not surprise you to learn that the authors and publishers who recognized the Internet's potential early on were in the computer book field. They were talking to one another online back in the day when you needed to know programming code to access the web. Business academics and science fiction writers were close behind them. Today, everyone is online—including your potential audience. And if you are the writer of fiction or nonfiction aimed at the teen market, quite simply, you can't afford *not* to be actively engaged online with your audience. Market research shows that most teens decide what to read next based on what they see online.

If you're serious about marketing online, having a website is a must, making it easy for someone to check your credentials and find out more about your book. You may also be thinking about starting a blog—think of it as an online daily journal—which can be part of your website. Check out the site of business book writer Penelope Trunk (www.penelopetrunk.com) to see how she showcases her blog alongside her web pages. The site is very easy to navigate as well as being clear and informative.

As you set out to connect with your audience online, keep in mind that you should focus on your specific audience. The beauty of Internet is that it allows you to pinpoint the individuals who are most likely to care about your book.

ONLINE BOOK MARKETING OPPORTUNITIES

Here are some of the many ways you can start to market your book online:

- Check the major bookseller sites to see if your publisher has uploaded your book jacket and other pertinent information. If the information about your book is missing, then track down the person at the publishing house whose job this is. If you end up sending the information yourself, then check each site for its submission guidelines.

- Any good reviews? Submit them to any online booksellers that will display them.

- Booksellers (both online retailers and the brick-and-mortar stores) send email newsletters to their customers. Ask your publisher about offering an excerpt or an article for booksellers to use.

- Some booksellers have blogs and invite authors to participate as guest bloggers. For instance, check out Powells (www.powells.com/blog) where you'll find hundreds of author guest blogs as well as Q&A's, exclusive articles, and other promotions. Talk to your publisher about getting you involved and say that you're willing to create exclusive content for the site.

- Amazon Connect allows authors to blog directly to the readers who have bought their books: The blog entries show up on the readers' homepages when they log on to Amazon. Conceptually, it's a very interesting idea, but in practice, many of the blogging authors lose the opportunity to draw readers into their work. If you participate, suggest that the reader visits you at your website so you can bring that reader into your circle.

- Look for book publishing discussion groups and join the ones that appeal to you. Take part in the many conversations about book marketing and exchange ideas. For information on how to find discussion groups, see page 216.

- Look for discussion groups related to the topic of your book. Join and start talking. By contacting special interest sites that would have a natural interest in your book, you can build an interested audience. Note that the protocol is to avoid blatant self-promotion. Your goal is to become part of the online community and build a natural fellowship with the group and earn the members' support. For more about online protocol, see page 217.

- Search for online newsletters, websites, blogs, and companies that relate to your book topic. Contact the sites and offer an excerpt from your book. (Make sure to let your editor and publicist know

what you are planning: Your publisher's subsidiary rights department has a vested interest in selling excerpts of your content so you
want to avoid accidentally undermining those efforts.) In exchange,
ask if the site is willing to link to yours so that you can pull in more
readers. If any of the sites conduct Q&A's with writers, see if they
would be interested in talking to you. Author Rosemary Harris
(www.rosemaryharris.com) set up an interesting promotion for her
first gardening-themed mystery, *Pushing Up Daisies*, with the Park
Seed Company. The website for this gardening catalog agreed to se-
rialize chapters from the book online and to sell the book through
its print catalog.

▪ Set up an electronic signature that includes information about your
book and your website's address. The information in your signature
will appear at the bottom of every email and posting that you send. (If
you do not know how to set up a signature, use your software Help
function, which will direct you to your toolbar.)

▪ Reach out to reading groups by offering an excerpt from your book
to give them a taste of your work. For more on finding reading
groups, see page 218.

▪ Offer to write for relevant newsletters or blogs. Many welcome relevant content. Type "guest blogger author" into your search engine
and you'll see how wide this opportunity is.

▪ Identify the bloggers who should receive review copies of your
book.

▪ If you already have an active and growing database of fans, offer
them a sneak online or email preview of your work, perhaps the first
chapter, just before the book is shipped to bookstores. Or offer a contest where you give away 10 signed copies of the book.

▪ Create a promotional video about your book (a book trailer or
video-podcast) that can be posted online. This doesn't have to be expensive to be appealing. (See more on how to make a book trailer on
page 242.)

■ Ask your publisher to sponsor a spot for your book in AuthorBuzz (www.authorbuzz.com). Through its weekly opt-in emailing list, AuthorBuzz sends information about new books to thousands of readers, librarians, and booksellers. The mailing might include excerpts, contests, a special message from the author—anything that you want to buzz your audience about. If your publisher won't pay for this, then you can also contact AuthorBuzz directly to set up the promotion yourself.

■ Ask your publisher to have your book entered in The Great American Book Giveaway (www.bkgiveaway.gather.com), a weekly drawing for free books that helps yours get noticed by thousands of readers and book clubs. Again, if your publisher won't do this you can set up the promotion yourself. (Contact meryl@mediamuscle.com.)

■ Dear Reader (www.dearreader.com) is a wonderful online book club that emails excerpts from books to members as a kind of literary sampler. Join the club—as a reader you'll love it—and you'll see the many promotional opportunities offered by the site's proprietor, Suzanne Beecher. Contact her through the site to receive instructions on how to submit a review copy of your book for the program.

ONLINE DISCUSSION GROUPS

With many thousands of discussion groups to choose from, you can find one on almost any topic. To get started, go to Google and click on "Groups." In the recreation area, you'll find "Books." Click there to see if any of the groups appeal to you. Or go to http://groups.yahoo.com and start exploring. When you click through to a discussion group's site, you'll find instructions on how to sign up.

Joining a group is free and you can unsubscribe at any time. You need to stay within the boundaries established by the group's administrator. The rules are clear when you sign up. Once you join, you'll start to receive emails posted by the other list members. The emails essentially take the form of an ongoing conversation. Some groups are more active than others and produce a flood of correspondence. You are under no oligation to chime in and can opt to read what's being said before jumping into the conversation. Generally speaking, you can't promote your book aggressively in a discussion group. If you do try to promote your book in an inappropriate way, you'll soon hear from other members. If you continue to abuse the privilege, then the administrator might eject you. You will understand the acceptable level of promotion once you spend a little time in the group.

One way to gain exposure in a group without breaching protocol is to ask the administrator if you may offer a free chapter of your book. (Again, make sure to alert your publisher about the content you want to give away so that you don't run afoul of the sub rights department. An alternative is to write an article about your book that you can offer instead.) You might suggest that interested readers can email you directly for the excerpt or go to your website where they can download it.

Mind Your Online Manners

There's a protocol to online behavior that has its roots in the very ethic that founded the Internet: It's a free medium but you need to respect it and others who use it.

When online, keep the following concepts in mind:

- Unlike watching television, where you are a passive media consumer, participating online is interactive, which means that you give as well as take.
- Go online and you are in public. So avoid getting into personal arguments. They spiral out of control and you will look bad. Very bad. It's okay to disagree with someone, but keep your argument to the facts.
- Initiate conversations by acknowledging or thanking the other person for their site or posting.
- Be yourself and be real. Avoid seeming like a shill selling your book. If you come off like a huckster, it's repellent.
- Reach out to bloggers yourself rather than have someone do it for you. That's part of being authentic and forming real connections with others.

- Read and understand the blogs you want to engage with before you try to participate. When you do make contact, indicate knowledge of the site just as you should with any other media. The fact that the Internet offers easy access doesn't mean you should be casual about your communication.
- Think of reaching out to others online as an electronic form of networking. When you network in your career, you're setting up relationships that are mutually beneficial. Bring that same mindset to your blogging relationships.

All of this advice is utterly academic when taken out of context. So if you haven't already, go online and start exploring the way other writers and individuals are using the web.

FINDING READING GROUPS ONLINE

Reading groups use the Internet in several ways. Some groups post their booklists on a website as a service to their members and then meet in person. The group called Mostly, We Eat has a website that welcomes non-members and offers a free email newsletter (www.mostlyweeat.org). Some reading groups are run entirely as email lists, meaning that members never meet in person. Instead, the members email one another and the dialogue takes place entirely online through the ongoing replies. Or else an online reading group might host live-time online chats and then post the conversation on its website. An example of this, on a grand scale, is the *USA Today* reading group, which posts questions for readers on its website and hosts online chats with the author of the featured book.

As reported in the *Atlanta Journal-Constitution*, Walter Mosley's publicist, Sally McCartin, contacted more than 250 online reading clubs by email and sent them advance copies of one of Mosley's early novels. Some of the clubs interviewed Mosley. Others added his book to their reading lists. The *New York Times* reported on how Donna Woolfolk Cross created an audience for her historical novel by marketing to reading groups. The book, *Pope Joan*, has more than 100,000 copies in print in its paperback edition. Her site, www.popejoan.com, offers a section dedicated to reading groups, encouraging the groups to contact her to set up an "appearance" by speakerphone. She offers a discount to reading groups if they purchase the book online through the site. Smart. In fact Cross's efforts are credited with motivating booksellers to begin offering speakerphone author events to reading groups that meet in their bookstores.

Several reading groups gained national prominence after being featured on some of the televised book clubs. Search for these groups online and you will come up with hundreds. Two of the prominent groups include The Pulpwood Queens (East Texas) and the Sweet Potato Queens Eating and Reading Club (Jackson, Mississippi). Try the books section of Yahoo! clubs at http://groups.yahoo.com. When you find groups that seem appropriate to the subject matter of your book, simply email the administrator or website manager to ask if you can send an excerpt or complimentary copy of your book for consideration. Let the host know that if the group selects your book, you would happily make yourself available by phone or in person for an upcoming meeting, depending on your location.

WEBSITES

A website can have multiple uses, and you may not even realize its full potential until you have one up and running. Author sites range from a few static pages of basic biographical information to full-fledged interactive blogs with daily posts and many pages of frequently updated content.

Most publishing houses lack the resources to set up a site for every author. In any case, it's better that you set up the site yourself so that you can control its content. (Don't think that your publisher's post of your book on its own site gives you sufficient web presence: After all, when was the last time you visited the site of a publishing house? 'Nuff said!)

Educate yourself about websites *before* you create your own. I can't emphasize this enough, because you can easily take the wrong path and end up wasting time and money.

Aim high: There are a lot of amateurish looking author websites and they don't do anyone much good. They have poorly scanned photographs, cluttered backgrounds, clunky and clashing fonts, poorly written text, and so on.

Start by checking out other author sites to see what features you would like on yours. Which ones make you curious about the author or make you want to buy their books or go back to their site again? If you come across a site you really like, send the author an email complimenting the site and ask for the contact information for the site's designer. As you dip your toe into online marketing, you'll find again and again that initiating conversations with individuals often starts best with a note of admiration or thanks. It will open many doors for you.

Plan on interviewing several web designers to get an idea for the range of services available. This is essential. Contact the owners of the websites they've created to check on their credentials. There are a lot of second-rate services out there and you'll need to do your research to avoid them. Think of it this way: You wouldn't undertake major construction in your home without getting bids from several contractors and architects. You should approach your web home the same way.

Here are some successful sites to start you browsing:

Lemony Snicket's site (www.lemonysnicket.com) displays his kids' books alongside fun (and creepy) interactive content. The homepage welcomes you with a warning to leave the site, "Warning: Do Not Enter: This site is very unpleasant." Snicket's droll and faintly sick humor is consistent throughout the site: Never does he drop his authorial voice. He also provides a printable poster, games, and a screensaver as well as an author biography and list of books. The site strikes exactly the right tone: It engages without overhyping and provides real content.

Another children's author who has created a content-rich site is Jan Brett (www.janbrett.com). She offers an impressively high level of interactivity for users, including contests for schools and libraries to win copies of her books and an author visit, email postcards, printable notecards and envelopes, coloring pages, and more. See also Kevin Henkes's site, www.kevinhenkes.com, where he offers games for kids, recipes for dishes mentioned in his books, and a mouse maze. Beverly Cleary's site, www.beverlycleary.com, has trivia quizzes based on her many books, and also an interactive neighborhood map where her characters live. Perhaps children's authors have a leg up when it comes to creating a playful site, as their books are inherently about learning as play. Authors of adult books could certainly adapt some of the engaging features of children's book sites.

Look at mystery writer Laura Lippman's site, www.lauralippman.com. While simple in design, it is also attractive and hugely informative. The site makes great use of hyperlinks—links embedded in the text—so that you can find out more information about the people or places that Lippman talks about. Isabel Allende has created a very personal site at www.isabelallende.com. Naturally there is information about all of her books here, but there is also a photo gallery of Allende with her family, and a page of frequently asked questions based on her fan mail. The homepage is beautiful.

The more interesting your site, the greater the likelihood that visitors will return or, even better, tell others about your site. Here are some more examples:

- Thriller writer Joseph Finder (www.joefinder.com) offers newsletters, a bio, interviews, updates on international sales and tours, and frequent giveaways, which encourages repeat visits.

- Paranormal novelist Sherrilyn Kenyon (www.sherrilynkenyon.com) writes several blogs on her site and recently posted a free short story in pdf format. Her publisher reports that it was downloaded 60,000 times within four months.

- Romance novelist Debbie Macomber (www.debbiemacomber.com) offers a content-rich site including readers guides and recipe contests. Here's her innovation: Because her novels take place in a knitting shop, Macomber posts a downloadable knitting pattern on her site and sends a knitting pattern to her fans at Christmas.

- The site for *Special Topics in Calamity Physics*, by Marisha Pessl (www.calamityphysics.com), is a gorgeously layered site, one that matches the complexity of this literary novel. The site also includes links to the book's MySpace and Friendster pages.

Like these authors, think of your website as a tool to keep your customers—your readers—happy. As with other forms of media, always consider the benefit to the end user.

Anything you can post on your site (or blog) that has viral appeal to readers is highly beneficial—like Macomber's knitting patterns. Viral marketing is when a concept, product, or service is so appealing that news of it spreads like contagion from person to person, who share it instantly and aggressively. It's an extreme form of word of mouth, where your customers become your biggest promoters. Think of Apple's success with the launch of the iPhone: Apple's customers created enormous anticipation for the product by talking about it constantly. When you're planning your site, spend some time thinking about what you can offer your readers—whether it's exclusive content or an interactive problem-solving game or quiz—to prompt them to tell others about it. (For an example of a book campaign that created viral marketing buzz, see page 237.)

Another consideration when planning your site is to try to "own" the topic you have written about. In other words, attract potential readers to your site by creating a destination built around their interests. For example, author Terrence Cheng made his site a resource for anyone interested in Chinese fiction, politics, and society, and particularly in the events that took place in Tiananmen Square in 1989, the starting point for his first novel, *Sons of Heaven*. The site included a discussion forum, information about current events, books, and writers related to China, as well as background about the book. Cheng started planning the site's design a full year before his book was published. He showed a designer 20 websites that he liked, not restricting himself to author sites. Then he and the designer focused on the elements that he would incorporate into his site. He gave the designer a flow chart on paper showing the content that he intended to include. Then the designer submitted his first screen, and the two worked together to refine the site. When Cheng's second novel, *Deep in the Mountains*, came out, Cheng adapted the website to focus on the young adult market for which this novel was written.

Here are some of the features that your website might offer:

1. A clean, uncluttered homepage with text that explains what your site offers, that shows your book cover and links to other clean, uncluttered pages and activities on the site. The more graphics you

have, the slower your site will be to download and the less likely users will stick around before clicking to another site.

2. An author biography and photo, and press release about your book.

3. A reading group guide to your book for bookstores and reading groups. For sample downloadable guides, go to www.reading groupguides.com and www.readinggroupchoices.com.

4. A book excerpt or other free content. Invite users to download and use your original article(s) providing that they credit you and your book. You will specify the credit line that they must run if they reprint your content.

5. A "counter" to track the number of visitors to your site, helpful to know if you want to impress your publisher with your web traffic numbers, but not essential. The counter should be hidden so that only you can access it. (Most publicly displayed counters look tacky.)

6. A link to buy your book. Set yourself up as an affiliate or associate with one of the online booksellers so that you get a percentage of sales when readers click through from your site to the retailer's site. Go to www.amazon.com, www.bn.com, or www.booksense.com to read the guidelines for affiliates.

7. A way to capture names and email addresses on an opt-in mailing list.

8. Contests. Give out free copies of your book or galley on a limited, while-supplies-last basis. You can offer the copies to, say, the first 25 users to register for the prize. This way you can capture all the contestant's names in your growing database. Promote the give-away to other sites to encourage linkage to yours.

9. Email newsletters, another excellent way to collect opt-in email addresses. Check out the newsletter archive on Lawrence Block's site (www.lawrenceblock.com).

10. Your speech-making credentials. Pages aimed at organizations for which you might give speeches should include the topics that you can address, any endorsements from organizations that have already hosted you, and a resume of your speaking experience.

11. A media center or press room with your press materials.

12. Links to other sites where you have contributed articles.

13. Links to related sites, making your site a resource and destination that users will bookmark.

14. A way for readers to contact you and to post comments.

15. A prompt for users to forward your website pages to a friend via email.

16. A schedule of upcoming appearances (and don't forget to take the schedule down when the appearances are done).

17. Your blog.

One last point: Make sure your website appears on your book jacket and any promotional materials.

CREATE YOUR WEBSITE

Creating a site involves a few steps:

- Registering for a domain name (or URL).

- Designing the look and writing the copy for the site, tasks that have important technological components as well as aesthetic ones.

- Finding a host server because once the site is built, it needs a place to sit.

- Linking the site to others and listing it in search directories.

Some web design companies offer domain registration, design, and hosting all in one package, with prices ranging from rock-bottom all the way to luxury class. But you will do your homework before making any decisions about which way to go.

Domain Name

You can register your domain name through any domain registrar for a nominal annual fee. The site does not have to exist yet in order for you to register the name. But unless you have a burning need to reserve a particular name, you can wait until you've selected a web designer who can help you with name selection and registration. Choose an address that makes your site easy to find. Most likely your book publicity will center on the title of your book so you might use that as your address. If you are building ongoing visibility through your own name or if you've written more than one book, then consider using your name in the domain. Like the title of your book, choose your domain name carefully. A long or complicated name will be hard for users to remember.

Design

You have an array of web design services and individual designers to choose from. Some services will offer you only a few pages and restricted add-on options. Others will offer an abundance of add-on features like a commerce capability (to sell your own books), games, and other interactive features. Compare them to see what appeals to your taste and budget. At this stage, remember, you are simply exploring.

Keep in mind that a web designer is not the same thing as a graphic designer. Kristen Powers (www.websitesbykristen.com), who designed novelist Jane Heller's website (www.janeheller.com), has a good FAQ section on her site that explains what a web designer does. Some designers offer ongoing service in the form of periodic site updates and expansion: Their work isn't necessarily a finite project that ends the moment your site is loaded onto the host server, so select someone you like and trust.

No matter who designs your site, it should accommodate future edits and add-ons. Updating your site is a must. There's nothing more frustrating for a user than connecting to sites that are clearly out of date.

Here are some options to explore:

■ Yahoo! offers a few interesting choices. For small business websites, go to http://webhosting.yahoo.com. Look at the demo to see what's involved in creating your site. It's simple and inexpensive, but you are restricted to the service's page templates. This may be right for you—or not. Check out also the personal website services at Yahoo! (http://geocities.yahoo.com) for more options. The site is filled with great information about setting up a site. Explore it thoroughly. If you set up a site on Yahoo!, you'll be assigned a web address like this: http://geocities.com/yourname. You can also buy another domain name and have it point to this site and even the geocities address so that your readers never see it.

■ Google offers a free website service. Go to http://pages.google.com and get started by following the instructions. (At the time of this writing, the service was still in the testing phase. The URL and pricing may have since changed.) Beyond Yahoo! and Google there are many other automated design and hosting services. Avoid services that post banner ads for other companies on your site and those with amateur-looking templates.

■ Hire a service that specializes in author websites like www .authorsguild.net or Authors on the Web (www.authorsontheweb .com). The latter offers the choice of templates or customized pages, and will also host the site. The service's email newsletter, the *Book Reporter*, draws readers to its own site, which is crammed with information, reviews, contests about books and publishing, and links to author websites. Therefore your own site benefits from a continual marketing effort to potential readers. Because Authors on the Web is a reader's environment, you are reaching a targeted audience—readers of quality fiction and nonfiction. Rates are higher than the do-it-yourself options, but still reasonably priced. You'll find a complete list of prices online. Another service that specializes in developing author sites is www.authorbytes.com, which also has an impressive roster of clients and offers podcasting services.

▪ Hire a designer to create your site. The designer does not need to specialize in author sites to be able to produce a good one for you. Remember: Good web designers don't just design—they also provide significant technology and marketing assistance. Fees range from a few hundred dollars to a few thousand. You'll pay more for a highly customized site with audio and video components and ongoing tech support. You will still need to find a host server, though the designer should be able to find or recommend one. If you are serious about your website and want a professional-looking forum to showcase your ideas and work, then working with a designer is the way to go. As a novice to online marketing, you can't possibly learn everything in time to create an effective, selling, appealing website.

You can easily find many website designers online, and their sites display their portfolios and, sometimes, their prices. Before you sign up with any designer, look at the sites they've designed, and ask for references and contact them.

▪ If you are graphically inclined you can design the site yourself using downloadable software. Dreamweaver is one popular website design program, complete with layout tools and text editing capabilities. If you go this route, consider working with a web copywriter to make sure you've created text and meta tags that will help your rankings. Then you'll need a host server, which can be found all over the web.

Web Hosting

There are many services that offer hosting. If you are not signing up for a host server through your designer or web service, then you'll need to do your due diligence to make sure that your selected host server is a reliable one.

SOME WORDS OF ADVICE FROM
A WEBSITE CONSULTANT

Karyn Zoldan of Bridge Marketing, a company that specializes in web copywriting and consulting, offers the following 10 dos and don'ts to consider before creating a website:

1. Do shop around. Start surfing and write down the URLs (website addresses) of sites you like and don't like and why. A good web designer should ask for this information just to get a clue about your expectations.

2. Do register your own domain name (yourbusiness.com) or if the web designer does, be sure you or your company is listed as "administrator." It's similar to owning a car and having your name on the pink slip. You don't want anyone else to own your website.

3. Do request that the web host or web designer provide you with the FTP host name, log in, and password. If you don't have this information and the host or designer dies or runs off to Hollywood, you have no way of ever accessing your site again.

4. Do read the contract carefully and know up front how much it costs to add additional pages and to update information. Are you paying a maintenance fee and if so, what does it include? Be sure you understand the procedure (and get it in writing) if you decide to change hosts or designers. How is it handled and how long does the process take?

5. Do focus on content. Web users want immediate gratification without sensationalism.

6. Don't get carried away by graphics. Remember, less is more with graphics.

7. Don't believe it if you're offered a free website, the deal of a lifetime, or that a website will get a million "hits" tomorrow. Realize that a website is another form of marketing with the best reach for the money.

8. Don't hire your neighbor's son to design your website. He may be a web whiz but can he design a site that's appropriate for your target audience?

9. Don't be held captive by cyber-babble gibberish. Ask questions and if your host or designer doesn't communicate in terminology you understand, find one who will.

10. Do update your site often. If you posted an event that happened in April and it's now May, your information is stale. Lack of updating content sends a message to customers that you don't care.

To Zoldan's 10 points, I add the following 5:

11. Does the service or designer optimize the site for search engines and then help submit your site to web directories? If not, will the designer explain to you how to submit the site yourself?

12. Once the site is built, can you easily edit content yourself or will the designer do that for you? If the designer will do that, then how quickly can changes be made for you?

13. Do other sites built by the service look good? Can you find them on search engines?

14. Has the service/designer created sites for other authors? Have you contacted those authors for references?

15. If you "outgrow" your site, and need to offer more pages of content, does the service offer "add-on" features, like a commerce capability or linking, for a reasonable price? Or can you add these embellishments yourself?

SEARCH ENGINES AND DIRECTORIES

Your designer will work with you to get your site noticed by search engines. This is also known as search engine optimization or SEO. Coming up with descriptive keywords and phrases that summarize what your site's about is the first step. This is because the description and keywords used on your website help identify your site to search engines. For example, if you've written a book on dog grooming, you want a user to find your site quickly through a search engine when they type in "pet care" or similar phrases. Make the description short and truly descriptive, rather than promotional. Search engines are continually changing their formulas for listing sites, and are relying less and less on keywords.

To get your site noticed, you'll also need to list it on web directories (see Yahoo! Directory at http://dir.yahoo.com as an example of what a directory looks like and how it organizes websites into categories.) Go to www.bridgemarketing.com for more excellent ideas about creating an effective website. For more advice about optimizing your site for search engines, see also www.highrankings.com by Internet specialist Jill Whalen.

Not all web specialists agree about how to optimize your site. Web designer Brian Perrin (www.abmarketworks.com), who created the terrific site for Mouth Public Relations (www.mouthpublicrelations.com), believes that much current discussion about SEO is a hyped up way to oversell services to people setting up websites. "There are, of course, things you need to do to make sure a site gets indexed," says Perrin, "but those are part of the normal design process and not an excuse to pad an invoice with additional services. As long as you design a site using valid, up-to-date code, make sure it has more than just art and animation on the homepage—the page must have textual content or search engines will ignore it—and then link to it from a site that is already well indexed by search engines, the new site will get listed. We make sure our sites are correctly designed for indexing and then we list each new site on our own site. That insures that Google and the other large search engines will have the new site listed within two weeks to a month. The other search engines eventually follow suit, on disparate time lines."

You Need a Break! Check Out This Site

For a tongue-in-cheek but helpful analysis of what makes a website good or bad, go to www.webpagesthatsuck.com.

Another significant factor that affects your site's rankings is having high-quality links to and from other sites to yours. One way to accomplish this is by having your article or book excerpt accepted on other sites with a link back to yours. Your time is well spent reaching out to sympatico bloggers and websites to get your content out in the world. And as multiple references to your site get noticed by the search engine web crawlers, your site moves higher in the search engine rankings.

Contact other sites directly and offer to cross-link, where you will link to their site and they link to yours. "If you sell bananas, you'd want to link to pages like Banana Importers Trade Association, 1,001 Banana Pie Recipes, or Healthy Eating," says Mark Gebbie, publisher of *The All-In-One Media Directory*, www.gebbieinc.com. "The idea is not to hook up with others who sell bananas, but others who are in some way related to bananas. People who eat them, research them, cook with them, promote them ('Banana Promotion Council'), paint them, whatever. When requesting cross-links, be polite and friendly. Perhaps begin by saying, 'Saw your site, and I'm very impressed with the work you have put into it.' Explain who you are, and why you would consider their link to be 'a fine addition' to your page. Suggest why your link may be of import to them, even if it is obvious. Send your URL and a few lines of text to go with it so they can link to you if they agree. As your page becomes more of a resource rather than an ad, it becomes a more attractive place for everyone concerned.

"To promote the Gebbie Press *All-In-One Directory*, I contacted public relations firms, advertising, marketing, promotion firms, freelance writers, photographers, journalists, and the like. As it is a media reference work, I've approached hundreds of newspapers, magazines, radio and television stations, and so on."

Mark Gebbie came up with another smart way to get his site linked to others. He started an award program. Because his site includes hot links to media outlets, he created a Station of the Month logo, which a number of the radio stations agreed to post on their sites, creating another link to Gebbie's site.

Some search engines won't even rank your site if you don't have quality links from other sites. Karyn Zoldan explains the importance of quality links and of working with legitimate web designers: "An author should never sign up to a 'link farm,' which will punish you forever," she says. "For instance, if the author is writing about weight loss, they don't need an unscrupulous consultant to come in and link this site to a car mechanic, a furniture maker, an ice-cream maker, etc. High-quality related links to reviews, weight-loss products that are mentioned in the book, and other resources mentioned in the book, press releases, and related blogs would be the way to go."

BLOGS

Like many features of the Internet, blogs can't be defined as one particular thing. Consider this explanation from Blogger (www.blogger.com):

> "A blog is a personal diary. A daily pulpit. A collaborative space. A political soapbox. A breaking-news outlet. A collection of links. Your own private thoughts. Memos to the world.
>
> "Your blog is whatever you want it to be. There are millions of them, in all shapes and sizes, and there are no real rules.
>
> "In simple terms, a blog is a website, where you write stuff on an ongoing basis. New stuff shows up at the top, so your visitors can read what's new. Then they comment on it or link to it or email you. Or not."

What a blog should not be: a flog. In other words, if your blog is simply a self-promotional book commercial then it will not engage other readers and you'll be talking to yourself online.

Much ink (and pixels) have been spent debating whether blogging actually helps sell books. This debate will be over quite soon as more authors demonstrate how their blogs have created effective platforms to promote their work and stimulate sales. For your decision about whether to start your own blog, the bottom line comes down to this: Do you have the time to commit to writing what amounts to writing a daily column, and then reach out to other bloggers and online communities so you can draw traffic to your blog? Unlike traditional websites, which tend to be more static, the appeal of blogs is that the content is refreshed at least daily if not more frequently. The blog gives you a forum to write about anything you want, and more important, to connect with readers. As David Carr, media critic for the *New York Times* describes it, having a presence online is an opportunity to build your tribe, the group of people who will follow you to your next book, too. Carr believes that book publishers (and authors) have a terrific opportunity to talk to readers about the story behind the book: Readers have an endless appetite to know how the author did it.

If you've got the time to write your own blog, the rewards can be great. Blogs give you the opportunity to:

- Reach and talk to your readers and build a dedicated fan base.

- Comment on current events, and so chance a break into the media mainstream.

- Link to other blogs to gain an audience.

Setting up a blog becomes easier by the day. For starters, check out Blogger or Yahoo! 360°, both of which offer free blogs. Or you can blog via your social networking accounts like Facebook, Gather, and MySpace. Or your web designer can set up a blog on your website.

Something else to consider about blogging: Do you think the potential readers for your book will be motivated to read your book when they learn about it on a blog? And how are those readers most likely to encounter your blog posts: Chances are, unless you already have an online platform or presence, your potential readers aren't going to find your blog. You may be better off at first by looking for opportunities to be a guest blogger on other people's blogs: You'll increase the chance of reaching new readers who are already visiting those other blogs. Plus your posting will link back to your website to draw those readers into your community. For instance, Barry Eisler is a thriller writer who contributed some very smart blog posts about the publishing business to the blog run by M. J. Rose called Buzz, Balls & Hype. I thought his comments were perceptive and they drew me into wanting to know more about his fiction. So I ordered his first novel, *Rain Fall*.

Being a guest blogger is akin to writing a guest editorial column for a newspaper. The *Huffington Post* is a good example of a powerful website that runs posts from all kinds of contributors. Head Butler is a smaller blog, but one with its own dedicated readership, which on occasion accepts guest blogs. Get to know the blogs that cover your field of expertise, and then get to know the bloggers by sending them feedback commenting on their posts. Once you've established a relationship you can ask if they are open to your contributing a guest blog posting. Why take the time to build a relationship with the blogger rather than just come out and ask to post on their site? Because you seem self-interested and pushy rather than engaged in the blogger's commentary. One blogger likens that approach to a drive-by posting—the author who shows up once, never to return, in it only for the book mention of the moment. PR firms are starting to offer blog tours as part of their services. Bear in mind that some bloggers will always be suspicious of an author reaching out through a representative rather than directly.

Given that getting involved in blogging is time-consuming, and that there are many thousands of blogs in existence, how can you discern which blogs are worth trying to write for? Start by going to www.technorati.com and www.alexa.com. These sites show the popularity of blogs by measuring traffic and how many other sites link to them. Search the topic of your book to see which blogs turn up. The rankings can help you decide which blogs might be worth pitching and getting involved with.

Then visit the blogs that you turned up in your search and check out their blogrolls—the lists of admired blogs that a blogger links to. As Mark Fortier of Fortier Public Relations explains, "You'll notice certain sites appearing on everyone's blogroll and this is a good sign that these are important ones. Getting good coverage on the number one blog in your subject area is often far more valuable than getting traction on several lesser blogs. Not only does the number one blog have the largest audience, but there's also a good chance that the lesser blogs will all read and link to your coverage there. I recommend studying the top blog in your area carefully to think about what kind of content might excite this blogger and what might be the most viral to give your book traction. There is certainly value to sending your book to a blogger and hoping they'll plug or review it. But it's better if you can turn a top blogger into a long-term cheerleader for your book by offering him or her exclusive viral content from your book. That helps this blogger maintain status with their audience as a destination. If you can make a blogger feel special and that you have a common interest or opinon and a common reason to benefit from the promotion of your book, then you may have just enlisted an extremely valuable partner. Book sales impact depends as much on what the blogger writes about your book as it does on who the blogger is." For a good example of how a viral campaign can work, see A Case Study on page 237.

Also consider how core the blog's readership is to the topic of your book. The blog might be a narrowly focused one but if it delivers readers who are committeed to your topic, it could be a good core group to start the buzz.

THE BLOGROLL

▪ **Bad Pitch Blog** (www.badpitch.blogspot.com): Check out this blog by two PR professionals who critique bad press releases. While the site addresses press releases coming from all kinds of professions, it's nonetheless a helpful guideline about what not to do in a book pitch or press release.

▪ Nancy Pearl's **Book Lust** is run by the librarian who founded If All of Seattle Read the Same Book, a program encouraging the entire city to read the same book at the same time and then discuss it in various groups and media. Now called Seattle Reads, the idea caught on around the country and today more than 50 cities have similar book programs. Known for her book recommendations, she has set up Book Lust as a wiki (a site where visitors to the site can add their own content such as book reviews) at www.booklust.wetpaint.com.

▪ **Booksquare** (www.booksquare.com) offers thoughtful and insightful coverage of books and publishing. The blog's tagline is "Dissecting the publishing industry with love and skepticism." Check out the archives for excellent pieces on the protocols of blogging called "How to Behave in the Blogosphere, the Easy Way" and "The Tupperware Party as the New Marketing Metaphor."

- The well-read **Bookslut** (www.bookslut.com) offers an opinionated blog about books and publishing. Recent great posts: Reviews of bad book cover art and a funny piece about celebrities who write children's books.

- **Buzz, Balls & Hype** (www.mjroseblog.typepad.com/buzz_balls_hype) is an essential resource for authors by novelist (*The Reincarnationist*) and marketer M. J. Rose. Its savvy approach to marketing books features among the most thoughtful publishing commentary around today. Guest bloggers appear frequently here, offering solid advice about advertising, publicity, and just plain getting through your day as a writer. Rose is an ardent advocate for writers and also frequently recommends books that she likes. She also created Author-Buzz (see page 216).

- **Galleycat** is an irrevrent and informative blog (www.galleycat.com) that reports on the daily happenings and news in book publishing.

- Guy Kawasaki's blog, **How to Change the World** (www.guykawasaki.com), will help you think like an entrepreneur. This former Apple Fellow is author of many books and describes himself as an evangelist, entrepreneur, investment banker, and venture capitalist. His blog is influential in the business, design, and academic communities, among others. Check out the book area on Kawasaki's site. His jacket design competition for *The Art of the Start*, his book about entrepreneurship, is inspired: Partnering with istock photo, he received 150 entries, one of which was chosen for the final cover and 70 of which were printed on the inside of the book's dust jacket.

- **Joe Wikert's Publishing 2020** blog (www.jwikert.typepad.com) covers book publishing as it relates to technology and the media. Written by a book publisher, its insights into the daily business of book publishing are thoughtful and entertaining.

- If you want to dig deeper into marketing, the theories behind it, and check out some innovative marketing campaigns, go to Diego Rodriquez's blog, **Metacool** (www.metacool.typepad.com). In his bio, this Stamford professor says he is "bummed out by bad marketing" and on the marketing link on the blog you'll find all kinds of examples of good marketing. Don't limit yourself to that section of the blog. You'll quickly find yourself drawn into the world of innovation and entrepreneurship that Metacool covers.

A SUCCESSFUL ONLINE CAMPAIGN: A CASE STUDY

Warner editor Rick Wolff credits author Robert Sutton's online marketing efforts for the success of his book, *The No Asshole Rule: Building a Civilized Workplace and Surviving One That Isn't*. As succinctly as the book title telegraphed the book's content, it also presented an inherent challenge to the publicity campaign: Which media would print the word "asshole?" Knowing that broadcast and print media might be reluctant to cover the book, the author and publisher went after online buzz to build attention for the book. Sutton, who is a professor at Stanford University, started his promotional activities a full year before the book's publication date. Why was this important? Because in the world of blogging (also called the blogosphere,) your credibility is your main calling card and it takes time to build your blog's presence and voice. As Sutton explains, it's important to be seen as an authentic member of the blogging community so that you don't seem like you've just dropped in to sell books before you head out of town again.

Sutton says, "I think there is no magic to this, it is all persistence, and even then, most books aren't hits even if you do everything right. The main thing that might be new is that the web and blogs and preorders all combine to mean that authors need to start working on buzz earlier than before." He launched his blog eight months before his book's publication to start talking about his ideas and invite readers to share their own workplace stories. You can see his posts at http://bobsutton.typepad.com.

He also sent early copies of the book to bloggers—about 75 of them—six months before the book's publication. Bloggers started talking about the book and preorders started ringing up at Amazon. Sutton says that on publication date, the book was number two in preorder ranking on Amazon. The beauty is that all the preorders, once filled, count as sales in one day. If your book is selling in sufficient numbers to qualify for bestseller rankings, then that surge of orders on one day can be very helpful. Naturally the early interest on Amazon signaled to the publishing house that they had a potential hit on their hands.

Mark Fortier of Fortier Public Relations worked on this campaign and talks about a viral marketing element that started some serious buzz. In this instance, the viral part of the campaign was an exclusive online self-diagnostic test offered to one of the most powerful business bloggers on the web, Guy Kawasaki, who had already posted an influential book review some months before pub date. The Asshole Rating Self-Exam (ARSE) was completed more than 100,000 times and counting. (Find it at http://blog.guykawasaki.com/2007/02/arse_the_asshho.html.) Fortier says, "This helped start a viral conversation that generated several blog postings a day for months."

Another important source of buzz for the book was a speaking appearance at an all-company meeting of the human resources consulting firm SuccessFactors, a small but influential group. As an experienced business speaker, Sutton arranged other talks with a few local companies and offered to give speeches in return for them placing orders for the book. And he also made some deals with speaking clients to give speeches for lower than usual fees if the companies ordered books in advance. (Sutton swears by the bookseller 1-800-CEO-READS when bulk quantities of books are needed in a timely way for events.)

All these efforts paid off: The book became a *New York Times* bestseller.

Sutton now has three blogs: his own site and two more housed at *Harvard Business Online* and the *Huffington Post*. After publication date, he kept his blogs going, not seeing them as a means to merely promote a book but rather as a meaningful and rewarding way to connect to readers and other people who are thinking about similar issues. He continues to add interactive features to his blog, such as the recent self-quiz to identify if you are an asshole when you travel.

A BLOG THAT LAUNCHED A TOUR

Seth Godin always seems to be on the cutting edge of figuring out smart marketing applications for new technology. Read his blog at www .sethgodin.typepad.com where he tried an experiment to see if his blog's readers could help create a successful book tour for *The Dip: A Little Book That Teaches You When to Quit and When to Stick*. Instead of his publisher choosing tour cities in advance and hoping that people would show up, he tapped into his blog readership to secure the largest possible committed audiences up front, selecting the final cities based on the known level of interest. The experiment worked and he went on to sell, 1,000-plus books in each of the seven markets.

"This is a much bigger story than one author visiting a few cities," writes Godin on his blog. "This sort of approach works for just about any marketer. If you don't have customers who are willing to organize this sort of event, what are you missing? It's easy to imagine doctors doing it when bringing a brain researcher to town. Or chocolate or wine fanatics welcoming a particularly talented vintner to their neighborhood. And it doesn't have to be an in-person visit. It could work just as well in sending people to a vibrant, important YouTube document on a politician, or a blog post about a new actuarial practice. It's taking the world (including me) a long time to get around the top-down, Oprah-driven mindset that comes so naturally." Godin concludes with a powerful lesson: "The takeaway for all of us is this:

1. Build a permission asset: a group of people that actually wants to hear what you're up to.

2. Create something (a product, a service, a story) that those people want to spread (not get paid to spread, but choose to spread) and get out of the way."

Godin's approach is a tactic that musicians caught on to long before authors, creating a community online—often on MySpace (www.myspace .com)—where they can share music and correspond with fans. As their profiles grow, they can target cities to visit to play a gig based on known enthusiastic fan bases. If authors and book publishers concentrated on cultivating fans (readers), then bookstore visits could be much more likely to have assured turnouts and be more financially remunerative for bookseller, publisher, and author alike.

SOCIAL NETWORKING

What is social networking? It's when individuals participate in an online community with other people who share their interests. If you join a social network, you'll create a profile, link to other profiles as a "friend," invite others to link to you, and post comments on other people's profiles.

MySpace.com and Facebook.com are perhaps the most well-known of the social networking sites. On MySpace, you can set up a web page that displays your interests and anything else you want to say about yourself. You can include text, video, audio, links, quizzes, surveys, lists of favorite books and music, and so on. MySpace users skew young, so the site can be a great way to connect with a younger audience. There are also countless reading groups and book reviewers housed on MySpace: Check out the book channel. It's a universe of its own, its key distinctive feature being its lively social connectivity and active commentary. The downside: It can take a while clicking around to locate the groups that interest you. Go to the homepage, click on the link to "books," and start exploring. Readergirlz is an example of a robust author site on MySpace. (Find it by searching from the MySpace homepage.) Readergirlz is a group of writers for teens who arrange a series of online promotions. The sites for the four authors who comprise the group are very active, intensely visual, and musical. Their audience enjoys media multitasking and these authors cater to that. Another example of how MySpace can generate interest in books: Search for PostSecret from the MySpace homepage. The visual nature of the PostSecret project (where people anonymously send postcards to the author, Frank Warren, that reveal their most personal secrets) lends itself to online display and online anonymity. The medium suits the message perfectly. The author has created a minimovie about PostSecret, which plays on MySpace TV. There viewers/readers can post their comments and share their enthusiasm (or criticism) for the film and book. This film is quite startling: It opens with the postcard confession, "Everyone who knew me before 9/11 believes I'm dead."

Aimed at an older audience than MySpace or Facebook, Gather (www.gather.com) is an impressive social networking site that has an active and well-organized book channel. Here, at any one time, you'll find authors sharing book excerpts and writing about their work, reviewers of all stripes posting reviews (and the caliber and sophistication of writing is impressive) advice on finding an agent, on promoting your book, live author chats, a contest to help an author help his publisher design his book cover (and why not come up with contests of your own?) amateur book reviewer contests, a first chapter competition, and so on. You can participate both as a reader and as a writer, meaning that you don't have to get involved in the site by talking about your own work. You can start by posting reviews and commentary about other books and so naturally start to build a community and readership on the site. You can start your own discussion groups or participate in others'. Check it out: It's free to join.

It used to be that writers felt like they had to be in New York City in the heart of book publishing in order to participate in the social and professional swirl around the New York book world. No longer. Communities like Gather offer an abundantly vibrant book community for anyone who lives anywhere who is interested in talking or writing about books.

Another great book community is www.librarything.com, which lets you catalog your home library or simply to catalog the books you've read or are reading. You can rate your books, and tag and organize your collection. Each book has a social information page, which tells you what other people think about the book, and the site also tells you who else has the same books in their library. You can find recommendations of books to read, explore other people's collections, and chat to other members online. If you are an author and post 50 books from your library, you are entitled to become a LibraryThing author and set up an author website. And by seeking out the readers who have your book in their library, you can reach out to the readers who like your work. In partnership with book publishers, the site distributes galleys to avid readers and encourages them to post reviews to start book buzz.

New communities are appearing online all the time. The right community for you can help you find your readers, so explore to see if you can find a space where you want to spend some time.

Don't force yourself to participate in a social network. If it's not for you then you'll find it challenging to participate in an authentic and productive way. This is a form of media that you should enjoy participating in. If you don't, then move on. There are plenty of other ways to reach your readers.

BOOK TRAILERS

Many successful websites, blogs, and online retailers are relying on video to attract users, a good reason to think about a book trailer for your book. While some publishers are producing book trailers, many authors are creating their own. (A book trailer is a video. It is sometimes referred to as a video-podcast. A podcast can be either an audio or video.)

For a book called *The Dangerous Book for Boys*, the publisher created an inexpensively produced video showing a father and son doing fun projects from the book together—it appears on Amazon. And in a stroke of great luck and good pitching, the video aired on *Today* and helped drive the book onto bestseller lists. For the book *Quirkology: The Curious Science of Everyday Lives*, author Richard Wiseman produced a series of engaging videos to demonstrate the nature of observation and predictability, which he posted on YouTube to reach a massive audience. (You can see the videos for yourself on www.quirkology.com.) Trailers don't have to be expensive to be effective. Working with freelancers, one of the major book publishers budgets about $1,000 to produce its trailers.

Author Brenda Coulter, who writes inspirational romance novels, created a book trailer for her novel *A Season of Forgiveness*, and discusses how she put her trailer together on her blog. (See her blog entry for June 4, 2007, at www.brendacoulter.blogspot.com.) Start by going to YouTube, Coulter advises, and search for "book trailers" to watch as many as possible to get a sense for which ones are appealing. Coulter estimates that she spent 40–60 hours putting the trailer together but it cost her only

$65.00 to purchase some music reuse rights. She used royalty-free images and music and did not have to buy any special software, instead using Windows Movie Maker, which came with her Windows software package. (Mac users can use iMovie.) When the trailer was finished, Coulter posted it on video-sharing sites including YouTube, MySpace, AOL Un-Cut Video, Google, as well as her own blog. She also found a site called GodTube, which yielded her 50 views in 24 hours. Creating a trailer for an illustrated book—say a graphic novel or a children's book—is a much easier proposition than for a nonillustrated book as the visual elements already exist. For a novel, like Coulter's, the book trailer is a little more demanding to create as it needs to present visuals and audio that suggest the book's atmosphere and plot.

Other examples: Go to www.bookvideos.tv to see the excellent trailer for Jeannette Walls's *The Glass Castle*, which perfectly establishes the premise and tone of this excellent memoir. Also see www.deborahleblanc.com and register on the site to check out her very effective book trailer for her novel *A House Divided*.

As is the case for most forms of promotion, creating a book trailer takes time. If you don't see yourself becoming a minimovie director, then you can hire someone to create a video for you. Remember: Creating the trailer is the first step; then you need to market it, by posting it to video-sharing sites and sending it to your contacts and other sites that might be intersted in linking to it. So if you're going to invest either the time or the money in developing a book trailer, be prepared to spend the time to market it.

Here's an example of a simple yet stunningly sweet video. *Frankie Manning: Ambassador of Lindy Hop*, a memoir by the dancer, was published on May 26, 2007, his 93rd birthday. As a promotion, his book publisher created a video, including fantastic clips of Manning performing over the years. Interspersed among the clips is a message telling the viewer to go buy his book on May 26 on Amazon to drive up the rankings on one day. It worked: The book reached number seven on Amazon, which, as noted before, doesn't necessarily indicate enormous sales volume for the book, but the unusual campaign did get the book noticed widely.

Don't bother creating a book video if it's not interesting and engaging. What's the point of investing time and money if the ultimate product does not attract viewers and make them want to share it? Five seconds of a title's screen credit can seem like eternity: The biggest mistake that authors are making in creating trailers is not understanding the faster pacing of film. (Who would have predicted 20 years ago that authors were supposed to become experts in all forms of media in order to sell their books!) Two book trailer services you can explore are to be found at www.authorbytes.com and www.expandedbooks.com.

EXTREME ONLINE MARKETING

If you find that you're grooving to your online marketing experiences, then you can take it another step. Second Life is the self-described 3D online digital world "imagined, created, and owned by its residents." What does this mean? That you can literally create another persona for yourself and participate in this electronic world, living a kind of parallel virtual life. And with more than 6.5 million "residents" of Second Life, you won't be alone. You choose an avatar (a 3D cartoon-like representation of your Second Life persona) and then go about your business in Second Life—attend movie openings, open a business, go shopping, fly a plane, get a date, take in a fashion show, and so on.

Second Life has its own market-driven economy: In this virtual life there is real money being made and lost. It's hardly surprising then that big business (Cisco, Dell, IBM) has crept into Second Life alongside the spirited entrepreneurial individuals who inhabit the place. Naturally there is an opportunity for authors. Some authors and publishers are using this virtual community to reach out to readers, and why not? For example, the Random House Group in the UK has set up a virtual book group in Second Life where members discussed Audrey Niffenegger's novel *The Time Traveler's Wife* at the first meeting. The book events take place on Elysian Island, which is focused on books, writers, and artists.

Another UK publisher, Penguin, brought William Gibson to Second Life to promote his novel *Spook Country*. The publisher screened a film related to the book, sponsored a competition to design an avatar for Gibson, offered giveaways, and set up an author reading and Q&A. As the person who coined the phrase "cyberspace", it was only fitting that Gibson take part in this type of book promotion.

Go take a look.

E-BOOKS

E-books were for one brief, shining moment about a decade ago the new Internet-based vision of book publishing: Readers would embrace an electronic form of books readable on portable devices and revolutionize the business of reading. While this has not yet happened, electronic books—which can be downloaded onto an e-book reader—offer a decent promotional opportunity for the printed form of books.

Several new e-book readers have recently come onto the market with enhanced capabilities and user-friendliness. As this market evolves, the devices will become part of a complementary delivery system to get books into readers' hands in several formats.

Three very different writers have exploited the promotional value of e-books. Through their experiences, you can see how an electronic edition of your own book might benefit you.

Go to horror novelist Douglas Clegg's site at www.douglasclegg.com. The site works beautifully to introduce new readers to Clegg's work as well as to provide fans with news about his new books and other activities. Clegg credits his website with rebuilding an audience for his work. When his book sales were dropping, Clegg began offering free electronic versions of his new work at the site. Readers who downloaded the free editions started going into bookstores to look for titles on his backlist. The downward trend in sales was reversed over the course of about 18 months, and his publishers began to reissue titles that had gone out of print.

Another writer who has shown that e-books can create a market for the printed editions of the work is Seth Godin. His book *Unleashing the Ideavirus* talks about how to turn your customers or clients into marketers for your business or product through powerful word of mouth (www .ideavirus.com). Before the printed edition of the book was available, he offered the book as a free download. The freebie created such enthusiasm and positive word of mouth that on the first day of the book's release in hardcover, it went straight to number five on Amazon. The first hardcover printing was 26,500 copies priced at $40 and at this writing, according to Godin, one million downloads were reported. Despite the fact that Godin had offered the content for free online, he created the market for the successful publishing of the hardcover edition of the book, and subsequently for the paperback. Godin says that he made *Unleashing the Ideavirus* available electronically to see if free online content might enhance rather than harm book sales, and help create a market of readers. He gave the book away in order to sell it.

Author M. J. Rose couldn't find a publisher for her first novel, *Lip Service*. So she self-published an e-book edition and then spent considerable time on marketing it to all the female-friendly sites she could find online. Her efforts caught the attention of Doubleday Book Club, which offered a print edition to its members. After that, Pocket Books offered her a contract for the book publishing rights. Go to www.mjrose.com for the full story.

ONLINE MARKETING—A SUMMARY

The Internet is your powerful and efficient research tool, and provides you with opportunities to build an audience for your book. A website is a must and gives you the platform to reach out directly to your audience.

You can:

- Join email lists and discussion groups about subjects related to your book.

- Make sure the online retailers have posted the appropriate marketing information about your book.

- Build an email database to which to market.

- Offer content to websites and blogs in exchange for mentioning your book and site.

When you create your website, keep the following points in mind:

- Look at other authors' websites to pick and choose the elements you like.

- Before you build the site, plan on how you will use and market it, both in the short and long run.

- Take a couple of hours to learn about web-building basics so that you can work constructively with your designer.

- Continually update your site so that your content appears fresh and relevant.

- Get your publisher to mention the site on all written materials, including the catalog page, press releases, and your book jacket.

- Submit your site to web directories.

- Market the site to your target audiences, reading groups, email lists, newsgroups, other related sites, organizations that might host you as a speaker, booksellers, and the media.

If you decide to set up your own blog, remember that daily fresh content is a must. An excellent, if not preferred, alternative to running your own blog is to seek guest gigs on other people's blogs so you avoid the pressure of a daily deadline.

As you participate in the many bounties that the Internet has to offer, respect the rules of engagement and stay open to the many new experiences, contacts, and relationships with your readers that await you.

SET UP YOUR OWN PUBLICITY

IN any number of scenarios you will become your own publicist to a greater or lesser extent. Perhaps your publisher is doing nothing to promote your book. Perhaps you want to supplement your publisher's national media efforts by targeting local media in certain markets. Or perhaps your book was published last season—or even last year—and your publicist is working on new projects, while you want to continue the media effort. If you have hired your own publicist, you may even assist his or her efforts. There is no rule book that says an author can't call the media. If your overextended publicist makes anxious noises when you propose a go at your own publicity, do not be disheartened. Do what you need to do. It's your book.

This is your action-plan checklist, some of which you may have already accomplished in the months leading up to your book's publication:

■ Find out what your in-house publicist is covering. Though the effort may be limited, it is nonetheless foolish to duplicate or to get in the way of the publicist's work. Remember: Throughout the campaign his or her support, however nominal, is essential.

■ Set your budget—just as if you were hiring a freelancer, your budget will be driven by the extent of the campaign that you desire. How much are you willing to spend on expenses like mailings, phone calls, photocopying, and travel? (See page 101 for a list of campaign costs.) Your expenses will be affected, naturally, by the cost of resources like photocopying, Jiffy bags, and postage, so factor those in accordingly.

- Formulate how you will position the book for the media and write a press release and/or pitch letter. (See page 115 for the rules on writing press releases. See Chapter 2 starting on page 43 for coming up with angles to pitch your book to the media.)

- Create a list of media targets with contact information.

- Develop customized pitch letters for the most important press contacts.

- Send copies of your book and press release to the media.

- Make follow-up calls.

When you get some publicity hits, report them to your editor and in-house publicist. This allows them to track your book's sales. If the publicity bookings are significant, such as a major national television show, then your publisher will ask the sales reps to call their accounts and perhaps get more copies into the stores before the appearance airs. If the publicity seems to be triggering reorders then you can certainly ask your publicist or editor for reimbursement for reasonable out-of-pocket expenses. Hard for them to say no when the book goes back to press as a result of your work.

WHAT YOU MIGHT GET FROM YOUR PUBLISHER FOR FREE

Chances are that you can persuade your publicist or editor to provide you with the following items, which will help offset your promotional costs:

- Reams of stationery or copy paper.

- Photocopying. Offer to provide the publicist with your press materials to have copied at the publisher's copy center. Provide them several weeks ahead of the date that you will need them: The centers are sometimes slow. If you live in the same city as your publisher, ask if you can come in to use the photocopier.

- Access to an empty office and a phone to make long-distance calls, if you live in the same city as your publisher.

- Editing consultation. Ask your editor and publicist if they are willing to review any press materials that you write.

- Facilities to mail review copies and postage. Your publicist might agree to stuff and send your mailing packets, or that you come into the office and stuff them yourself. The publishing house may cover the postal expense for you.

- Reimbursement for travel expenses. If you book yourself on a major national television show, your publisher will likely pay your expenses.

- Media mailing lists. Your publicist can print out media lists for you, both in the form of "call sheets" and mailing labels. Call sheets are the pages you will use to take notes on your follow-up calls and include complete information about the media contacts: names and addresses, the show's ranking in the market and booking preferences, phone numbers, and email addresses. (Note that some publicists will not share their mailing lists and discourage authors from contacting the media. This is not always a thoughtless decision on their part. Some authors are loose cannons and should be kept from doing any damage! You can discuss with your publicist how you've thought out your pitch and won't say anything to producers that is potentially foolish. Point out that you can research the information anyway. If you still can't get your hands on the media lists, try talking to the publicity director or your editor for help. Failing that, you're on your own.)

- Free advice. Ask your publicist and editor what they think of your media strategy and if they have advice or criticism about your approach.

- Invitations to the book party you are throwing for yourself, or that a friend is throwing for you. Publishers will sometimes pay for the invitations and your publicist may invite local media, or at least identify the right media to invite.

■ Books. Tell your publicist that you are using them for publicity purposes and not giving them away to your friends. As long as your publisher sees your publicity efforts paying off, they will probably continue to supply you with promotional copies.

■ Jiffy mailers and envelopes. Some publicists and editors and editorial assistants might provide you with these for your book mailing.

Bear in mind that your publisher will not give you these goodies for an unlimited time. Unless your book has become newsworthy or unless the sales are still strong, you will likely wear out your welcome a few months following publication date.

DEFINE THE EXTENT OF YOUR CAMPAIGN

If you have limited time but a lot of confidence and/or media experience, focus your effort on a few targeted press opportunities with the biggest potential payoff. These would include national radio and television shows, nationally syndicated columnists, leading metropolitan newspapers, especially those affiliated with syndicates, and top local radio and television shows.

For media novices, starting out small makes sense, and the easiest path of entry into the world of media is radio. Radio producers are fairly accessible people, and even when rushed, they will usually hear out your pitch and give you a quick yes or no. With the recent growth of satellite radio, there are many new venues to approach. Start by pitching talk show producers at top radio stations (100,000-plus listeners) in major markets and to syndicated radio programs. Send your release to a group of 25 stations to start practicing your pitch and your follow-up technique. Do these interviews from your home or office or in studio if you're in the same city. Keep this effort alive as long as you like: The pool of media is virtually endless. According to *Talkers* magazine, there are 5,000 radio talk show hosts in the United States. If you prove to be a good guest, some radio stations will have you back on air again within a few months. Also pitch your local print and television shows, and then branch out into pitching the national television programs as you gain more confidence.

Before you approach the big-time TV shows, get some television experience under your belt by pitching local cable shows. With regard to the performance quality of guests, cable is less demanding than the national network shows. When you appear at the station, ask if the producer will kindly send you a copy of your segment on DVD once it airs. Providing that your appearance was a decent one, this DVD will help you book yourself on other shows. You can also post links to your television appearances on your website. Do not send your only copy to other stations—they will certainly misplace it. Make duplicates. As you gain experience in booking yourself, you can approach the larger media with confidence.

If you send your pitch mailings out in small batches, you can limit the project to manageable blocks of time. You will fine-tune your pitch in the follow-up calls from your first mailing before you commit time and money on a mass mailing.

If you're uncomfortable with the idea of radio or television interviews, but your pitch is nonetheless a topical one, you might conduct a print campaign to feature reporters and syndicated columnists nationwide. You might start by targeting, say, the top 50 newspapers in the United States and Canada, and then branch out from there as your time allows.

Be aware that some reporters are loath to entertain calls directly from authors. They can be downright rude if they perceive you as amateurish or a waste of their time, particularly if you are a self-published author. You can help overcome the media resistance by presenting yourself in a professional manner, and by understanding the media before you pitch them. Sometimes there is a plus side to doing your own publicity. Preferring to talk to an author than to a "flak" (the journalist's derogatory nickname for a publicist), other reporters will be open to hearing from you. Your naturalness may seem endearing and your amateurism may work to your advantage.

GET THE CONTACT INFORMATION
FOR YOUR MEDIA TARGETS

If your publicist won't supply you with media lists, then you can find the names and addresses of the media online and from media directories such as Bacon's, Burrelle's, and Gebbie's *All-In-One Media Directory*, which are often available at your local library. Media lists are also available through www.literarymarketplace.com in the public relations services section.

To find print contacts, use the newspaper websites listed on page 130. In addition, a great site for locating radio stations is www.radio-locator.com to search stations by ZIP code, city, state or province, format, and call letters. Click to www.npr.org for a link to all the National Public Radio stations nationwide, and many of the sites will give you information about the shows' producers. Get a feel for commercial talk radio from the industry's trade magazine at www.talkers.com. Click onto the Heavy Hundred section of the archives to find an annotated list of the top 100 talk radio hosts, contact information, and links to their websites. The site also sells a radio media directory.

The website www.radiopublicity.com sells a radio media list database for the top radio shows in the United States. The site and database is run by Alex Carroll, an author who over the years has booked himself on hundreds of radio programs to promote his book, *Beat the Cops: The Guide to Fighting Your Traffic Ticket and Winning*. His experience in the media led to the sideline of selling his publicity expertise and radio databases. If you are planning to concentrate on booking many radio interviews for yourself, and if you've already done a few radio interviews and know that you are effective on air, then this radio database may be a worthy purchase. Talk to your publicist about the quality of the department's own radio media list. If the list could use some updating, ask if your publisher would pay for the cost of the list so that they can adapt it for their own use as well as give you a copy.

I also like another resource offered at the same site. If you are booking interviews yourself, you will probably find Carroll's downloadable book, *The Radio Publicity Manual*, to be very helpful. The book reveals hundreds of terrific tips to setting up an effective interview: the worst day and time of the week to do interviews (Friday afternoons, because you lose the audience that would have spread word of mouth about your book in the workplace), how to present yourself in the best possible way to get a radio booking, and tips on selling your books to listeners through a toll-free number. The book is particularly helpful if you have an interest in selling your book directly to consumers.

FOLLOW-UP CALLS AND THE PROTOCOLS FOR DEALING WITH THE PRESS

Once you've done a mailing, do not sit back waiting for the phone to ring off the hook with many anxious producers calling to book you as a guest. This will not happen. These people get hundreds of press releases every day. They have scant time to sort out which among the pile might offer a promising guest. For a recent mailing from my office to 150 radio stations, only four producers called to book the guest. For the dozens of other interviews, we initiated the calls ourselves. (In many cases, you can call the radio station without having sent any material. Pitch the idea on the phone and the producer will know right away if the topic is right for the show's audience and if you could be a good guest.)

Start to make follow-up calls within a day or so of when you think your press release has landed on producers' desks. To get through the list of producers fairly quickly, plan on setting aside an hour or two a day for a few days to work through the list. If your calls are met with instant rejections, then reconsider your pitch or your approach. Ask the producer or reporter why he or she is not interested in your idea: The answer can help you refine your pitch or your strategy. Are you calling in midafternoon when daily print reporters may be on deadline and less tolerant of interruptions? Or are you calling radio producers while the show they produce is on air? Have you targeted the right reporter or show? Are you presenting your ideas in a long-winded way and not getting to the point fast enough? Is your pitch off base? Fine-tune and practice your pitch, then try again. If you're still meeting resistance, you might try talking to a publicity firm about a couple of hours of consultation to help you get on the right track.

Tami DePalma and Kim Dushinski, partners of MarketAbility, a public relations firm that handles book campaigns, say, "In making follow-up calls, your goal is to be pleasantly persistent. Realize that each media contact needs good stories, solid information, and credible experts just as badly as you need media coverage. Every reporter, producer, and editor has a certain number of column inches or airtime to fill. You just might be the solution—if you know how to present yourself." On their site, www.marketability.com, they offer the following excellent advice for people who are making their first publicity follow-up calls:

- Sometimes you have to force yourself to get started on follow-up calls. Once you get started, if you are not communicating effectively after five to seven calls, consider starting over later in the day or tomorrow.

- If you are nervous or hesitant, make a practice call to someone you know but pretend they are a media contact. Start speaking exactly as you will on a real follow-up call.

- At the beginning of every call, always ask if you have reached them at a good time. If not, *do not try to sell your story anyway!* Just because you have them on the phone right now does not mean you need to grab them while you can. Ask them what day and what time would be better. And *let them go!*

- *Call back when you say you will!* The media is amazed by how often people say they will call back, never to be heard from again. This is a big lost opportunity. You've sparked an interest. Do not let the fire go out now.

- At one time, voicemail was used to screen people out. Not anymore. It is absolutely necessary and often used to screen the good stories in! Do not be afraid to leave voicemail messages. When you do, leave your name, company name, and phone number at the beginning *and* the end of the message so they don't have to rewind to get your contact information.

- On voicemail, mention that if you don't hear from them in a given time period—at least a week from the original call date—you will probably try them again later. Then, rather than pestering them, you are simply fulfilling an obligation. Keep voicemail messages short.

■ When you reach them in person, but they have not made a decision for whatever reason, ask them, "Would it be appropriate to call you back next week?" Then ask what a good day and a good time to call are. Keep track of this information.

■ Smile with every phone call. Yes, you are bound to get cranky people who are on strict deadline. It will happen. Smile even bigger and ask them when a better time would be to call, then call them precisely at that moment! You may be surprised what a difference a deadline can make. They will probably be a whole new person.

■ Rejection is the best way to sell your next contact on your story. What about your story didn't they like? Was it too visual? Not visual enough? Too much or too little content for the length of their show? Do they like the story but just need an opposite opinion to balance yours? Would it fit the format of any other columns or shows?

■ Evaluate your rejections. What valid information have you received? Was the reviewer just having a bad day, a bad year, and a bad life? Was he or she simply on deadline? How can they help you improve your pitch?

The callback scripts below are adapted from MarketAbility. DePalma and Dushinski suggest that you start by calling any media contacts who are obvious matches for your story idea first. These are easier calls to make and will get you on a roll. Adapt these scripts for your own book pitch and work from them while you make your calls.

"Hi. This is [your name], author of [your book]. Have I reached you at a good time? I have an idea for a feature/news story that will interest your audience. [Briefly state your idea.] Would you be interested in receiving specific information that makes it a story?

"Great! What's the best way for me to get it to you, mail or fax or email? What's your current address/fax number/email address? Could I call you back [in a few hours if you're faxing or emailing, in a few days if you're mailing]? What will be the best time on that day?"

Follow-up calls should be made very shortly after you expect that your pitch has arrived at the office of your media target.

"Hi. This is [your name], author of [your book]. [Give new information or a new angle to the story you talked about earlier.] You probably received this information via mail/fax/email a few days/hours ago. Does it sound like something that will work for your show/publication?"

If you get a reporter's voicemail, leave a message. Many times reporters screen their calls so if you leave your pitch on their voicemail, you may get a call back.

"Hi. This is [your name], author of [your book] at [your phone number]. I have an idea for a feature/news story that will interest your audience. [Briefly state your idea.] I will be mailing/faxing/emailing you specific information that makes it a story. I'll call you back [in a few hours if you're faxing, in a few days if you're mailing] to see what you think of the idea and answer any questions you have. If you'd like to reach me, please call me at [phone number]."

WHEN A PRODUCER OR REPORTER SAYS YES

Once you've got the reporter or producer's interest, you're nearly home free. But some people make crucial mistakes at this stage and lose the media opportunity. So follow these simple guidelines to complete the transaction and get the coverage you've been planning for.

▪ When a producer or reporter returns your call and leaves a voicemail message, call back as soon as possible. If you postpone calling, the reporter may lose interest and move on to another story. Or you might miss the reporter's deadline and fail to get into their story. The media move quickly.

▪ When you connect with the reporter, ask for the deadline. Send any follow-up material that the reporter needs well in advance of the deadline.

▪ Ask what the article is about. The reporter will not have read your book and may be calling you for a quick comment. In other words, the reporter is probably not writing an article about your book alone. It is up to you to contribute a point of view that helps the reporter flesh out his or her article.

▪ After your interview, ask the reporter to identify you as the author of your book. Although your book may not be the focus, the title should be mentioned in the piece. Spell your name and your book's title for the reporter.

▪ If the reporter wants to interview you immediately but you do not feel sufficiently prepared, schedule the interview for later in the day or on another day, if the reporter's deadline permits. The exception is when you've positioned yourself as an expert on events in the news: In that case you are obliged to make yourself available at a moment's notice.

▪ When arranging an interview, get the reporter's phone number and email address in case you need to call back to reschedule or cancel for any reason.

▪ If you're concerned about how you are quoted, do not ask a reporter for a copy of the article before it has appeared in print. Reporters can't do that, as stories can be killed or delayed at the last moment to make space for other articles or breaking news coverage. Sending you a copy of the article before it runs is considered a breach of ethics. However, you may ask the reporter to read your quotes back to you before the piece is filed. But don't exercise this option unless your subject matter is sensitive or complex. Otherwise, you've earned the reputation as a cumbersome source and not one that the reporter is likely to turn to again, unless you are the leading expert in your field.

■ After you've given an interview to a print reporter, ask when the article is expected to run. On the day the article is supposed to appear, check the paper's website to see if it ran. If not, drop an email to the reporter or call to ask when it might appear.

■ Keep track of your forthcoming interviews in an organized format, so that you don't accidentally forget them.

■ When you arrange to set up a radio interview that will take place by phone, take down all the following information: name of host, name of producer, live studio phone number, producer's phone number, the city or town in which the station is located, the time of the interview in the station's time zone and in yours, whether the station is to call you or if you are to call the station (in which case ask for their 800 number), whether the interview is live or taped, how long the interview will last. Ask the producer about the host's manner with guests. Is it an irreverent approach, a conservative, humorous, or intellectual spin? Will the host mention your publisher's 800 number so that listeners can order the book? If so, note that on your schedule and write the number down, too. A day before the interview, you will call the producer to reconfirm the interview and all the pertinent information. If you're scheduling multiple interviews for yourself, then keep an interview itinerary similar to that of a tour itinerary. (See the appendix on page 295 for an example.)

Clipping Services

Do not waste your money on a clipping service. These are companies that will send you press clippings about your book for a fee. The volume of press clippings for one book is too small to make the service worthwhile, and the press clips are readily available directly from the newspaper websites. Find articles also by typing your book title into search engines.

THE EMAIL PITCH

Many reporters prefer to be contacted by email, and pitching them this way is acceptable if you follow certain protocols. If you do not have a relationship with the reporter, send a quick query asking if they'd like further information about your book. Make the query's subject line succinct and informative, such as: New Book Says Pets Improve Their Owner's Health. (Note that the subject line should probably be the same as your press release's headline.) In the body of the email, mention the highlights of your book and invite the reporter to email you if he or she wants further information.

Keep the body of the email short, confined to one screen view if possible. Do not cut and paste your two-page press release into the email screen. And *never* send an attached file unless invited. With sensitivity to viruses, most reporters will not download your files unless they've specifically asked for them. If they want more information they will let you know.

Do not send mass emails in which you have copied other reporters' names into the address field or the cc field. This is a serious breach of media etiquette. Do not do a blanket emailing just because the technology is capable of doing so. Instead, make your correspondence targeted and to the point. Your contact information should include your phone number, as your email address alone is not sufficient. When reporters pursue a subject, many prefer to call.

Be cautious of online press release distribution services that send press releases to the media. The service may tell you that the media recipients have opted to receive the emails. Well, I would question the kind of reporters who opt to receive email press releases. Serious reporters at most newspapers don't need them—they already get so much mail.

IDENTIFY ONGOING MARKETING OPPORTUNITIES

Political and cultural events propel certain books and authors into the limelight. Backlist titles bubble up in the popular press all the time. Definitions vary but essentially a book becomes backlist about a year following publication. As long as the information in the book is of perennial or renewed interest, there is a continued market for it. For instance, when George W. Bush became president, Paul C. Nagel, the author of *John Quincy Adams: A Public Life, a Private Life*, was invited to appear on interviews even though his book had been published four years earlier. Why? Because Adams was the only other son of a former president to become president.

Periodically, a film or television program will refer to a book, suddenly bringing it back into vogue for a time. The television drama *The Sopranos* mentioned *The Art of War*, the ancient text on strategy by Sun Tzu, bringing that book into the fore again with a sudden flurry of attention. And the film *Shakespeare in Love* brought attention to all things Shakespeare for a while. President Clinton's reading list one summer included a novel by Walter Mosley, as reported prominently in the *New York Times*. If you're the beneficiary of one of these chancy and unexpected events, then good for you. But you can also deliberately create some momentum around your backlist book, to keep the book alive in the market and in print. Although the world likes "new," as long as you are presenting ideas and information that fit the media's needs, you can continue to publicize your book no matter how long it has been in print. Many publishers will keep a book in print even at low annual sales volume if they know that the author is an active promoter. Here are some ideas to keep your book moving:

- If you are visiting cities on business or for pleasure, make time for a book signing as part of your visit. (Call the bookstore six to eight weeks or more in advance of your visit so your event can get on the store calendar.) If you have the time, create a full market push for the book in that city. Do this by contacting the local media and sending out press releases four to six weeks before you arrive in town. If you have less advance notice before your trip, you may have to forego the bookstore event but you can book some media for yourself.

- Look for articles about individuals who might take an interest in your book. For example, say you've written a book on early child development and you come across an interview with someone who believes in the charter movement for elementary school kids. Write to that person expressing support for his or her point of view and enclose a complimentary copy of your book. Depending on the individual's status within their own organization, you may suggest that they invite you to speak at a forthcoming meeting. Thus, you are building the circle of people who are aware of your book as well as building your professional credentials. The book becomes a way to network. You can also contact the reporter of the article to say that you enjoyed it and to express your own point of view on the subject. In your correspondence, include your contact information and credentials so that the reporter can get in touch with you for a follow-up story, which you can even suggest.

- Send out periodic topical releases about your book.

- Certain titles lend themselves to evergreen promotion. Cookbooks are one example of this, and well-timed press releases (summer grilling recipes, ideas for Halloween treats, holiday recipes, leftover turkey recipes) can help keep the book alive in the print media.

- Pitch yourself for seasonal stories related to the subject of your book. For example, if you are an author of a book on dating or relationships, then pitch the idea that the holidays are the loneliest time for singles. Support the pitch with a statistic from, say, the American Psychiatric Association revealing that singles seek therapy more frequently in November and December. Then describe your prescription for singles to cope with the holiday blues and mention your book.

- Radio interviews conducted by phone are a cost-effective and time-efficient way of maintaining a public profile. They are relatively easy to set up. Give yourself a reasonable goal, say, two or three interviews a week to keep the momentum going.

- Let your editor and publicist know immediately if breaking news happens that connects with the subject of your book. (Don't assume that they'll make the connection themselves.) You or your publicist should write a press release or media alert to advise the press about your expertise. Depending on the circumstances, your publicist may even contact the national media to arrange interviews.

■ The Internet offers infinite opportunities to reach your target audience. Set aside a little time each day to identify and reach out to appropriate sites, links, and discussion groups.

■ Position yourself as an expert in your field. Drop a note to newspaper and magazine reporters who cover your beat and explain your credentials. Even if they end up contacting you for an interview that's not directly connected to your book's topic, your book's title will be mentioned in the piece.

SET UP YOUR OWN PUBLICITY—A SUMMARY

If you will be doing your own publicity bookings, you are limited only by the time available to you. You can conduct an ongoing campaign indefinitely—there are thousands of radio stations and newspapers to pitch. As you get comfortable with the mechanics of doing publicity, you might find a rhythm that blends into your normal schedule where you are pitching and conducting several interviews a week. As you gain confidence, you can graduate to pitching the national television media.

If you are doing your own publicity you will:

■ Set a budget.

■ Define the extent of your campaign.

■ Refine your pitch.

■ Research the media to contact.

■ Pitch the media in batches to keep the project manageable on an ongoing basis.

■ Report any positive results to your publisher.

With publicity, there are no guarantees about the kind of exposure you will get. But certainly you are creating opportunities for yourself that can deliver significant rewards.

PARTING THOUGHTS

BEING an active and smart participant in your own marketing and publicity campaign will help create paths to your own success. By continually promoting your book to the media, you may stimulate ongoing sales and keep your book in print. Your efforts, though they may not seem to deliver immediate benefits, will pay off in other ways that you might not anticipate.

- You will improve your book's sell-through, creating a success of your book in the minds of booksellers even if they didn't order many copies. Booksellers view a book as a success if they sell all the copies they bought whether they ordered two or ten of them. This helps your publisher advance higher numbers of your next book.

- Your efforts for the hardcover edition of your book might promote a significant increase in sales for your book's paperback edition.

- Your interviews might lead to a large corporate bulk purchase because someone at the company heard you on a radio interview. Or you might receive invitations to speak at events or to be interviewed by other media.

- You will create a track record with the media, which gives you ammunition to sell your next book to a publisher.

■ You will find readers entirely as a result of your own efforts.

■ You will develop a way of thinking about marketing your work that will be helpful to you in many other areas of your life.

In some ways, being a first-time author is like being a stranger in a strange land, an immigrant venturing beyond the familiarity of home. You've arrived at the golden mountain and to your eyes, every new experience is an opportunity. You are an entrepreneur who is willing to take risks, explore possibilities, and be bold about it. With this drive and attitude, success is bound to follow.

Good luck!

RESOURCES

A DIRECTORY OF SERVICES FOR AUTHORS AND PUBLICISTS

BOOK FAIR DIRECTORIES

Go to www.booktv.org, the online complement to Book TV on C-SPAN 2. The site includes a full listing of book fairs as well as other useful information about author venues.

Go to www.loc.gov/cfbook/bookfair.html, the Center for the Book at the Library of Congress, for a selection of book events around the world.

Go to www.shelf-awareness.com/news.html for a list of and links to book fairs around the United States.

Go to www.short-fiction.com for a great listing of book fairs around the United States.

BOOK FAIRS, FESTIVALS, AND LUNCHEONS

Arizona Book Festival
Phoenix, Arizona—Spring
www.azbookfestival.org
Celebrates the Southwest. Events with authors and activities for children.

Austin International Poetry Festival
Austin, Texas—Spring
www.aipf.org
Poets, performances, and slams.

Baltimore Book Festival
Baltimore, Maryland—Fall
www.baltimorebookfestival.com
Readings and talks by authors, and cooking demonstrations.

Banff Mountain Book Festival
Banff, Alberta, Canada—Fall
www.banffcentre.ab.ca/mountainculture
Specializes in the literature of the outdoors, and includes seminars and readings.

Black Expo
Search for "Black Expo" online to find sites for expos nationwide, including Dallas, Houston, Indiana, Los Angeles, Missouri, New York, and Philadelphia. The expos offer entertainment, author seminars and signings, career seminars, and vendor booths.

Border Book Festival
Las Cruces, New Mexico—Spring
www.borderbookfestival.org
A weeklong festival. Includes writers, artists and storytellers, vendors, panels and workshops for adults and children, and readings and performances.

Boston Globe **Children's Book Festival**
Boston, Massachusetts—Fall
www.bostonglobe.com/promotions/childrenbookfest
A series of readings and literary luncheons staged at various locations throughout the city.

Buckeye Book Fair
Wooster, Ohio—Fall
www.buckeyebookfair.com
Features many author appearances.

Bumbershoot Literary Arts Festival
Seattle, Washington—End of summer
www.bumbershoot.org
Part of Seattle's biggest public arts and music celebration. Includes author
appearances.

Detroit News Book and Author Luncheon
Detroit, Michigan—Spring
Invites five authors annually. Audience members pay in advance for tickets.

Fall for the Book Literary Festival
Fairfax, Virginia—Fall
http://fallforthebook.org
Sponsored by George Mason University, the Fairfax County Public Library,
and others, this street festival includes storytelling, author talks and panels,
poetry slams, events for children, and cooking demonstrations. The events are
held in the city of Fairfax and at the George Mason University campus.

Great Salt Lake Book Festival
Salt Lake City, Utah—Fall
www.utahhumanities.org
Includes author appearances and seminars on papermaking and other book arts.

Harbourfront
Toronto, Ontario, Canada—Fall
www.readings.org
If you are lucky enough to get yourself invited to Harbourfront's annual
reading festival in October, then you should be very happy. The Book Festival

is the dream event for authors, with packed audiences, long lines of people buying books, a liberal entertainment budget, and lots of opportunities to meet your fellow writers. The focus of the festival is literary, and audience members buy tickets to attend up to one year in advance. Sign up on the site to get a free reading schedule newsletter by email. The Harbourfront website includes contact names and numbers, as well as links to other reading venues and writers' festivals in Canada. Also includes information about Canadian awards and prizes and links to literary journals.

Harlem Book Fair
New York, New York—Summer
www.qbr.com
Panel discussions, readings, storytellers, musicians, and other entertainment.

Kentucky Book Fair
Frankfort, Kentucky—Fall
www.kybookfair.org
Kentucky's primary literary event raises money for public libraries and hosts as many as 150 authors.

The Latino Book & Family Festival
Spring and Fall depending on the city
www.latinofestivals.com
The festival is produced by actor Edward James Olmos and is a weekend-long event held in Hispanic markets including Chicago, Houston, Inland Empire (southern California), Los Angeles, New York, Phoenix, and San Diego. Features author appearances and educational and family programs.

Los Angeles Times Festival of Books
Los Angeles, California—Spring
www.latimes.com/fob
A large and well-attended fair that includes more than 75 panel discussions with authors and about 300 authors. The fair helps to raise money and awareness for literacy.

Miami Book Fair International
Miami, Florida—Fall
www.miamibookfair.com
A very well-organized and vastly enjoyable weeklong fair of author events, cooking demonstrations, and children's activities.

National Book Festival
www.loc.gov/loc/cfbook
Author events and street festival sponsored by the Library of Congress.

New York Is Book Country
New York, New York—Fall
www.nyisbookcountry.com
Citywide author events for adults and children. Includes several formal book and author luncheons sponsored by the *New York Times* and other organizations.

Novello Festival of Reading
Charlotte, North Carolina—Fall
www.novellofestival.net
Readings, lectures, and a book fair. North Carolina's largest annual book event.

Printer's Row Book Fair
Chicago, Illinois—Summer
www.printersrowbookfair.org
The largest outdoor literary event in the Midwest, this fair offers literary programs and vendors of new, used, antiquarian, and specialty books. Events include music, storytellers, and children's storybook characters in costume.

San Antonio Express-News Book and Author Luncheon
San Antonio, Texas—Fall
The luncheon invites six authors, including those who may be of high local interest.

Sarasota Reading Festival
Sarasota, Florida—Fall
www.sarasotareadingfestival.com
Contact information varies annually and is posted on the site. Up to 250 events with authors, including readings and panel discussions, sponsored by the *Herald-Tribune*.

Small Press Book Fair
New York, New York—Spring
www.nycip.org
Includes bookmaking and printing demonstrations, readings, and workshops featuring panels of authors and their publishers.

Sonoma County Book Festival
Santa Rosa, California—Fall
www.socobookfest.org
Readings and book signings for adults and kids.

Southern Festival of Books
Nashville, Tennessee—Fall
www.tn-humanities.org/festival
Includes both southern and national writers, with exhibits and author panels.

St. Petersburg Times Festival of Reading
St. Petersburg, Florida—Fall
www.festivalofreading.com
Author events and events for children.

Tennessee Williams/New Orleans Literary Festival
New Orleans, Louisiana—Spring
www.tennesseewilliams.net
Includes readings, workshops, panel discussions, and a book fair.

Texas Book Festival
Austin, Texas—Fall
www.texasbookfestival.org
Features many authors in lectures and readings, as well as cookbook author events.

Vegas Valley Book Festival
Henderson, Nevada—Fall
www.vegasvalleybookfest.org
Author events and events for children.

Virginia Festival of the Book
Charlottesville, Virginia—Spring
www.vabook.org
Features writers in panel discussions and talks, and a vendor's fair.

BOOKS AND RELATED READING

How to Get Happily Published
Judith Applebaum
HarperCollins, 1998

This book explains the full publishing process and what the author should do to get involved.

Rule the Web
Mark Frauenfelder
St. Martin's Griffin, 2007
An excellent book that helps you use the Internet to your full advantage.

Unleashing the Ideavirus
Seth Godin
Hyperion, 2001
Download this great book about viral marketing at www.ideavirus.com. It will inspire you to think creatively about marketing your own work.

1001 Ways to Market Your Books
John Kremer
Open Horizons, 2006
Geared to the self-published author, this book is packed with many great ideas for authors and examples of what other authors have done to market their books. Kremer's site, www.bookmarket.com, offers good book publicity and marketing advice.

Trash Proof News Releases
Paul Krupin
Direct Contact Publishing, 2001
Free downloadable e-book available from www.trashproofnewsreleases.com that shares many examples of well-written press releases and discusses successful press release writing techniques.

Guerrilla Marketing for Writers
Jay Conrad Levinson, Rick Frishman, and Michael Larsen
Writers Digest Books, 2000
Offers many ideas for how to market your book. I like the authors' get-with-it, no-nonsense approach.

Grants and Awards Available to American Writers
PEN American Center
This book lists more than 1,000 grants and contact information. Available through PEN (www.pen.org) and other book retailers.

Buzz Your Book
M. J. Rose and Douglas Clegg
Available as a downloadable e-book. Filled with strategies for coming up with a marketing plan for your book and how to implement it. See www.buzzyour .com, Amazon, or www.pigeonholepress.com.

Jump Start Your Book Sales
Marilyn and Tom Ross
Writers Digest Books, 1999
Full of great ideas for sales and promotion. Aimed at the self-published author but filled with plenty of advice that's pertinent to the author with a publishing house.

Plug Your Book: Online Marketing for Authors, Book Publicity through Social Networking
Steve Weber
Weber Books, 2007
An excellent, in-depth discussion about online book marketing.

BOOKSTORE DIRECTORIES

American Booksellers Association
www.bookweb.org
Lists members of the American Booksellers Association. The site includes addresses and bookstore websites.

Barnes & Noble
www.bn.com
Locate any store in the chain.

Books-A-Million
www.booksamillion.com
Locate any store in the chain.

Booksense
www.booksense.com
The site for independent booksellers. Use the ZIP code locator to find stores in any town you will be visiting. (The list will include independents only, not chains.)

Borders
www.borders.com
Locate any store in the chain here.

New England Booksellers Association
www.newenglandbooks.org
Offers regional bookseller news as well as a good store locator for the region.

LIBRARIES

www.nlc-bnc.ca/canlib/epublic.htm
Links to libraries throughout Canada.

www.publiclibraries.com
Links to libraries throughout the United States.

MEDIA DIRECTORIES AND MEDIA LINKS

Bacon's Media Directories
http://us.cision.com/products_services

Burrelle's
www.burrelles.com

Gebbie Press: The All-In-One Media Directory
www.gebbieinc.com

Literary Marketplace
www.literarymarketplace.com
The site includes many free searchable databases, though some services are restricted to paid subscribers. The media directories include producer contacts.

Matthews Media Directory
www.marketwire.com
Specialized directories and mailing lists for Canadian media.

PubList
www.publist.com
A free database of 150,000 magazines, newspapers, journals, newsletters, and periodicals worldwide.

NEWSPAPERS
News Voyager
www.newspaperlinks.com
Search for local newspapers.

StudyWorld
www.studyworld.com/college_newspapers_online.htm
Search for college newspapers.

NewPages.com
www.newpages.com
Search for alternative weeklies and periodicals.

RADIO
***Talkers* magazine**
www.talkers.com
The trade magazine of the talk radio industry. Click on the "Heavy Hundred" section of the archives to find an annotated list of the top 100 talk radio hosts, and a brief description of their shows and contact information. The site also sells a radio media directory.

Radio Publicity
www.radiopublicity.com
Offers several radio media packages. If you can't find radio media lists for free, then these more expensive radio media databases are up-to-date and downloadable on mailing labels and as call sheets.

Radio-Locator
www.radio-locator.com
Search for stations by ZIP code, city, state or province, format, and call letters.

National Public Radio
www.npr.org
Links to all the NPR stations nationwide, and many of the sites will give you information about the shows' producers.

SYNDICATED COLUMNISTS
Blue Eagle Commentary
www.blueeagle.com

Headline Spot
www.headlinespot.com/opinion/columnists

TELEVISION
GovSpot
www.govspot.com/pulse/talkshows.htm

MEDIA TRAINERS

CMG Productions
New York, New York
www.cmgproductions.com
A full-service communications firm including media training. Its services are oriented to businesspeople, so authors of business books will be comfortable in this environment.

Harrow Communications
Oakland, California
www.prsecrets.com
Susan Harrow offers marketing consulting and media coaching to cover any interview situation. Fees are $1,000 minimum for a five-hour session. Her site also offers a newsletter and terrific publicity tips.

The Newman Group
New York, New York
www.newmangroup.com
Has a specialty in training authors. The site has contact information and explains all the media services offered.

Parkhurst Communications
New York, New York
www.parkhurstcom.com
Offers speech and media training and specializes in work with authors. Contact Bill Parkhurst.

Joel D. Roberts & Associates
Los Angeles, California
joelroberts@mac.com
A former radio interview host who offers media training to authors and others.

ONLINE MARKETING RESOURCES AND SERVICES

AuthorBuzz

www.authorbuzz.com

A service that puts authors directly in touch with readers.

Bridge Marketing

www.bridgemarketing.com

This site offers a wealth of information about setting up a website, the importance of key words, and how to choose a website designer.

Dear Reader

www.dearreader.com

A wonderful site for readers and authors. Offers excerpts from books and a variety of book promotions.

The Great American Book Giveaway

www.bkgiveaway.gather.com

Contact Meryl Moss at meryl@mediamuscle.com to submit your book.

A weekly contest for a free book that helps expose yours to potential readers.

High Rankings

www.highrankings.com

Offers web consulting services and good background information about setting up your site. Includes free articles on keywords and search engines by web copywriting specialist Jill Whelan.

How Stuff Works

www.howstuffworks.com

The Internet section offers great information about websites and search engines.

Library Thing

www.librarything.com

A social-networking site centered on listing the books you own and have read.

Net Read

www.netread.com

Offers authors the ability to notify local media about their appearances and events. You can also sign up for emails notifying you of events in your area. This is a good way to learn about author events and venues.

What's Next Online
www.whatsnextonline.com
A site that offers services for building and promoting websites, as well as tips for writing press releases and conducting PR professionally.

PERIODICALS, BLOGS, AND ONLINE NEWSLETTERS

The American Journalism Review
www.ajr.org
As well as offering selections from the *Review*'s content, the site links to newspapers, magazines, newswires, and TV and radio sites nationwide (as well as internationally).

Authors on the Web
www.authorsontheweb.com
Free email newsletters that cover new books, and news of authors and publishing. Also offers contests and other features.

Bad Pitch
www.badpitch.blogspot.com
This entertaining blog critiques bad press releases.

Booklust
www.booklust.wetpaint.com
The wiki run by librarian Nancy Pearl.

Bookslut
www.bookslut.com
An irreverent blog with author interviews and commentary on the publishing business.

Booksquare
www.booksquare.com
A thoughtful blog about the publishing industry. Particularly insightful about blogging, online marketing, and electronic media.

Bookselling This Week
www.bookweb.org
The free email newsletter for booksellers from the American Booksellers Association.

Columbia Journalism Review
www.cjr.org
Offers its own online content as well as links to newspapers, magazines, and
TV stations around the country.

Galley Cat
www.galleycat.com
Part of Media Bistro, this daily summary and commentary on publishing news
is a must-read for publishers and authors alike. Subscribe for free online.

Library Journal
www.libraryjournal.com
The monthly trade magazine for the library market.

Metacool
www.metacool.typepad.com
The tagline for this blog is "Thoughts on the art and science of bringing cool
stuff to life." Here you'll find Diego Rodriguez's observations about marketing,
design, and technology, among other things. The site will draw you in.

The Publicity Hound's Tips of the Week
www.publicityhound.com
Practical publicity tips from a PR specialist.

Publishers Lunch
www.publisherslunch.com
Free daily email with publishing industry news and gossip.

Publishers Weekly and PW Daily
www.publishersweekly.com
The weekly trade magazine for the book industry also offers a free daily email
newsletter. The site offers industry news, reviews, and interviews from back
issues of *Publishers Weekly*.

School Library Journal
www.slj.com
The monthly publication for the school librarian.

Writers Weekly
www.writersweekly.com

Angela Adair-Hoy, the coauthor of *How to Publish and Promote Online*, offers a useful forum and resources for writers looking for editorial and marketing ideas. Subscribe to the free weekly e-newsletter.

Yahoo! News
http://dailynews.yahoo.com
Go to the literary news section of this site to find current publishing news stories and an eclectic though helpful list of links.

PRESS RELEASE SERVICES

Bridge Marketing
www.bridgemarketing.com
This Internet marketer will review and write press releases, among other services.

Elance
www.elance.com
Allows you to post your press release project for writers to bid on. The writer's credentials and rates, and a feedback and rating system are displayed on the site.

Press Release Writing
www.press-release-writing.com
Shows sample press releases and offers press release writing services.

PUBLICITY CONSULTANTS AND PUBLICISTS (FREELANCE AND AGENCIES)

As a former publicity director, I have hired some of these agencies and I also freelanced at Goldberg McDuffie Communications some years ago. Most of the agencies prefer that potential clients contact them through their websites because the websites address many frequently asked questions about their services. You can find an even more extensive list of publicity firms at www .literarymarketplace.com. (Register for free and go to the advertising and marketing link, then to the public relations services link.)

Book Promotion 101
www.bookpromotion101.com
Bella Stander's intensive seminars for authors teach the basics of book promotion. She is also available for individual consulting. See also her blog

http://readingunderthecovers.blogspot.com as well as the excellent resources
for authors section on her site.

Carol Fass Publicity and Public Relations
New York, New York
(212) 691-9707
www.fasspr.com
FASSPR@aol.com
The agency handles PR campaigns for all kinds of fiction and nonfiction
books. The agency's fiction work includes a specialty in mystery novels.

Fortier Public Relations
New York, New York
(212) 675-6460
www.fortierpr.com
mark@fortierpr.com
Mark Fortier's firm specializes in the promotion of business authors and
thinkers.

FSB Associates
Basking Ridge, New Jersey
(908) 204-9340
www.fsbassociates.com
An agency that specializes in web-based book and author marketing services in
all topic areas.

Goldberg McDuffie Communications
New York, New York
www.goldbergmcduffie.com
The agency offer, services for books in all subject areas, including literary
fiction and serious nonfiction. The agency will not take on self-published books,
but will work directly with authors who have a publisher.

MarketAbility
Arvada, Colorado
www.marketability.com
Tami DePalma and Kim Dushinski are the partners of this book publicity and
promotion firm that represents publishers and authors of business, lifestyle, self-
development, and women's titles. Their site offers free articles about publicity,
including how to work with your publicist, how to pitch the media, and what
your media kit should include.

Morse Partners
New York, New York
(212) 861-2397
(212) 517-5652
www.morse-partners.com
Rose Marie Morse and Katy Keiffer's agency handles literary fiction, general nonfiction, high-end cookbooks and gardening books, art and photography books, thrillers, and mysteries.

Meryl L. Moss Media Relations
Westport, Connecticut
(203) 226-0199
www.mediamuscle.com
This agency conducts campaigns for books in all subject areas and offers a full range of publicity services as well as a speaker's bureau. The agency will often book speaking engagements as part of a publicity tour, and works directly with authors as well as publishers.

Mouth Public Relations
New York, New York
(212) 260-7576
www.mouthpublicrelations.com
Headed by Justin Loeber, this boutique agency publicizes books in all categories and also offers special event planning and media training.

One Potata Productions
New York, New York
www.onepotata.com
Headed by Diane Mancher, who has directed the publicity departments for several publishing houses, the agency handles nonfiction of all types—whether cookbooks, biography, health, gay/lesbian, as well as commercial fiction. Query by email and specify when your book will be published, what it is about, and what sort of publicity you are looking for.

Planned TV Arts
New York, New York
www.plannedtelevisionarts.com
The Planned TV Arts division of the PR agency Ruder Finn specializes in book publicity. The tip sheet section of their website offers many useful tips about the media.

PubInsider.com
Los Angeles, California
www.pubinsider.com
Jeff Bowen's agency offers publicity consulting to coach authors how to do
their own publicity, as well as full-service publicity campaigns. Bowen focuses
on nonfiction titles with an emphasis on self-help, spirituality, business, and
education books.

Raab Associates
Westchester, New York
(914) 241-2117
www.raabassociates.com
This firm, headed by Susan Salzman Raab, specializes in marketing children's
and parenting books. The site has great information about publicizing children's
books.

Judy Spagnola
Cherry Hill, New Jersey
www.book-trends.com
info@book-trends.com
Spagnola promotes romance novels and mysteries to independent booksellers.
Romance and mystery writers can query by email.

YC Media
New York, New York
(212) 609-5009
www.ycmedia.com
The agency specializes in cookbooks and works directly for publishers, and
less often directly with authors. The principals, Kim Yorio and Caitlin
Friedman, will consult authors to help them formulate a publicity strategy.

PUBLISHING AND WRITERS ASSOCIATIONS, NEWS, AND RESOURCES

American Booksellers Association
www.bookweb.org
Offers links to sites specializing in writers resources and other industry groups.
Lists the regional book shows with contact names and numbers. Includes a
bookstore search directory. Subscribe to *Bookselling This Week* here.

ASJA (American Society of Journalists and Authors)
www.asja.org
A membership group that offers guidance for freelance nonfiction writers and journalists.

The Book Report Network
www.authorsontheweb.com
www.bookreporter.com
www.kidsreads.com
www.readinggroupguides.com
www.teenreads.com
Headed by Carol Fitzgerald, the network offers a community for readers and writers, with links to authors' websites, recommended reading, news of the publishing industry, message boards, articles about reading and writing, and more. The site also offers services for writers such as website building and hosting.

Canadian Booksellers Association
www.cbabook.org
Information and news for Canadian booksellers. Also posts the dates of the annual convention.

Christian Booksellers Association
www.cbaonline.org
News and information about the Christian book market.

Connecticut Authors and Publishers Association
www.aboutcapa.com
A group of published and self-published authors, and publishers, with regular meetings and presentations.

Horror Writers Association
www.horror.org

Media Bistro
www.mediabistro.com
This site for media professionals has a "how to pitch" area that talks about pitching specific media. Great advice with concrete leads.

Mystery Writers of America
www.mysterywriters.org

New England Booksellers Association
www.newenglandbooks.org
Offers regional bookseller news as well as a good store locator for the region.

Northern California Independent Booksellers Association
www.nciba.com
The directories area has great links to local literary groups and libraries.

Novelists, Inc.
www.ninc.com
A resource for fiction writers that offers publishing information and writers networking. Offers advice on contracts, taxes, incorporating, and other business matters, as well as discussions about writing.

International PEN
www.pen.org
The mission of this writers' fellowship is to advance literacy, promote reading, and defend free expression. You'll find good information here about events and resources.

Poets & Writers
www.pw.org
The site for the monthly magazine *Poets & Writers* offers publishing advice, online services, panel discussions, and awards.

ProfNet
www.profnet.com
A service that notifies publicists of dozens of press leads twice daily by email. The leads are queries from reporters who are on deadline and looking for experts to interview on all kinds of topics. The subscription is expensive for an individual but certainly affordable for a publicity department or for several departments to share in a larger publishing house.

Readerville
www.readerville.com
Offers many friendly, smart online forums about books and publishing.

Reading Group Choices
www.readinggroupchoices.com
Features downloadable reading guides and interviews with authors.

Romance Writers of America
www.rwanational.org

Science Fiction & Fantasy Writers of America
www.sfwa.org

Sisters in Crime
www.sistersincrime.org

Society of Children's Book Writers and Illustrators
www.scbwi.org

Southern Independent Booksellers Alliance
www.sibaweb.org

NEWS AND RESOURCES
www.antion.com
A source of advice on giving speeches and presentations.

www.bookbrowse.com
Offers reading recommendations and news of the publishing industry. Also offers excerpts from current popular literature, author interviews, and reading-group guides.

www.bookfinder.com
A free search service for new and used books.

www.bookspot.com
The associations section of this site offers great links to all kinds of resources and organizations for writers as well as information about awards. The site is particularly useful for its links to e-newsletters and e-zines in genre and other categories. For instance, the pages on African-American writing link to Blackwriters.org and to Black Women in Publishing.

www.bookwire.com
Offers useful links to industry services.

www.modernpostcard.com
A service that produces custom postcards for budget prices.

www.pageonelit.com
A literary site that includes news, book recommendations, essays, author interviews, tips for writers, and contests.

www.prplace.com
This site offers good links to PR services, publications, and databases. It includes free listings of top newspapers and TV and radio outlets, though these do not include names of producer contacts.

www.shawguides.com/writing
A free online guide to writers' conferences around the United States.

SPEAKER'S BUREAUS (LECTURE AGENTS)

Literary Marketplace (www.literarymarketplace.com) has a good listing of lecture agents. The two agencies listed below specialize in authors and arrange speaking engagements at corporations, trade associations, colleges, religious organizations, and more.

Authors Unlimited
New York, New York
www.authorsunlimited.com

The Chelsea Forum
New York, New York
www.chelseaforum.com

WEBSITE CONSULTANTS, DESIGNERS, AND SERVICES

AB MarketWorks
www.abmarketworks.com
Website design as well as design for other marketing materials.

AuthorBytes
www.authorbytes.com
Website development service with a specialty in author sites.

Authors on the Web

www.authorsontheweb.com

Website development service specializing in creating and hosting author sites.

AuthorsGuild.net

www.authorsguild.net

Offers website templates and hosting for reasonable prices.

Bridge Marketing

www.bridgemarketing.com

A website content, copy, and consulting company. Contact Karyn Zoldan.

Expanded Books

www.expandedbooks.com

Creates book videos.

Literati.net

www.literati.net

Builds, hosts, and markets author websites.

Register.com

www.register.com

Budget web building and web-hosting capabilities.

VeriSign

www.verisign.com

Budget web building and web-hosting capabilities.

Websites by Kristen

www.websitesbykristen.com

See the site for a good overview about web design and search. Contact Kristen Powers.

APPENDICES

SAMPLE PRESS RELEASE

FOR IMMEDIATE RELEASE: **Contact:** Name
                                              Senior Publicist
                                              (212) xxx-xxxx
                                              name@sterlingpublishing.com

Join the Zen-Cleansing Revolution with
Five Everyday Ingredients to Help You Achieve a Spotless Nirvana

A New Book Shows How

(July 23, 2007—New York, New York) Inspirational cleaning guru Michael de Jong writes with humor and a Zen-like spirit as he reveals how five safe, all-natural products can be used to clean just about anything in your home. **CLEAN: The Humble Art of Zen-Cleansing** (June 2007; Sterling/Joost Elffers Books) shows how baking soda, borax, lemon, salt, and white vinegar can take care of most household cleaning needs, eliminating the need for costly and environmentally harmful commercial products.

"Zen-Cleansing is a great way to let go of the drudgery associated with cleaning, and it's as simple as using five down-to-earth ingredients," says de Jong. "What's truly amazing is that their combinations create what I call 'catalysts for cleanliness.' With so many environmentally unfriendly cleaners on the market, it's time for people to do their part to make the world a safer, cleaner, and frankly more beautiful place."

Each ingredient's uses are covered alongside dozens of clever tips, while a handy alphabetized directory makes it easy to locate the cleaning information you need. With its graphically stunning and easy-to-use design, **CLEAN** helps you find your spick-and-span center.

Conceptualized and designed by legendary publishing visionary Joost Elffers—the force behind such bestsellers as PLAY WITH YOUR FOOD and THE 48 LAWS OF POWER—this wonderful guide will help get your house shipshape without harming the environment or your health.

ABOUT THE AUTHOR
Author and artist **Michael de Jong** did his "clean" investigations while polishing, dusting, washing, wiping, rinsing, scouring, and scrubbing for others. He currently lives, writes, and makes art in the New York City area.

CLEAN: The Humble Art of Zen-Cleansing by Michael de Jong
- Sterling /Joost Elffers Books • ISBN: 1-4027-4766-7
- Price: $7.95 (Canada $10.95) • Pages: 136 pages, Hardcover, 5 × 6
- Pub Date: June 2007
  www.zencleansing.com
  For the Zen-Cleansing video see www.youtube.com/zencleansing

SAMPLE PITCH LETTER

The second paragraph of this letter lists the talking points in bullet format. I prefer this style as it highlights the salient discussion points for the interviewer. In this instance, the interview subject is not the author of this book, which is a perfectly acceptable approach if the author is not available for interviews.

July 26, 2008

Dear Producer/Interviewer:

I am writing to suggest an interview with Cookie Washington, an entrepreneur featured in TURN YOUR PASSION INTO PROFITS: START THE BUSINESS OF YOUR DREAMS, by Janet Allon. In the last recession, many people who lost their jobs started their own businesses, turning what seemed like bad news into the success of their lives. In this current economic downturn, your audience will want to know:

- When to switch careers and launch a business.
- How to tell if you've got a marketable product or service.
- The five most important qualities/resources needed to launch a business.
- How to avoid the top three pitfalls in the start-up years.
- How to find seed money.

TURN YOUR PASSION INTO PROFITS features 35 successful women entrepreneurs who reveal what you need to know to start your own business. In this tenuous business climate, going it alone can be a risky venture. Cookie Washington, who markets her line of custom clothing and accessories out of her home in Charleston, SC, can explain why she decided to take the plunge, the risks she took, and how she's beating the odds. I'll call soon to discuss having her as a guest on your show.

Sincerely,

Name of publicist
(212) xxx-xxxx
jdoe@janedoe.com

SAMPLE MEDIA ALERT

MEDIA ALERT
INVITATION FOR COVERAGE

Contact: Jane Doe
(212) xxx-xxxx
jdoe@janedoe.com

AUTHOR OF NEW BOOK ABOUT PREVENTING CAR THEFT TO DEMONSTRATE ANTITHEFT TECHNIQUES

WHAT	A demonstration of new theft-prevention techniques
WHO	Frankie Franks, car expert, mechanic, and author of EVERYTHING YOU NEED TO KNOW ABOUT YOUR CAR, will reveal new low-cost methods to prevent car theft. Police sergeant Bill Myers will join him to discuss the most common types of car thefts in Daytona.
WHERE	Parking Lot of Barnes & Noble bookstore at 2655 Laramie Road
WHEN	Thursday, July 25, 2008, from 12:00 noon to 1:00 p.m.
NOTES	Over the past 10 years, author Franks has been developing fail-safe techniques to prevent car theft. His advice is endorsed by the police department of Daytona and the American Automobile Association.
INTERVIEW	Franks will be available for interview before and after the demonstration on July 25 and 26. To arrange an interview beforehand, contact Jane Doe at (212) xxx-xxxx.
PHOTO OP	Frankie Franks and police sergeant Bill Myers will demonstrate five simple car protection features that anyone can afford.

#

SAMPLE TOUR SCHEDULE

The following tour schedule shows the media portion of the itinerary only. The schedule provided by your publicist will also include information about hotels and escorts. This particular schedule shows that the author conducted interviews by phone before arriving in Columbus to help promote in advance his bookstore and university appearances.

Thursday, May 23
ADVANCE PHONE INTERVIEWS TO PROMOTE YOUR EVENTS ON MONDAY AND TUESDAY IN COLUMBUS

9:30 a.m. to 10:00 a.m. CST Live, by phone	**SUBURBAN NEWS PUBLICATIONS** 5257 Sinclair Road Columbus, OH 43229 Contact: Kathleen Radcliffe (614) xxx-xxxx *You are to call Kathleen. Mention your bookstore and university appearances next week.*
1:30 p.m. to 2:00 p.m. CST Live, by phone	**COLUMBUS MESSENGER** 3378 Sullivan Avenue Columbus, OH 43204 Contact: John Matuszck (614) xxx-xxxx *You are to call John. His article will run prior to your events in Columbus.*

Monday, June 3
COLUMBUS

8:15 a.m. arrival **8:30 a.m. to 9:15 a.m.** Live, in-studio	**WLVQ-FM** *Wags & Elliott Morning Show* Two Nationwide Plaza, 10th Floor Columbus, OH 43215 Contact: Dan Orr (614) xxx-xxxx

10:10 a.m. to 10:45 a.m.   **KHOW-AM**
Live, by phone   *Peter Boyles Show*
                                      4695 South Monaco Street
                                      Denver, CO 80237
                                      Host: Peter Boyle
                                      Contact: Greg Dobbs
                                      (303) xxx-xxxx
                                      Backup studio number (303) xxx-xxxx
                                      Peter will call you at the Columbus Hilton.
                                      Mention your forthcoming event in Denver.

1:05 p.m.   **WOSU-AM** (NPR)
Live, in studio   "Open Line"
                                      2400 Olentangy River Road
                                      Columbus, OH 43210-1027
                                      Host/Contact: Fred Anderle
                                      (614) xxx-xxxx

4:10 p.m. to 4:30 p.m.   **WTVN-AM (ABC)**
Live, in-studio   *John Corby Show*
                                      1301 Dublin Road
                                      Columbus, OH 43215
                                      Host: John Corby
                                      Contact: Joe Bradley
                                      (614) xxx-xxxx

6:45 p.m.   **WBNS-TV (CBS)**
Taping at bookstore   *Evening News*
                                      Will come to B&N and tape an interview to run
                                      on either 10:00 p.m. news or the next morning.
                                      Contact: Angela Pace
                                      (614) xxx-xxxx

7:00 p.m. to 8:00 p.m.   **BARNES & NOBLE**
Discussion & signing   Easton Town Center
                                      4005 Townsfair Way
                                      Columbus, OH 43219
                                      Contact: Amy Mann
                                      (614) xxx-xxxx

Tuesday, June 4
COLUMBUS

8:00 a.m. arrival	**ONN OHIO NEWS NETWORK**
8:15 a.m.	*Morning News*
Live, in-studio	770 Twin Rivers Drive
	Columbus, OH 43216
	Host: Mike Kallmeyer
	Contact: Jeremy Naylor
	(614) xxx-xxxx

9:50 a.m. arrival	**WSYX-TV (ABC)**
10:00 a.m. to 10:15 a.m.	*Newsmakers*
Taped, in-studio	1261 Dublin Road
	Columbus, OH 43215-7000
	Contact: Carol Luper
	(614) xxx-xxxx

11:45 a.m. arrival	**WCMH-TV (NBC)**
12:00 p.m.	*Newschannel News at Noon*
Live, in-studio	3165 Olentangy River Road
	Columbus, OH 43202-1518
	Contact: Sean Seagroves
	(614) xxx-xxxx

4:00 p.m.	**JOHN GLENN INSTITUTE FOR PUBLIC**
Book talk & signing	**SERVICE AND PUBLIC POLICY**
	THE OHIO STATE UNIVERSITY
	400 Stillman Hall; 1947 College Road
	Columbus, OH 43210
	(Parking at Ohio Union Garage)
	Contact: Debbie Merritt
	(614) xxx-xxxx
	Talk, followed by Q&A, reception, & book signing.
	The Film Theatre holds 300. Books to be sold by
	campus bookstore.

INDEX